THE MUTUAL FUND
WEALTH BUILDER

THE MUTUAL FUND WEALTH BUILDER

A Profit-Building Guide for the Savvy Mutual Fund Investor

DICK FABIAN

McGraw-Hill
New York   San Francisco   Washington, D.C.   Auckland   Bogotá
Caracas   Lisbon   London   Madrid   Mexico City   Milan
Montreal   New Delhi   San Juan   Singapore
Sydney   Tokyo   Toronto

Library of Congress Cataloging-in-Publication Data

Fabian, Dick,
    The mutual fund wealth builder : a profit-building guide for the
savvy mutual fund investor / by Dick Fabian.
       p. cm.
    ISBN 0-07-136247-9
    1. Mutual funds.   2. Investments.   I. Title.
HG4530 .F26 2000
332.63'27—dc21

                                                                  00-046463

McGraw-Hill

A Division of The **McGraw·Hill** Companies

1 2 3 4 5 6 7 8 9 0   AGM/AGM   0 9 8 7 6 5 4 3 2 1 0

ISBN 0-07-136247-9

Printed and bound by Arcada Graphics Martinsburg.

McGraw-Hill books are available at special quantity discounts to use as
premiums and sales promotions, or for use in corporate training programs.
For more information, please write to the Director of Special Sales, Professional Publishing, McGraw-Hill, Two Penn Plaza, New York, NY
10121-2298. Or contact your local bookstore.

 This book is printed on recycled, acid-free paper containing a
minimum of 50% recycled, ⊗ fiber.

C O N T E N T S

PART 2
Compounded Growth Revisited   33

Chapter 4

The Blueprint for Wealth   35

Chapter 5

Creating Spendable Income   59

PART 3
Understanding the Investor   63

Chapter 6

Investor Observations   65

Chapter 7

Chapter 8

Chapter 9

The Basics of the Plan   113

Chapter 10

The Domestic Fund Composite Trading Plan   123

Chapter 11

Getting Started with the DFC Plan   139

PART 4-2

Implementing the Fabian Compounding Plan: The Advanced Course   151

Chapter 12

The Multiple Composite Trading Plan   153

Chapter 13

Implementing the MCP Plan   167

PART 6
Observations to Ensure Success   215

Chapter 17

Successful Thinking   217

P R E F A C E

The following is a presentation made by the author at a Money Show in Orlando, Florida, on February 3, 1999. There were over 10,000 people in attendance.

"I have something personal I want to share with you . . .

As a result of my 30 years in the field of finance and after I have worked with thousands of individual investors, do you know what is the most important thing I learned? It is that the power of compounded growth is the cornerstone that can enable every adult in America to become wealthy, and with the tools that are available today in the mutual fund industry, everyone should be working to attain 20 percent compounded growth.

It was over 30 years ago when a man, a little older than I, sat down and explained to me about the power of compounding. That was the beginning of my investment career in the mid-1960s.

Now when anyone asks me what my mission has been over the past 30 years, I tell that person it has been to teach as many people as possible about the positive impact that compounding can have on their lives.

There are some cultures who give credence to the concept that when an elderly member of their community dies, that is the equivalent of a library burning down. Well, before this library burns down, I have decided I want to leave a legacy.

I have 15 grandchildren and one great-grandchild. My legacy, using compounding, will be that all of them, after a 25-year period, will have $1 million after taxes.

Not everyone is aware that an individual starting an IRA at age 40 and simply contributing $2,000 a year—by realizing 20 percent compounded growth on that investment for 25 years—their retirement account would be in excess of $1,000,000. And $2,000 a year for 25 years is only $50,000.

For my grandchildren, for the first part of our legacy—that is, my wife and I—we are giving each of them $50,000, spread over a 5-year period. I know it would serve no worthwhile, long-term purpose to just give our grandchildren money if they are not also taught what to do with it. Therefore, the second part of my legacy is this book I am writing for them and for others to use.

The book contains both the philosophical and investment information that they will need to know in order to assure themselves that their individual accounts will grow in value, over 25 years, to at least $1,000,000 after taxes.

When you think about it, 25 years is not really a very long time, particularly when I realize that it was 22 years ago when I first started my Newsletter.

It is important that my grandchildren learn four things:

- To set, as their investment goal, a specific compounded growth rate. For them it is 20 percent compounded.
- How to search the entire world to know where the most appropriate investment opportunities are being offered at all times.
- How to establish and then how to use a performance yardstick to know they are always maximizing growth.
- To always have working *all* of their available investment dollars.

What I have just described for them is exactly what my book is all about.

There is still one more thing I want my grandchildren to learn. I want them to understand that the major benefit of having wealth is not just to have the ability to buy anything and everything you want. Instead, I want them to realize early on that having wealth has an ongoing, daily, uplifting influence on their lives.

One of the great joys of wealth is sharing. Because of this, I am asking each of them, at a minimum, at some time during the next 25 years, to give $50,000 to someone else and at the same time, share our compounding story with them. In that way, this legacy can go on indefinitely.

Thank you for sharing this personal time with me.

INTRODUCTION

BELIEVING CAN MAKE IT SO

I believe everyone can become a self-made millionaire based solely on the gains from their individual investments. Unfortunately, the vast majority of people do not share my view because, for most people, their personal life experiences contradict me. In fact, their view to the contrary is so strong, most of them would refuse to even listen to anyone advocating my belief.

Because of this negative reaction, my first objective must be to find a reason for these skeptics to be willing to open their minds and listen to what I have to say. My next objective is to eventually convert the skeptics into believers. I say *eventually* because, realistically, this can only be done one step at a time.

My first conversion step is to convince you that I have the credentials to justify your attention. To fulfill my objectives, I must demonstrate my qualifications. Part of this demonstration is to show how I meet the requirements of two of my axioms. (An axiom is a self-evident truth.) I have accumulated many of these self-evident truths during my career—in Part 3, I list 10 of them. There I describe their relevance in helping people reach their financial goals.

One of my axioms is this: Never take investment advice from anyone who has little or no money.

My 30-plus years in the investment arena has enabled me to become a multimillionaire. The largest portion of my net worth is liquid. Liquid assets are those that are immediately available for investing. You cannot immediately invest the equity in your house. This equity is considered a nonliquid asset.

Another one of my axioms: Never follow investment recommendations from anyone who does not have his own personal money in the same investments that he is recommending to you.

My entire career has been built around only using mutual funds. In the mid-1960s I was a licensed stockbroker and exclusively sold mutual funds. In 1970, for reasons I explain later, I surrendered my stockbroker license and became a Registered Financial Advisor with the Securities & Exchange Commission. I then began managing money for individuals, corporations, and pension plans, on a fee basis, once again using only mutual funds.

During 1974 and 1975, the ability to telephone-switch mutual funds was first introduced. This meant, with a single phone call—usually toll-free—individuals could "switch" their mutual fund investments from market-oriented positions into money funds and back again. Beginning in 1976, I took advantage of this new service for my management clients. Because I wanted to share this new, simple, investment process with others, I wrote my first book in 1976 entitled *How to Be Your Own Investment Counselor.* As a result of my book, the media called me the Father of Mutual Fund Trading. Over 300,000 copies of the book are in circulation.

As a by-product of the book, in 1977, I started publishing *The Fabian Mutual Fund Newsletter.* The function of the newsletter was to help investors to implement the simple plan I outlined in the book. Douglas Fabian, my son, in 1985 became the editor of the newsletter, which is now called *Fabian Investment Resource.* The newsletter's investment results have far exceeded my initial expectations. In August 1997, the Fabian newsletter received Mark Hulbert's "Best Market Timing Award" covering the previous 17 years.

To show how everyone can become a self-made millionaire, I have divided my book into six parts.

Part 1   Here I outline my credentials. I review both my investment beliefs and my investment philosophy. I explain the reasons why those who have a desire to become a self-made millionaire would have an interest in reading what I have to say.

Part 2   In this section, I review the magical powers of compounded growth. Knowing mathematically what compounded growth is differs from knowing how to apply it to your personal life. I include compounding growth tables to enable readers to track their individual investment goals. I also show how to use compounding to create spendable income from investments after retirement.

Part 3   Here I discuss the investor. In every financial transaction there are two components: the investor and the investment. There is no such thing as a poor investment—only poor investors. I believe this is the most important part of the entire book. Unfortunately, those future unsuccessful investors most likely will choose to skip Part 3. They will be anxious to start reviewing what I have to say about the investing details.

In Part 3 I review 10 of my axioms for investing. It is one thing to learn how to invest. However, it is just as important to learn about the things that hinder successful investing.

Part 4 It has always been the my philosophy to share with everyone all the details of the investment strategies we follow. To enhance the probabilities that you, as an investor, will realize the maximum long-term benefits from compounding, any investment plan you decide to use must be simple to understand and easy to follow. Because this is so important, I share with you everything about the ongoing, simple Fabian Compounding Plan I first introduced in 1977. (Throughout this book, I refer to my compounding plan as this, the, or my compounding plan.)

The plan can be started with as little as $1,000 or with more than $30 million, making it suitable for both small and large investors. I include the year-by-year performance results since inception of the plan. In addition, I share with you the expanded version of my compounding plan I use for the clients of my money management company.

After the reader is familiar with the two procedures I first outlined and therefore has an insight into my uniquely simple investment philosophy, I then describe how to incorporate these steps with a personalized plan for them to follow.

Part 5 Here I talk with my grandchildren. My special message to them will be valuable for all other readers as well—both young and old. One of my suggestions is to encourage them to form a "Master Mind Group" as recommended by Napoleon Hill in his book *Think and Grow Rich.*

I want each of them to become a financial mentor for that special person to whom they will be giving their $50,000. In this role, they will be sharing my compounding story with them.

Part 6 There are some observations about investing that only have value *after* one understands all the steps of an investment approach. It is then time to outline how to develop an ongoing financial lifestyle. I want to point out the investment signs to look for to ensure success, as well as the areas to avoid. I expect that these observations will enhance the probability that everyone who reads the book can become a self-made millionaire.

It is my hope that after reading the book you will agree with the comments made by an attendee of a six-hour seminar that I videotaped several years ago. He said: "As you can tell just by looking at me, I have been around for some time. I am retired and have been living off my investment income for the past 12 years. I would like to thank you and call to the attention of this group here today that this has been one of the most mature and sensible presentations that I have ever heard on investing money. If I were to ever write a book, I would be able to identify with all of the things that I have done wrong with investments as you have been pointing out to us. I read *Forbes,* I have been to the seminars, and this is the most down-to-earth presentation on how to manage money I have ever been to. Again, I want to thank you, and I would like to tell this group here to pay attention to what you have to say. You have a great message."

PERSONAL BACKGROUND

Let me begin by telling a little about myself. I have been active in the financial community for over three decades. In 1976 I wrote my first book, *How to Be Your Own Investment Counselor.* Over the years, because of my success in helping individual investors to accumulate wealth, I was the subject of articles in the *Wall Street Journal, Barrons,* the *New York Times, Money* magazine, *Forbes, USA Today,* and many other publications. In addition, I have been a featured speaker at many of the large investment conferences held around the world. I have appeared twice on "Wall Street Week" and several times on various networks.

Presently, I am the Chairman of Fabian Financial Services, Inc., a financial money management company. The firm is licensed with the Securities & Exchange Commission as a registered financial advisor. Individual and corporate clients pay us over $6 million annually to have us personally manage their money. As you can see, money is my business.

My experience has taught me that to really understand any person, you should first learn what he believes. Knowing his beliefs makes it easier to accept how and why he says and acts the way he does. Throughout the book I explore with you all of my beliefs.

WHY THIS BOOK WAS WRITTEN

You might say this book was 30 years in preparation and one year in the making. It is a culmination of my personal experiences working with individual investors plus the ideas of others, whom I paraphrase often. Many things you find in this book you have seen or heard before. However, what I offer is a personal perspective, along with strong beliefs and a never-ceasing desire to share with others. I am people-oriented.

America is the land of plenty, and we all want to participate in the good life. Well, based on what I believe, all of us have the capability to fulfill that wish for the good life . . . if only we were wealthy. I read that the late Malcolm Forbes had a plaque on the wall of his house that read: "People who say money can't buy happiness must be shopping in the wrong store."

"I know it would serve no worthwhile, long-term purpose to just give our grandchildren money if they aren't also taught what to do with it. Therefore, the second part of my legacy is this: I am writing a book for them and for others to use.

"The book contains both the philosophical and investment information that they will need to know in order to assure themselves that their individual accounts will grow in value, over 25 years, to at least $1 million after taxes."

—Excerpt from Preface

PART 1
Fundamental Concepts

C H A P T E R   1

People's Wealth Expectations

Have you any idea of what people think of their chances of becoming wealthy? Visualize this with me if you will: You are walking down the street and you arbitrarily stop someone and ask them, "Would you like to become wealthy?" The probabilities are high they will answer, "Sure, of course I would like to become wealthy." Then you ask them, "Do you think you will ever be wealthy?" Most likely they will answer, "No."

There is a simple reason for their answer, and it is important to understand. They think that they are not going to become wealthy because, for them, they believe it is not possible. We all respond to life as we perceive it be.

What I am attempting to do is to show the importance of the word *believe.* Everything we are and everything we do is consistent with what we believe. Another interesting thing about what we believe is that even if what we believe is not true, we still behave as if it were true.

The reverse is also true. By this I mean we cannot accept something we do not believe, even if it is true. For example, it really is possible to become wealthy based on your personal investments alone. In fact, you can even become a self-made millionaire.

I cannot guarantee that everyone who believes it is possible for them to become wealthy will become wealthy; however, without any reservations, I can guarantee that for everybody who believes they cannot become wealthy, it becomes a self-fulfilling prophecy. They never will become wealthy.

Going back to the person we stopped on the street. He said he would like to become wealthy, but he doesn't believe it's possible. Therefore, his only solution, if he is ever going to become wealthy, is to change his financial beliefs.

One of the objectives of my book is to help people to change their false financial beliefs.

MY BELIEFS

I want to share with you some of the things I believe. See Figure 1-1.

Your age and your present financial status will have an influence on whether or not the things I believe will be important to you. Check to see if the acceptance or rejection of my beliefs could have an impact on your life. Feel free to accept my beliefs or reject them. Feel free to challenge them and to challenge the conclusions I make based on what I believe.

WORKING HARD WILL NOT MAKE YOU WEALTHY

During my financial career I have been most helpful to investors because I am first people-oriented and then market-oriented. I do not know how to predict the market—no one does. However, it is easy to predict people's behavior, because we all do the same things for the same reasons.

All through our lives we have been told that hard work and perseverance are necessary for financial success. I think it would be hard to find anyone who does not believe this. Further, we receive reinforcement of this belief every day, both in our own lives and the lives of others. Because everybody believes this is true, anyone who wants financial success works hard and is persistent. Yet, for most people, following this process by itself does not result in attaining wealth.

While we were growing up, we believed it was important for us to eventually qualify for a good job and/or become part of the professional work force. We believed this enhanced the probability that we would be well paid—that is, attain financial success. In school we worked hard for high grades to be admitted to the "better" colleges. In college we worked hard to be one of the highest achievers in our subjects because we believed that would open the most lucrative doors in the workplace. Finally, if the future potential within a particular company appeared to be great enough, we were willing to start at the bottom of the ladder. We did this because we believed that hard work and perseverance would carry us up to the top—

FIGURE 1-1

I Believe That . . .

- The older we become, the level of health care available to us is in direct proportion to the amount of liquid assets we possess.
- Time is the most important ingredient in the formula for accumulating wealth. The total formula is **Compounding + Time + Money = Wealth.**
- The power of compounding is the eighth wonder of the world.
- Compounding can turn insignificant amounts of money into enormous sums.
- The easiest process that our government gives us to accumulate wealth is our IRA.
- The highest financial priority for all working individuals is to maximize their contributions to whatever tax-qualified plans are available to them.
- Everyone can be his or her own investment counselor.
- There are some things people will do, there are some things people won't do, and the things people know they should do fall into the category of things they won't do.
- No one will make a long-term commitment to anything unless they are motivated.
- All of our actions are controlled by what we believe to be true— whether or not in reality it is true.

- Most of us perceive ourselves as being part of the crowd and are reluctant to be considered "different."
- Our children will not take our financial advice *but* they will follow our financial example.
- People do not give serious consideration to their financial future until well after 50 years of age.
- At age 65 or older it is even more important to seek growth on your investments than to settle for interest and dividends.
- Everyone must have a specifically defined investment plan to follow while working to attain this goal.
- Investing must not interfere with one's quality of life and must not cause disharmony in the household.
- It is essential that your investment plan be simple to understand and easy to follow.
- Today is the first day of your financial future.
- In order to have a significant impact on your future quality of life, a substantial portion of your total available investment dollars must be put to work to attain your financial goals.

FIGURE 1-1

I Believe That... *(Continued)*

- Fewer than 10 percent of Americans had liquid financial assets—cash, savings, checking accounts, certificates of deposit—over $40,000 in 1980, when Congress boosted the deposit guarantee limit from $40,000 to $100,000.
- Americans save less than anyone in the world.
- A shocking number of people earning $50,000 and up don't save. The average "rich" family with an income of $50,000 to $75,000 has assets including stocks, bonds, and bank accounts (excluding equity in their houses) of only $11,000.
- Only 16 percent of the population who qualify for an IRA have one.
- Nine out of ten divorces are related to money matters.
- Only 5 percent of the population in America can put their hands on $10,000 when they're 65 years old.
- The individual investor generally thinks that almost everyone else knows more about investing than he or she does.
- The individual investor seeks advice from any and all sources and avoids relying on his or her own judgment.
- The most common theme encountered in a series of in-depth interviews is that many would-be investors are baffled by the mass of information coming to them.

- One of the barriers facing individual investors is the lack of clear, basic, and straightforward decision-making information.
- Interestingly, even though many people want more advice, they still do not want financial matters to take up a lot of their time.
- Individual investors are afraid to reveal how little they know or understand about investments.
- Low-yielding bank accounts are maintained despite the desire of many investors to take advantage of the higher returns they know are available.
- The amount of liquid wealth we have is the most important ingredient in determining our quality of life.
- Women are more emotionally suited to be successful investors than are men.
- The financial manager in a marriage has a responsibility to prepare his or her spouse to handle their finances if he or she dies first.
- After retirement the relationship that ensues with your children is influenced by their perception of your wealth.
- A large percentage of men who retire at age 65 will live an additional 20 years.

FIGURE 1-1

I Believe That . . . (*Continued*)

- Most people do not have a financial goal.
- The reason many people have not been successful with their investments is because they have no financially successful role model to follow.
- Many people believe they are not meant to be wealthy.
- America is a financial candy store. Those with money may enter and enjoy. All others simply look through the window and wish.
- Mutual funds are not the best investments; however, they are the simplest investments that I know of that have the potential to attain my financial goal.
- People pay too high a price to avoid risk.
- Any problem that can be fixed with money should not cause stress.
- Once people become keenly aware of the power of compounded growth, if at anytime in their lives they know that they do not have compounding working for them, they will feel cheated.
- Unless you can imagine your future better than your past, you're dying.

- Buy and hold is not a prudent investment approach.
- Dollar cost averaging is not a humanly doable act over the long term.
- When we have clear goals and are focused on them, our concentration can be sustained.
- When we are uncertain about our goals, it is hard to bring our will to bear on them and easy for our concentration to wander.
- Understanding the power of compounding is what makes us believe that we can be wealthy.
- The attainment of your financial goal is much more important than any investment you may use. The goal always comes first—the investment vehicle always plays a secondary role.
- Everyone with a goal to accumulate wealth from his or her investments over the long term should maximize the use of tax-deferred opportunities.
- Once we set a specifically defined financial investment goal, we must believe it is achievable.

over time. This logic is persuasive, yet for most people, it does not result in wealth. See Figure 1-2.

POSITIVE THINKING WILL NOT MAKE YOU WEALTHY

Sometime during your life you heard about the power of positive thinking. No doubt, at one time or another, you even attempted to apply positive thinking to something that you felt was very important, such as wanting to become wealthy. Then, lo and behold, what you thought about, as positively as you could, failed to materialize. As a result, over time, you stopped believing in the power of positive thinking. However, the truth is, positive thinking does work, provided you really believe that whatever you are thinking positively about is achievable for you.

FIGURE 1-2

Source: Copyright ©1999 by Mike Shapiro. Used by permission of Mike Shapiro.

As Dr. Maltz points out in *Psycho-Cybernetics* (see the "Three Important Books" section later in the chapter), once someone sets a meaningful specific goal, instantly he or she starts thinking about all of the reasons why it will not be possible to attain it. Do not fool yourself; it happens to everyone who sets a significant goal. So as you set your goal, you must answer two questions:

1. Do I believe it is possible for me to reach the goal?
2. Do I believe in the reasons that have entered my mind that could prevent me from reaching the goal?

Human nature dictates that *we will always behave* in response to what we *believe.* Therefore, if we decide to believe in the reasons that can prevent us from attaining our goal, then no amount of positive thinking is going to enable us to succeed.

If hard work with perseverance and/or positive thinking cannot enable us to become wealthy, then where else can we look? From my experience the best answer to that question is *the power of compounded growth.* Compounding, plus a simple plan to follow, will enable you to maximize its benefits. This is what gives everyone the potential to become a self-made millionaire.

I AM A MILLIONAIRE

I do not say I am a millionaire simply to brag. I say it because I want you to know from whom you are getting money advice. You would be surprised at the number of people who have little or no money and still give advice on this all-important subject. Because I believe this concept is so important, it is one of my Fabian Axioms of investing: Never take investment advice from anyone who has little or no money.

Yes, I am a millionaire. However, I can remember a time in my life when I was not as financially well off. I am 70-plus years of age, and having lived this long, I find there are some advantages to maturity.

One advantage is, I have already lived through the things many of you are now experiencing. This makes it possible for me to relate to your present situation. I recall my earlier years and remember how I felt and how I reacted to my personal environment. I did all of the conventional things. After I was discharged from the U.S. Navy at the end of World War II, I completed college and got married. With that college degree I thought I was very fortunate. I was led to believe that having a college degree would help me become wealthy. It didn't. As the years went by, my wife Marie and I had five children. It was rough going at first, but later on it seemed that things were acceptable financially. Though, deep down, I was not really satisfied.

You see, I knew that I was just surviving and just getting by. Not getting ahead financially. At some point in almost everyone's life, he or she looks around and thinks: *I live in America, the greatest country in the world. There are unlimited economic opportunities and benefits here. Other people are enjoying almost all of these benefits, but I'm not.* Then comes the inevitable question, "Why not?"

Going through this thought process does not happen in just one day. It evolves over time. But the longer and harder you think about it, the more convinced you become that something is wrong. But you do not know exactly what it is.

DEFINITION OF THE HERD

Well, I finally figured it out. And, please, do not take offense at what I am about to say. I can tell you what is wrong. The truth is, we are all part of the herd. The herd is made up of all those people who are just surviving. Think about what has been emphasized to you since the day you were born. You first heard it from your parents. You were constantly reminded of it all through school, and it continues to this day in your adult life. You were taught that you must learn to be compatible with all the people around you. You were taught to conform and not make waves. As time went on, your experiences and observations confirmed the advantages of conforming. After a while, you realized that the path of least resistance was to follow the herd and not step out of line. That way, no one picks on you. Once you realized that conformity was the path of least resistance, you figured out how to survive like everybody else. And that is about all most of us ever do. We just survive.

Rationalization helps us to continue to accept just surviving. We look at everyone around us, the rest of the herd, and we say, "Well, this is the way it is supposed to be." Think about your immediate world. Not many others have much more than you. No one on your street has a house that is much different than yours. Most everyone you know has an adequate automobile and adequate clothes, and takes a vacation once a year. But the fact is your friends and neighbors are not wealthy, are they? Yet, you know that there are some people's lives that are very different. So sooner or later, you finally ask, "What must I do to separate myself from the herd . . . from all those people who are just surviving? How do I become wealthy? Is it even possible for me to become a self-made millionaire?"

I am sure your desire for something better led you to this book in the hope of finding your answer. Well, the answer is really quite simple. The answer is, you have to be different than the majority of the people in the herd. Different? Yes. But in what way? Not externally. You do not have to become a maverick. To be different from the herd, just change something inside. Change your thinking. The way to change is to first decide you really do want to become wealthy and believe you can. No one even has to know that you are thinking differently. The only one who needs to know that you have decided to take advantage of the economic benefits America has to offer is you.

Converting this desire into a goal is the hardest single step in the entire process of wealth building. Once this is accomplished, I will provide you with step-by-step instructions on accumulating wealth. The steps are really quite simple. Anybody can follow them in just a few minutes per week. But first you have to decide, once and for all, that you truly do want to become wealthy and believe it is possible.

THREE IMPORTANT BOOKS

I want to recommend three books, which I believe everyone who truly wants to reach his or her financial goals should have in his or her financial library. Each book should be read like a textbook, with the important items highlighted. The books are as follows:

- *Psycho-Cybernetics* by Dr. Maxwell Maltz
- *The Richest Man in Babylon* by George S. Clason
- *Think and Grow Rich* by Napoleon Hill

I will be referring to these three books during our time together. Each one of them should be read at least three times. The first time through, read the book quickly to get the general idea of the author's message. The second time, read it a bit slower. The third time, underline those passages that you believe are important. And then once or twice a year, go back and review each book. If nothing else, just read the sentences you had underlined.

In *Psycho-Cybernetics,* Dr. Maltz talks about the importance of setting goals. Did you know that all of us have always attained *every goal* we truly wanted? Let me repeat that. We always attain every goal we truly want. What's more, do you know that any goal you do not specifically ask for you will not attain? This is the tragedy of life. Most people do not understand the goal-seeking mechanism that operates within us all. The truth is, we get everything we want. Dr. Maltz calls this internal goal-seeking device our *success mechanism*. Its function is to guide us to every goal that we strongly desire.

THE CONSCIOUS AND SUBCONSCIOUS MIND

Dr. Maltz explains that we have two levels of consciousness: the conscious mind and the subconscious mind. The physical environment around us and our emotional response to that environment determine what is in our conscious mind. Being aware of this, we can then determine and control the specific thoughts and ideas that occupy our conscious mind. The subconscious mind, however, works quite differently. It functions on its own, and it serves to bring us either the things we want or perhaps what we do not want. At any rate, it finds the ways and means to solve the problem or attain the goal, even though we are not consciously aware of its internal workings.

The subconscious mind is highly discerning when selecting the goals it will work on. Let me give you an example. If I were to ask you, "Would you like to become wealthy?" I am sure the answer would be "Yes, of course I would." Well then, why aren't you wealthy? If what Dr. Maltz tells us is true, that all our past goals have been fulfilled, then why has your desire for wealth not been fulfilled? The fact that you are not wealthy can only mean that you had not properly set that goal—to attain wealth. Or at the very least, you had not made it clear to your subconscious mind that this goal was highly important to you.

Let us examine the workings of the subconscious further and then make some observations. As time goes by, whether or not we think about it in these terms, we seek to fulfill our dreams and desires—some large, some small. The subconscious does not care which of these tasks it will work on. To make its determination, it continually asks one question: Which of your present desires or dreams is the most important to you emotionally? The word *emotionally* is the key. When you want something badly enough, you become intensely enthusiastic about it. When this happens, your subconscious mind then has a clear signal to work to fulfill that desire, using its maximum power. In *Think and Grow Rich* Napoleon Hill says that the only thing that stands between you and a million dollars is how badly you want it.

The subconscious mind is very efficient, and it only acts on what you truly want. That is why it is so important to give it clear signals. With a clear, emotionally positive signal, the subconscious knows exactly what you want, and it goes to work to ensure that you get it.

DESIRE PLUS BELIEF CAN MAKE IT SO

So the first and the most important step is to decide that you really do want to become a self-made millionaire. After all, everyone knows the advantages of wealth. Accomplishing this goal will have an impact on every other aspect of your life. Perhaps you are thinking, *But I already know that I want to become wealthy, and I have previously set this as a goal.* Well then, what's the problem? Why haven't you achieved the goal? I will tell you what most likely went wrong. The problem is, you presently do not believe it is possible for you to become wealthy. Sure, you would like wealth. You have even thought you had set this as a goal. But your current belief, even if you are not consciously aware of it, is that wealth cannot be yours. You see, you cannot fool the subconscious. If you do not believe it is possible to attain wealth, then, for you, it becomes a self-fulfilling prophecy.

Here is an example of how this goal-fulfilling process works. Suppose you say, "I want to run a mile in two minutes. That is my goal." That is fine, except your subconscious will not help you attain this goal because you know that running a mile in two minutes is not humanly possible. You do not believe that it can be done and neither does your subconscious. It's that simple. Fortunately, we can fix your beliefs regarding wealth because it is, in fact, humanly possible for you to become wealthy on your own. Since we are going to change your current beliefs, let us examine how you developed your false beliefs in the first place.

Consider for a moment how we arrive at any belief. Is it not true that we are either conditioned to believe or have physical evidence to support a belief? For example, assume that you are feeling ill and decide to see a doctor. You have been conditioned to believe from parents, teachers, friends, and the media that doctors are trained to diagnose and treat your illness. This belief in the doctor's skill puts you at ease in his or her presence. In many cases, just seeing the doctor has a healing effect. After making a diagnosis, your doctor may prescribe medication or suggest an operation. Although you may dislike taking medication or having an operation, you follow the doctor's advice, believing he or she knows best and that the prescription or operation will make you well.

Here is another example. How did we come to believe that the airplane you intend to board would actually fly? You may not know how to build or fly an airplane, but you have been conditioned to believe that airplanes really can fly. When you arrive at the airport, you see planes landing and taking off. This is physical evidence. Therefore, based on prior knowledge, as well as current physical evidence, you believe the plane on which you have a reservation will indeed fly. With this belief, you feel safe getting on board.

Unfortunately, these simple luxuries of mass conditioning and physical evidence are not available when it comes to accumulating wealth. The evidence is simply harder to come by. The role models are scarce or nonexistent. The procedures to attain wealth are not taught by parents, educators, clergy, or the media, nor are they readily available from any other source. So it is no wonder that your belief is one of "I cannot become wealthy" instead of "I can become wealthy." You literally have no positive conditioning and no physical evidence to support a belief in achieving wealth.

Fortunately, I can change this conditioning so that you will be able to come to believe that wealth can be yours. And once you believe it is possible to become wealthy, the experience will prove to be very exhilarating. At that first moment, you will feel immeasurably better about yourself. And everyone around you will immediately notice the change.

THE POWER OF COMPOUNDED GROWTH

Let us now turn this concept into reality. I want you to become aware of the one simple tool that can make the fulfillment of your financial goal possible. Once you see how this simple tool functions and how easily you can put it to work, you will immediately start believing in the possibilities of your future wealth. And that, of course, is the first step.

The history of the world shows that the laws that govern the accumulation of wealth have been in existence for thousands of years. Money is plentiful for everyone who understands these laws. In the realm of wealth building, everything begins with one simple tool, and that tool is the power of compounded growth.

In Part 2, I walk you through a thorough examination and explanation of the power of compounded growth. Also included are tables and examples showing the results of different investment amounts over various periods of time using 20 percent compounded growth.

Once you make the decision you truly want to become wealthy, that you are going to break away from the herd, then you cannot ignore the laws that govern the accumulation and protection of wealth. The truth is: *Thou shall not become wealthy without compounding.* Over the three decades I have worked in the financial arena, I have been continually amazed at how few people really understand the power of compounding. They may understand the definition of compounding—that it is growth on the original principal, plus growth on the growth. But do they understand how to relate compounding to their lives? Obviously, they do not. Otherwise, far more people would be wealthy. How about you? Do you know what compounding can do for you?

You should be aware that compounding has the ability to turn trifling amounts of money into enormous sums. For all of us who have experienced the power of compounded growth, we call it the eighth wonder of the world. Compounded growth is a mathematical law that operates in our universe, and it is free to everyone who chooses to use it. In case you ever wonder, compounding was created on the same day they invented gravity.

SETTING A MONETARY GOAL AND AN INVESTMENT GOAL

It is important to bring the power of compounding into your personal life. The way to do this is to first set a monetary financial goal—that is, the specific amount of money you wish to accumulate within a specified period of time. There does not have to be a maximum amount, but there must be a minimum. Each individual must decide specifically how much money he or she wants to accumulate in a given time period. The minimum, however, must be at least $300,000 by age 65 or at retirement. This is the least amount everyone needs to enable them to generate spendable income for their retirement years. (I discuss creating spendable income in Part 2.) However, do not shortchange yourself and fail to strive to become a self-made millionaire.

Once you have set a monetary goal, the next step is to set an investment goal. An investment goal is not a specific amount of money. Rather, it is a specific rate of compounded growth that will help you attain the specific amount of money you desire. As such, it then becomes your financial ruler. This is a very important tool.

Once you are able to decide on the specific amount of money you wish to accumulate and also state the specific rate of compounded growth you will use to work for that money, you have two big advantages. The first advantage is that at any time you can stop the clock and measure your progress. This will enable you to see if you are on target to reach your monetary goal. The second advantage comes when you can see that you are in fact on target. Believe me, the emotional aspects of wealth building are far more important than the physical aspects. Knowing that you are on target builds your confidence and keeps you motivated to stick with your plan. Why? Because this positive feedback is just what your subconscious needs to let it know that the wealth-building process is, in fact, working. In *Psycho-Cybernetics,* Dr. Maltz describes how important feedback is in working toward any goal.

Feedback helps the subconscious to make any necessary adjustments as it guides us to the target. You have to stop periodically and check your progress, or you will not know if you are on target. The goal is your financial ruler. Always keep in mind: The personal amount of money you are going to work to attain is what is most important. That is the destination. The path you follow to get there is secondary.

CHAPTER 2

Compounded Growth

THE INVESTMENT GOAL

Here is the Fabian Investment Goal expressed in its entirety: *20 percent annualized compounded growth over the long term. When I say the long term, I mean the rest of your life.* Perhaps when hearing this for the first time, 20 percent compounded growth does not sound like very much. But consider this: When you compound, what you are actually doing is building growth on top of principal and growth on top of the previous growth. Simply put, that is growth on growth.

It works like this: When you compound at 20 percent annualized growth, at the end of the first year, obviously your average annual growth is 20 percent. But after that, your average annual growth gets better and better each following year. After five years, you actually realize an average annual growth of 30 percent per year on your initial investment, not just 20 percent. And over 10 years, you actually realize an average annual growth of 52 percent per year on the initial money invested. Yes, that's right, 52 percent per year. Now how does that sound? Does that not get your adrenaline running? When you look at the compounded growth table in Part 2, you will see for yourself what I am saying is true. Can you see how an annual growth of 52 percent each year over the next 10 years, on the total amount of money that you could find to put to work today, could have an impact on helping you to become a self-made millionaire?

PUTTING MONEY TO WORK

It must be obvious to everyone that attaining wealth in the future requires that we put money to work now. Without at least a trifling amount of money to work with, even the tremendous power of compounding does not have the ability to function. I want to emphasize that I am not going to ask you to make any great money sacrifice or ask you to do something that would force you to alter your lifestyle. To prove this, we are going to walk through a specific example together. At the conclusion, you decide if I fulfilled my promise.

Whenever I speak at an investment conference, I always ask the audience, "How many of you here today have an IRA—that is, an Individual Retirement Account?" Most often, only a small number of hands are raised. And almost everyone who raises his or her hand is over 40 years of age. Both of these facts are surprising and important. In the first place, an IRA is one of the greatest wealth-building vehicles available to us. It is even better now that Roth IRAs are available. They are offered to us, free of charge, from the federal government. A Roth IRA allows invested dollars to grow tax-free and at retirement be withdrawn free of income taxes. In spite of these benefits, only a fraction of the population who are qualified to use one actually do. The last time I checked the figures on this, approximately 16 percent of those who are eligible to contribute to an IRA actually do so.

We can learn something interesting about people from this. First of all, we learn that most people do not even consider doing anything about their financial future until they are over 40 years of age. You and I would not dispute the advantage of starting on the road to riches when young. Yet, what do we observe in real life? Virtually everyone waits until they are age 40 or older to begin. Fortunately, starting at age 40 or later still gives you plenty of time to accumulate wealth, even if you use just an IRA. At one investment conference, after I asked the question about how many people had an IRA and observed the ages of those who responded, I went on to explain the power of compounding. There was one woman in the audience, about 40 years old, who seemed to be hanging on to every word. I could see that she was relating to my specific compounding example.

What I said went like this: Since most people decided to wait until age 40 to begin thinking about their financial future, let me show you an example of what can still be accomplished at that time in one's life. Let us assume that at age 40, the one and only investment a person uses to fulfill his retirement objectives is to open an IRA. He continues to fund it each year until retirement at age 65. Remember, I said, he is doing nothing else. No sacrifices. He is not gong to deprive himself of the little luxuries of life. He is not going to become a martyr. Just $2,000 per year deposits—only $167 per month. I am sure everybody can see themselves doing that, provided they believed this one step would enable them to take care of all of their retirement needs . . . in style.

At this point, the woman was nodding her head in agreement. Her eyes really opened up wide when I told her that by just putting $2,000 each year into an IRA, starting at age 40 and provided it grows at 20 percent annualized compounded growth, at age 65, the total value of the IRA account would be over $1 million. That's *$1 million at retirement*. Look at the IRA Growth Table, shown in Figure 2-1, to see the year-by-year progress working toward the retirement objective.

Do not allow yourself to become inflexible about your long-term goals. The object of a goal is to set a specific target to shoot for. But it is likely that over a 25-year period the actual result will not be exactly 20 percent compounded. It could be more or it could be less. In our IRA example, if the actual growth worked out to be 23 percent compounded, your final accumulation would be over $1.5 million.

If on the other hand, the actual growth worked out to be 17 percent compounded, your final accumulation would be almost $700,000. There is nothing wrong with that, is there?

Now let me ask you another question. If you had been in the audience at that investment conference when we discussed the IRA, would you have been nodding your head in agreement? Do you think that perhaps you could, without any great sacrifice, fund your IRA each year? This amounts to just $167 each month ($167 × 12 = $2,000). That is not an impossible task. Working with the investment goal, the simple step of using an IRA has the power of potentially making everyone a self-made millionaire over a 25-year period. Now do you see how everyone can attain wealth through compounding? Are you beginning to see how you can separate yourself from the herd? Attaining wealth is not a feat that is the exclusive province of smart, lucky, or dishonest people. It is available to everyone who will set a goal, believe in that goal, and follow a simple plan to attain it.

At this point in our discussion, don't concern yourself about how you are going to work to attain 20 percent annualized compounded growth. I will give you all of the details on how to work for our goal in Part 4.

FIGURE 2-1

Becoming a Millionaire Using Your Roth IRA

Age	Deposits	20% Growth	Year-End Value
40	2,000	400	2,400
41	2,000	880	5,280
42	2,000	1,456	8,736
43	2,000	2,147	12,883
44	2,000	2,977	17,860
45	2,000	3,972	23,832
46	2,000	5,166	30,998
47	2,000	6,600	39,598
48	2,000	8,320	49,917
49	2,000	10,383	62,301
50	2,000	12,860	77,161
51	2,000	15,832	94,993
52	2,000	19,399	116,392
53	2,000	23,678	142,070
54	2,000	28,814	172,884
55	2,000	34,977	209,861
56	2,000	42,372	254,233
57	2,000	51,247	307,480
58	2,000	61,896	371,376
59	2,000	74,675	448,051
60	2,000	90,010	540,061
61	2,000	108,412	650,474
62	2,000	130,495	782,968
63	2,000	156,994	941,962
64	2,000	188,792	1,132,755
Totals	50,000	939,870	

Note: Assumes IRA contribution is made at the end of the year.

A WOMAN'S PERSPECTIVE

I especially want to relate my story to everyone that believes wealth and financial security are only for the rich or white-collar workers. In addition, recent trends continue to show that women are seeking their financial independence.

The interesting thing about money is that it is not sexist. It works the same for men and women. In fact, when both husband and wife start IRAs at age 40 and if they attain the my Investment Goal, by the time they retire, their combined accounts could be worth over $2 million. Still, here is something a woman can do all by herself with just $167 per month savings.

THE BENEFITS OF KNOWING YOU CAN BECOME A SELF-MADE MILLIONAIRE

Let us look at the side benefits that come to everyone, men and women alike, who follow my approach. Once you believe that compounding will do for you the things I am describing, your life will immediately reflect this belief. The interesting thing about the way we react to money is that when we believe that money is on its way to us, it has the same emotional effect as if we had it in our hands right now. Therefore, when you believe that you have the capability to produce, all by yourself, $1 million tax-free with a Roth IRA by the time you retire, you will respond emotionally to that $1 million now.

Knowing you will be financially secure in the future will immediately change your attitude about yourself, and your self-image will improve now. Never again will you feel intimidated by the petty things that have adversely affected you in the past. Your financial peace of mind will enhance your present quality of life. You can even be more daring about accepting new opportunities knowing that you have a plan in place for your future financial security.

The more you can relate to compounding, the easier it will be for you to see that compounding is your key to wealth. I told you earlier about George S. Clason's book *The Richest Man in Babylon.* There you will find many examples of how compounding leads to wealth and also how a lack of compounding leads nowhere, at least where money is concerned. We all have different financial abilities and different time frames to work with, depending on our age. I include "Blueprint for Wealth Examples" in Part 2, with reference to the compounding data tables to show how you can arrive at the future value of money. I also supply a blank Blueprint for Wealth Certificate so that you can set in writing your personal financial goal.

You Must Be in Control

We have all heard the expression "if you want something done right, do it yourself." Since one of the most important aspects of your life is the financial side, it only makes good sense that it is handled properly. Logically, then, you must always be in control. Let me ask you a question. Up until now, how have you been handling the financial side of your life that directly affects everything else . . . where you live . . . how you live . . . how much free time you have . . . your peace of mind . . . your self-esteem, and so on? I am sure that you have a job and you go to work every day. In fact, many people go to work every day even though they strongly dislike what they do. But that is not the question. Your job allows you to survive, and everyone in the herd does that. What I want to know is how you handle the financial aspects of your life over and above day-to-day survival?

Are you depending on your parents for your financial future? Is it not possible that you could be written out of the will? Maybe your parents will outlive you. Are you depending on your employer for your financial security? The company could suffer a decline, change owners or management, or move out of your area. Any number of things could cause a change in your employment status and your income. Perhaps you are counting on your spouse, a friend, or a relative to take care of the financial side of your life. Ask yourself now, do any of these approaches offer true security? Are they absolutely dependable? You know they are not.

Some people feel secure and say that they rely on a financial advisor to look after their finances. Unfortunately, quite often we see headlines in the newspaper exposing the inept or crooked financial advisor who mishandles or steals his clients' money, often to their financial ruin. A while back, the papers were filled with stories about the financial disaster experienced by a famous basketball star whose playing career was drawing to a close. After working with a financial manager, all he could show after years of investing were losses in the millions and several lawsuits. And why? All because everything was just taken care of for him.

So even if you believe that you are now in control of your financial destiny, are you really? Do you rely on a stockbroker, a banker, a financial planner, or some other financial salesperson? Do you invest according to what the financial press recommends or what some investment guru forecasts for the future of the stock market? And speaking of investment gurus, this reminds me of the real estate specialist who was featured in *Money* magazine several years back. He eventually went broke and filed for bankruptcy as a result of following his own advice.

I continually remind clients, however, that they are still responsible for their investment dollars. To fulfill this responsibility, they must closely monitor, at least monthly, the status of their individual account.

I AM NOT A GURU

One reason I object to being called a guru, something the financial press likes to call me, is that so many so-called gurus end up broke. So, do not think of me as a guru. That implies I have some secret plan or complicated moneymaking scheme, which I don't. What I do have is something that is much more important than that. It is called common sense. What I am talking about here is complete control by you, not me. I do not want your money. I want you to take control, and that is why I am going to teach you how to handle it by yourself and handle it right. It only makes good sense, if you truly want to become wealthy, enhance your quality of life, and avoid becoming a victim: You must absolutely take control of your own finances.

From time to time, I meet with individuals and we discuss the wealth-building fundamentals. Usually, they make the statement: "Okay, I will change my thinking. I really do want to become wealthy. But what do I do next?" My answer to them is "Look in the mirror. Make a promise to the image you see there to never depend on anyone else when it comes to your money." This is the same advice I am giving you. Promise yourself that you will always be in control from this day forward. Once you make this commitment, no one can ever stop you from succeeding. No one can ever take your money away from you. Once you decide to take control of your financial destiny, becoming rich is just a matter of following a few simple steps. You will learn these steps shortly.

Before we go on, are you aware that there is a consolation prize for those people who are unwilling to assume the full responsibility and control over their own finances? They have one luxury. To be sure, it is an expensive luxury. You know what it is? They can blame someone else when they fail. But, remember, the opposite is also true. When you are in charge and you succeed, you and you alone can take 100 percent of the credit for that success. And, believe me, that is a fantastic feeling.

WHAT HAVE WE LEARNED SO FAR?

Let me summarize what we have learned so far. You are in the process of using the language of the subconscious mind to set in place a high-priority goal to accumulate wealth. You have promised yourself to always maintain personal control of your wealth-building process. You now know, and therefore believe, that accumulating the wealth that you desire is possible because you know about the power of compounded growth. You know that compounding turns trifling amounts of money into enormous sums. You have already adopted, or as you learn more about compounding, you will adopt, the Investment Goal of 20 percent annualized compounded growth over the long term. You are also going to follow another of my Axioms for investing: Always have working, to attain your goal, all of the investment dollars you have available.

Philosophy of Investing

UNDERSTANDING THE PHILOSOPHY OF INVESTING

Now it is time to begin the search. Time to find the plan to use to work for our investment goal. How do you proceed to find the specific path you will follow to work toward your investment goal of 20 percent annualized compounded, long-term growth? Note I said, how do you *proceed?* There are steps to be taken.

Take the time to understand and gain a thorough working knowledge of compounding. That is the key to the entire wealth-building process. As you become more keenly aware of the workings of compounded growth, it will become obvious to you that it takes time to maximize the benefits of compounding. You already know that at the end of 5 years, with 20 percent compounding, you actually average 30 percent gain per year on the original investment. Over 10 years, my compounding goal yields an average annual growth of 52 percent per year on the amount of money you started with. I did not point this out earlier, but over 15 years, your average annual growth is 96 percent per year. It keeps getting better year after year. The longer you compound, the greater your returns. This is as it should be. Your goal is for the long term, for the rest of your life. No longer are you thinking about short-term results. Now, since you are planning to use the power of compounding to enhance the quality of your life, for the rest of your life, the specific investment plan you adopt to work for your goal must be simple. Let me repeat that and let me emphasize it.

KEEP IT SIMPLE

Your goal must be simple. Before I explain why, let me ask you a question. Over your lifetime, how many resolutions or promises to yourself have you made that you stuck with for 1 or 2 years, let alone, 10 years? I am sure I know the answer, none. Except perhaps your marriage. And for some, maybe the marriage did not last. As an astute observer of people, I know that there are things that people will do and there are things people will not do. People will only continue to do things over the long term that are easy to live with. Therefore, the plan that you select to use to work for your goal must allow you to feel comfortable, over the long term, or you simply will not stick with it.

Let us examine some of the requirements such an investment plan must have. The plan you select must be easy to understand and simple to follow. Your plan should not take up a great deal of your time. For example, daily monitoring over a long period is unrealistic. A few minutes per week is more like it. We have all lived long enough to know that our emotions affect our actions. Therefore, the plan you follow must not cause stress or anxiety. If it does, you will not stick with it long enough to reap the benefits of long-term compounding. The plan must not cause you to change your lifestyle. It must not interfere with your occupation nor cause disharmony in your household. Let me remind you of a previous promise you made. Your plan must at all times be under your control. You must believe your plan has the potential to give you 20 percent annualized compounded growth. You cannot depend on others. One final ingredient that will enhance the probability of your success is this: You must have a plan that offers liquidity, so you can get to your money in the event of an emergency or for other investment opportunities.

Based on your own life experiences, won't you agree that if any of the requirements listed above are not met, it will increase the probability that you will not stick with the plan long enough to maximize the benefits of compounding? To succeed over the long term, the plan you adopt must be comfortable for you to use over the long term. Only with a high comfort level will you remain committed long enough to attain the wealth you desire.

UNDERSTANDING YOUR INVESTMENT PLAN

Some time ago, Robert Prector and I were featured speakers at an investment conference in Los Angeles. To those of you who do not know of Bob, he is the highly respected editor of a financial newsletter, *The Elliott Wave Theorist*. At this conference, he made some comments that I want to share with you now. In discussing how to be a successful investor, he said, "You must have a specific and clearly defined plan to follow, and you must have the discipline to stick with that plan. It must be a plan you have thought through in its entirety, so that if someone asked you how you made your investment decisions, you could explain it in detail. And if asked again in six months, the answer will be exactly the same." Heed Bob's advice.

Remember what was said earlier. Even before you start the plan, just believing that it is possible to become wealthy greatly enhances your self-image and has a positive effect on how you respond to the people and events around you. You can imagine then what your emotional response will be like after your plan has been implemented and you have tangible evidence that your plan is on target to reach your goal. Take a few moments and fantasize about how great that will be.

Now, let me make a few observations about investment plans. Once you decide to attain the 20 percent investment goal, it is very comforting to know that there are many different paths you can follow to reach your destination. This means that you do not have to burden yourself trying to find the best plan. That is impossible anyway, because what someone might consider the best plan today may not be the best plan next year, next month, or perhaps even next week. So take the pressure off. Do not look for the best plan; just seek out an appropriate plan. Any plan that has the potential to attain your goal and will also be comfortable for you to follow over the long term will do just fine. Remember, the only thing that really matters is that you attain the goal. The goal comes first and the path you follow to get there comes second.

LET US NOW DISCUSS RISK

There is one last subject we have to cover before we move on to Part 2. I am sure this final question has been lurking in your mind as I have discussed your path to riches—particularly when I mentioned you must always have all of your available investment dollars working. This is your "serious money." Let's not beat around the bush. Let's get it right up on the table for everyone to see, and then we can handle it once and for all. What I am talking about is risk.

Life itself is a risky business. Risk taking is a large part of our daily living. Because we want to be successful in accumulating wealth, we must understand our own personal reaction to placing our serious money at risk. To begin, I cannot think of one single thing a person can do with his or her money that is 100 percent risk free. You can hide it under the mattress, but then a burglar might break in and steal it or your house might burn down. Passbook savings accounts and CDs seem pretty safe, but there have been times when some banks and savings and loans closed up. Although it is true that federal insurance covers many of the people affected in these clo-sures, that insurance doesn't extend to the shrinking effects of inflation. And what's more, earning 4 or 5 or 6 percent in a bank account will not be a high enough return to enable you to become a self-made millionaire.

You can put your money in real estate, but then it is tied up. You have no liquidity. And real estate also has its risks. Nothing is entirely risk-free. But that is okay, because you and I have learned to live with various degrees of risk everyday. There are some risks that we will not take under any circumstances. There are others we are willing to take because of the rewards they offer, provided these risks do not turn us into emotional wrecks.

The question of risk is so important that I am actively engaged in dealing with it almost everyday. Remember that I have a group of investors who have entrusted us to personally manage their money. All of these peo-ple need to have their questions regarding risk answered. The best way for me to explain how I determine the risk potential for our clients is to review the philosophy of the investment plan I follow.

I believe the first thing we should do is to come to an agreement of what we mean by risk. Since we are talking about investments, no doubt we can all agree that risk means the chance that exists of losing all or part of the money we currently have invested. Based on this definition, an investor could come to the conclusion that he or she is safer (the reverse of risk) using investments that historically give up gains at a slower rate dur-ing market declines. At the same time, however, realizing that these same investments do not grow as fast as others do during market advances. An example would be using a growth and income mutual fund versus using an aggressive capital appreciation mutual fund. We can therefore say there are some investors who are more risk-adverse rather than more growth-oriented.

My personal outlook on risk when it comes to investing is governed by the amount of control I am able to maintain. To me the investment strat-egy with the highest risk is "buy-and-hold." Once investors accept a buy-and-hold approach, they give up control because they cannot protect themselves in a significant market decline. Their investment boat is going to be carried along by the random direction of the winds and the tides because it has no rudder. For me, since I am a trend follower, my investment boat has a rudder. This enables me to steer around obstacles that could hinder me from reaching my investment destination.

Let me begin with a little background of the plan I follow. In the beginning, I tested many investment approaches and eventually settled on the one I use today. The specific stock market plan I follow uses mutual funds. In Part 4 I will tell you everything you ever wanted to know about mutual funds and my compounding plan.

I do not believe that mutual funds are the cleverest investment or that they are the best way to make money. Even though they have been proven to be very popular for many years, I do not use mutual funds for these reasons. I use mutual funds because they are the simplest vehicles I have found that have the potential to attain my goal. Their simplicity enables me to use them comfortably over the long term, thus reaping the tremendous benefits of long-term compounding. Remember, by *long term,* I mean the rest of your life.

Because my plan has specific rules for both buying and selling, the risk factor is automatically handled. I am then able to concentrate on maximizing growth as I work toward attaining 20 percent compounding.

SUMMARY—THREE LAWS TO FOLLOW

Before concluding Part 1, let me review the three laws to follow to accumulate wealth.

Law #1 *You must decide that you really and truly do want to become wealthy.* Without making this declaration and truly believing it is possible, it will never happen. Remember what we learned earlier from Dr. Maltz. We fulfilled every goal we truly desired. So make the decision now that you truly want to become wealthy.

Remember your goal should be no less than $300,000 of liquid assets. I say *liquid assets* because this will be the money used to generate spendable income. You should set a much higher goal, but use $300,000 as the minimum you should accumulate by age 65 or at retirement. Once you have a specific goal set in your mind and the belief that it is possible for you to attain it, your subconscious mind will guide you straight to that target. Therefore, why not make it your goal to become a self-made millionaire?

Law #2 *Adopt a compounded growth rate capable of enabling you to accumulate your desired future wealth.* As I stated earlier, most people do not know how to set a realistic investment goal, so I suggest you adopt mine: 20 percent annualized compounded growth over the long term. This is a realistic investment goal. As I mentioned before, I do not care what plan you use. Always remember that the goal comes first. How you get there is secondary.

You now have the wealth-building steps in your possession. They are now a part of your conscious mind. It is my pleasure to share this valuable information with you. But now the rest is up to you. If it were your desire to build a house, first you would obtain a blueprint, and then you would buy the materials needed to actually build the house. This is what you must do now. In order to build a strong financial house, you must have a strong foundation and all of the materials needed to fulfill your desire. For this reason, I want to remind you of the three books mentioned earlier—*Think and Grow Rich, The Richest Man in Babylon,* and *Psycho-Cybernetics.* Read each of them at least once a year.

Law #3 *If you do not have a specific plan to follow, do exactly as I do.* I have lived long enough to know that no one does anything unless they are motivated. If I can get you to understand how the power of compounded growth can impact your life, how it can add to the quality to your life, I believe this will serve to motivate you to follow the simple steps I recommend to enable you to become a self-made millionaire.

So now, it is up to you.

To conclude, here is a brief story from *The Richest Man in Babylon:*

In order to develop a more even distribution of wealth among the cities of Babylon, the king asked the richest man in Babylon to teach the populace how to accumulate wealth. This he gladly agreed to. Upon concluding his lessons with those chosen to learn his secrets of accumulating wealth, the richest man in Babylon asked his pupils what they had learned. The answers fell into three categories.

First, there were many that said that the Goddess of Luck had favored this rich man and because they believed they could not be as lucky as he so they could not expect to succeed.

Next, there were those who complained of having no money and if the rich man had more than he could use, would he just give them some, then maybe they could employ the lessons he had taught them.

Finally the third group said nothing, for they had learned and understood. This group left and went on to build up great fortunes.

I hope you will respond as this third group. With the information given to you here, you will have every opportunity to enhance your understanding, which will also greatly enhance your confidence and, in turn, lead you to success.

In closing Part 1, I would like to share with you a letter that I had received: "Just a note to say thanks for sharing your wisdom. As a result we have not only improved our own quality of life, but that of our kids and also an aging parent. Thank you again for your help."

Now let us go on to Part 2 and discover why compounded growth is the eighth wonder of the world.

PART 2

Compounded Growth Revisited

CHAPTER 4

The Blueprint for Wealth

I will now discuss the most important element of this book. Through compounding, everyone can reach this goal using only the growth from his or her personal investments.

At first, this may seem hard to believe, but the process to follow, to become wealthy, is really quite simple. To build wealth, it is not necessary to start with a great deal of money or to take big risks to net big returns. The secret is using the passage of time to multiply your money. Bull markets come and go. Returns rise and fall. But time inevitably marches on. And since time is going to go by anyway, why not let it work for you to fulfill your financial goals?

In order for everyone to become wealthy, based only on their own investments, there are just two steps to be taken. First, you have to become virtually fully invested. In fact, this is one of my Fabian Axioms for investing. You will learn shortly that, for some people, being fully invested means saving just $113 per year.

Most people are not aware of this, but there are only a small number of individual investors who ever become virtually fully invested. By being fully invested, I mean putting to work 90 percent or more of the total number of dollars that one could make available for investing. I personally meet this definition.

We discussed earlier that for everyone to become wealthy based on his or her own investments, there are two requirements. First, you have to be fully invested. Second, you have to strive to attain a high compounded growth rate on all of your investment dollars.

THE HISTORY AND MAGIC OF COMPOUNDING

Let us now learn the details of the power of compounding and how it can bring financial abundance to everyone's life. Let's see what it is, how it works—its history and its magic. You will truly marvel as you become aware of what appear to be magical powers. Most important, though, you will learn how to use this simple tool, free to everyone, to fill your cup to overflowing and bring happiness and tranquillity to your life and the lives of those around you. That is quite a promise, isn't it?

WHAT IS COMPOUNDING?

Albert Einstein once described compounded growth as "the greatest mathematical discovery of all time." The world's most successful wealth builders have used it, and it is at the heart of my compounding plan.

Compounding multiples your money exponentially by earning you a return—not just on your original investment but also on the gains you make, year after year. In simple terms, compounding is growth on both your original principal and the growth you have previously earned from that principal. This creates an even larger sum to invest, which produces an even greater profit and further increases your investment capital.

Everyone is familiar with simple interest. With simple interest you just multiply the interest rate times the principal amount. For example, if you start with $1,000 and earn 20 percent simple interest annually, at the end of the first year, you will have $1,200. Now, for the first year, 20 percent compounded earnings are the same as simple interest. But that's where the similarity ends. Henceforth, you will earn 20 percent not only on the original principal but on your interest earnings as well. That is, you will earn 20 percent on the original $1,000 and also on the $200 previously earned interest. By the end of the second year, you will have $1,440 ($1.20 \times \$1,200 = \$1,440$). Likewise, by the end of the third year, your $1,440 will have grown to $1,728.

Let us now compare simple interest with compound interest. At 20 percent simple interest, the earnings on $1,000 will be $200 per year, so in three years you will have $1,600. With 20 percent compounded annually, however, your original $1,000 will grow to $1,728. This is an increase of

$128. Perhaps that does not sound like a whole lot more, but hold onto your coins because miracles do lie ahead.

In a moment, we will be looking at actual examples of the tremendous power of compounding and what it can do for you. First, however, let us take a glance back at history.

> If you have not acquired more than a bare existence, it is because you either have failed to learn the laws that govern the building of wealth, or else you do not observe them.
>
> —*George Clason from* The Richest Man in Babylon

THE HISTORY OF COMPOUNDING

History shows that the ancient Babylonians were the first to make wide use of the power of compounding, and as a result, they amassed tremendous wealth. The city of Babylon was the largest and richest city of its day—and its day extended for thousands of years. We still marvel over the advanced Babylonian civilization, a civilization that produced our first engineers, mathematicians, scientists, and financiers. Every schoolchild knows of the immense wall that protected the city, of the irrigation canals that brought forth the abundance of crops, and of the extraordinary hanging gardens that were a tribute to a people as interested in beauty as they were in science and trade.

Historians tell us that the Babylonians were well in advance of the rest of the known world in the field of mathematics. One of the most important archaeological finds of this century uncovered thousands of Babylonian clay tablets, long buried in the Asian desert, just north of the Persian Gulf. These engraved tablets, which the Babylonians used for writing just as we use paper today, depict everyday life in the great city. One tablet, remarkably well preserved after almost four thousand years, tells of the power of compounded growth and specifically the time it takes a fixed sum to double at 20 percent compounded annually. The answer: just under four years. The Money Doubles Table, shown in Figure 4-1, displays the amounts of time it takes for money to double in value at different compounding rates.

Today, in our modern technological age, we know many wonderful and useful things, but none more practical than how to make money

FIGURE 4-1

MONEY DOUBLES	
Compounding Rate	Years Required
5% ➤	14.4 years
7% ➤	10.2 years
10% ➤	7.2 years
12% ➤	6.0 years
15% ➤	4.8 years
17% ➤	4.2 years
20% ➤	3.6 years
25% ➤	2.9 years

grow—something the ancient Babylonians knew well before us. The laws that govern the accumulation of wealth have been in existence for thousands of years and are literally chiseled in stone. If you truly want to be rich, you cannot ignore them.

Returning to our Babylonian friends, we find that they put considerable effort into the study of compounding. Elaborate tables were established showing the results of compounding at various interest rates over extended periods. One reason for the serious interest in compounding was that the Babylonians maintained strict laws governing usury—that is, the laws that prevented moneylenders from charging unusually high interest rates for loans.

Much later, in early Christian history, the Pope found compounding a subject of serious interest, since usury was a sin. At one point, because of the abuses of certain moneylenders, the term *compounded interest* assumed a negative connotation, since the power of compounding resulted in an extremely unpleasant experience for the unlucky borrower.

Later, beginning with the Renaissance, several noted mathematicians, including Edmund Halley, William Oughtred, and Jacques Bernoulli, addressed the subject of compound interest. With the flowering of business in the sixteenth and seventeenth centuries, the business side of mathematics, in which compounded interest played an important role, was developed in greater detail. Formulas were developed for computing compound interest biannually, quarterly, monthly, and daily. Eventually, a formula was developed for computing interest compounded for an infinite number of periods—or at every instant.

In 1926, George S. Clason, a successful businessman and author, published the first of a series of pamphlets on thrift and financial planning, using parables set in ancient Babylon to illustrate his points. These pamphlets were distributed widely and helped millions to achieve more financially abundant lives. Eventually, these parables were published collectively in *The Richest Man in Babylon*. See if you recognize the principles that we've been discussing in the following quote from Mr. Clason's book:

> *A part of all you earn is yours to keep . . . Every gold piece you save is a slave to work for you. Every copper it earns is its child that also can earn for you. If you would become wealthy, then what you save must earn and its children must earn. That all may help to give you the abundance you crave.*

Mr. Clason's book is a classic on how to build and preserve wealth. If you have not yet read it, I suggest you do so now. If you read it years ago, read it again. As you can see, some of the sharpest minds in history were seriously interested in the power of compounding, and for good reason, too, since compounding has the power to convert trifling amounts of money into enormous sums.

THE POWER OF 20 PERCENT COMPOUNDED GROWTH

As I said earlier, my personal investment goal is to work to attain 20 percent annualized compounded growth on my investments over the long term. Again, by the long term, I mean the rest of your life.

So, my goal and your goal, if you choose to be among the special group of people who will become wealthy from the growth of their personal investments, should be at least 20 percent annualized compounded growth. I am convinced that compounding is the cornerstone that can create wealth for everyone.

Let me show you in detail why I believe so strongly in the power of compounded growth. Please turn to the 20 percent Annualized Compounded Growth Table shown in Figure 4-2. This table shows the effects of an initial $100,000 investment achieving 20 percent annualized compounded growth from 1 through 25 years.

FIGURE 4-2

20% Annualized Compounded Growth Table
Compounding + Time + Money = Wealth

This 20% compounded growth table shows the dramatic effects of long-term compounding on an initial investment of $100,000. Note that the average annual gain after the first year is 20%, but each year after that the return is higher. In five years, the average return is 30% per year; in ten years, the average return is 52% per year; and in fifteen years, the average annual return is 96% per year on the initial investment.

Year	A	B	C
1	$100,000 + 20%	20.00%	$120,000
2	120,000 + 20%	22.00%	144,000
3	144,000 + 20%	24.27%	172,800
4	172,800 + 20%	26.84%	207,300
5	207,300 + 20%	30.00% *	250,000
6	248,800 + 20%	33.10%	298,500
7	298,500 + 20%	36.90%	358,300
8	358,300 + 20%	41.25%	429,900
9	429,900 + 20%	46.22%	515,900
10	515,900 + 20%	52.00% *	620,000
11	619,100 + 20%	58.46%	743,000
12	743,000 + 20%	65.97%	891,600
13	891,600 + 20%	74.61%	1,069,900
14	1,069,900 + 20%	84.56%	1,283,900
15	1,283,900 + 20%	96.00% *	1,540,000
16	1,540,700 + 20%	109.30%	1,848,800
17	1,848,800 + 20%	124.62%	2,218,600
18	2,218,600 + 20%	142.35%	2,662,300
19	2,662,300 + 20%	162.88%	3,194,800
20	3,194,800 + 20%	187.00% *	3,840,000
21	3,833,700 + 20%	214.31%	4,600,500
22	4,600,500 + 20%	246.39%	5,520,600
23	5,520,600 + 20%	283.68%	6,624,700
24	6,624,700 + 20%	327.07%	7,949,600
25	7,949,600 + 20%	378.00% *	9,550,000

A = The value of the investment at the beginning of each year.

B = The average annual growth for each year. It is computed by subtracting the initial investment from the value at the end of any year and then dividing that figure by the initial investment. Next, to arrive at a percentage, multiply your answer by 100 and divide by the number of years you have held the investment. (See example below.)

C = The value of the investment at the end of each year after the effect of 20% growth.

*   Rounded

*Example using year 10

1. (6,191.74 - 1,000)/1000	= 5.192
2. 5.192 x 100	= 519.17
3. 519.17/10	= 51.92%
4. Rounded	= 52.00%

Most important here are the percentages shown in column B. This column shows the average annual growth at the end of each year on the original investment. Obviously, at the end of the first year, the average annual return is 20 percent. Now look at the fifth year. Here you see that an equal growth of 20 percent each year results in an average annual growth of 30 percent on the initial investment.

Now look at the tenth year. Here you see that the average annual growth is 52 percent each year on the initial investment.

To further illustrate the significance of my last statement, let me ask you a question. Which would be more meaningful to you: 52 percent growth on *all* of your current investment dollars for the next 12 months, or 52 percent growth *on those same dollars* for each and every year for the next 10 years? Of course, you would prefer that growth rate over 10 years. Trying to achieve 52 percent growth on any investment in any one year is extremely difficult, if not impossible. This is like hitting a home run.

Because I believe so strongly in the powerful effect compounded growth can have on people's lives, I find myself talking about it all the time. But whenever I make the statement to people about 52 percent annual growth on your current investment—for each and every year over the next 10 years—you know what happens? Almost everyone gives me a blank stare, shakes their head, and tells me they just do not see it the same way I do.

To help you further understand, let us take a moment to look at how 20 percent annualized compounding works from another vantage point. Please turn to the group of Annualized Growth Tables, shown in Figure 4-3. Let us review this page by first looking at the second table, the 10-year period. In this table, each line represents one year. On each line we show the amount of the original investment of $100,000 taken from the 20 percent Annualized Compounded Growth Table in Figure 4-2.

Since I said that 20 percent compounding over 10 years gives a 52 percent growth for each and every year on the original investment, I ask you, what is the result of a 52 percent growth on $100,000? The answer is $52,000. Therefore, you see $52,000 for each and every year on the table in the average annual growth column.

Finally, we add up the average annual growth figures for each of the 10 years. The total is $520,000. We then add in the amount of the original initial investment—in this case, $100,000—and arrive at an overall total of $620,000.

Now once again look at Figure 4-2. This table illustrates—year by year, step by step—how an initial investment of $100,000 grew each year

FIGURE 4-3

Annualized Growth Tables

5 Year

Year	Original Investment		Average Annual Growth of 30%
1	$100,000	=	$30,000
2	$100,000	=	$30,000
3	$100,000	=	$30,000
4	$100,000	=	$30,000
5	$100,000	=	$30,000

Total Annual Growth = $150,000
Original Investment = $100,000
TOTAL = $250,000

10 Year

Year	Original Investment		Average Annual Growth of 52%
1	$100,000	=	$52,000
2	$100,000	=	$52,000
3	$100,000	=	$52,000
4	$100,000	=	$52,000
5	$100,000	=	$52,000
6	$100,000	=	$52,000
7	$100,000	=	$52,000
8	$100,000	=	$52,000
9	$100,000	=	$52,000
10	$100,000	=	$52,000

Total Annual Growth = $520,000
Original Investment = $100,000
TOTAL = $620,000

15 Year

Year	Original Investment		Average Annual Growth of 96%
1	$100,000	=	$96,000
2	$100,000	=	$96,000
3	$100,000	=	$96,000
4	$100,000	=	$96,000
5	$100,000	=	$96,000
6	$100,000	=	$96,000
7	$100,000	=	$96,000
8	$100,000	=	$96,000
9	$100,000	=	$96,000
10	$100,000	=	$96,000
11	$100,000	=	$96,000
12	$100,000	=	$96,000
13	$100,000	=	$96,000
14	$100,000	=	$96,000
15	$100,000	=	$96,000

Total Annual Growth = $1,440,000
Original Investment = $100,000
TOTAL = $1,540,000

20 Year

Year	Original Investment		Average Annual Growth of 187%
1	$100,000	=	$187,000
2	$100,000	=	$187,000
3	$100,000	=	$187,000
4	$100,000	=	$187,000
5	$100,000	=	$187,000
6	$100,000	=	$187,000
7	$100,000	=	$187,000
8	$100,000	=	$187,000
9	$100,000	=	$187,000
10	$100,000	=	$187,000
11	$100,000	=	$187,000
12	$100,000	=	$187,000
13	$100,000	=	$187,000
14	$100,000	=	$187,000
15	$100,000	=	$187,000
16	$100,000	=	$187,000
17	$100,000	=	$187,000
18	$100,000	=	$187,000
19	$100,000	=	$187,000
20	$100,000	=	$187,000

Total Annual Growth = $3,740,000
Original Investment = $100,000
TOTAL = $3,840,000

25 Year

Year	Original Investment		Average Annual Growth of 378%
1	$100,000	=	$378,000
2	$100,000	=	$378,000
3	$100,000	=	$378,000
4	$100,000	=	$378,000
5	$100,000	=	$378,000
6	$100,000	=	$378,000
7	$100,000	=	$378,000
8	$100,000	=	$378,000
9	$100,000	=	$378,000
10	$100,000	=	$378,000
11	$100,000	=	$378,000
12	$100,000	=	$378,000
13	$100,000	=	$378,000
14	$100,000	=	$378,000
15	$100,000	=	$378,000
16	$100,000	=	$378,000
17	$100,000	=	$378,000
18	$100,000	=	$378,000
19	$100,000	=	$378,000
20	$100,000	=	$378,000
21	$100,000	=	$378,000
22	$100,000	=	$378,000
23	$100,000	=	$378,000
24	$100,000	=	$378,000
25	$100,000	=	$378,000

Total Annual Growth = $9,450,000
Original Investment = $100,000
TOTAL = $9,550,000

Compounding has the power to convert trifling amounts of money into enormous sums.

In order to realize the maximum benefits of compounding —
IT TAKES TIME.

by 20 percent and eventually attained a value of $620,000 at the end of 10 years. This is the same figure shown on the table in Figure 4-3.

Does this not prove, therefore, that 20 percent annualized compounded growth over 10 years yields the equivalent of a 52 percent growth each and every year on the original investment? To truly understand the power and benefits of compounding, it is very important that you are able to answer "yes" to this question.

Now let me ask you another question. If you truly believed that you could get a 52 percent growth each and every year for the next 10 years on all of the investment dollars that you put to work today, how much money would you commit? Think about your answer to that question for awhile!

With the tremendous power of compounded growth, who needs to run unnecessary risks? If you can achieve a 52 percent gain per year for 10 straight years, isn't that the same as hitting 10 home runs? Sure it is. Do not try to reinvent the wheel. Instead, go about making money the easy way. Allow the miraculous power of compounding growth to do the work for you. Doesn't that make sense?

It is my hope that you now will see how compounding has the power to convert trifling amounts of money into enormous sums. Look at Figure 4-2 again, and you will see that everyone can become a self-made millionaire in just 13 years with an original investment of $100,000 achieving 20 percent annualized compounded growth.

For further proof of the power of 20 percent compounding, look again at Figure 4-3. There you see that the growth each and every year on any original investment works out to be 96 percent with 20 percent compounding. On the 25-year table, it works out to be 378 percent growth each and every year on the original investment.

This is what makes it possible for an IRA started at age 40, adding $2,000 each year and achieving 20 percent compounded growth annually for 25 years, to result in the investment growing to over $1,000,000 at retirement. Refer again to Figure 2-1 in Part 1.

And remember, $2,000 a year over a 25-year period adds up to *only* $50,000. Once again we see that compounding has the power to convert trifling amounts of money into enormous sums.

INTELLECTUAL VERSUS EMOTIONAL ACCEPTANCE

During my many years in the investment arena, I have always been more people-oriented than investment-oriented. I do not know how to predict the market . . . nor does anyone else. However, it is really easy to predict the behavior of people because we all do the same things for the same reasons. Therefore, as a student of people, there is something we must discuss at this point.

Without a doubt, we respond differently when we accept a new concept intellectually and when we accept that same concept emotionally. Here is a case in point. With the mathematical evidence we have walked through regarding 20 percent annualized compounded growth, intellectually you can accept the growth results that you see because they are mathematically correct. However, having worked one-on-one with many individual investors over the years, I know that if someone accepts the power of compounding only on an intellectual level, it will not serve to motivate them to commit all of their investment dollars to strive to reach the Fabian Investment Goal.

My objective, then, is to get you to accept the results of compounding *emotionally.* We only respond to an idea emotionally when we can personally relate it to our daily lives. So when we are first exposed to the idea of actually achieving 20 percent compounded growth, we hesitate because, emotionally, we cannot relate to this on a day-by-day basis. I understand the dilemma. I have dealt with it many times in the past.

To overcome this dilemma, what I must do is reduce the 20 percent annual growth into smaller increments. How about monthly? To do this, we divide 20 percent by 12 months. This gives us an average of 1.67 percent per month. So now, instead of concerning ourselves with working for 20 percent each and every year, take the pressure off and strive instead for just an average of 1.67 percent growth per month. Usually the first thought that crosses people's minds when they hear that we are striving to get 20 percent annualized compounded growth using mutual funds is that this can only be accomplished by investing each year in the top four or five highest-performing mutual funds. In reality, nothing could be further from the truth. For instance, in the eight-year period, 1990 through 1998, each and every year there were hundreds of individual mutual funds that produced gains higher than 20 percent per year. Go to the library and verify for yourself that this is true. At the library ask to see the year-end edition of *Barron's,* the *Wall Street Journal,* or *USA Today.* A quick glance through the mutual funds listings will confirm that what I have just said is in fact true.

Even more important, you can verify for yourself *today* that there are many mutual funds right now that are on target to attain our goal. Let us assume, for purposes of an example, that on May 30 of any year (you can do this at any time, regardless of the date), you want to see for yourself just how many individual mutual funds are on target to reach our goal. Since the date is May 30, that means five months of the current year have elapsed. By multiplying 5 by the average monthly growth rate of 1.67 percent, the result is 8.35 percent. Next, look at the mutual fund listing in any daily newspaper that includes the year-to-date growth percentage for each mutual fund. Personally, I find the mutual fund listing in *USA Today* to be one of the easiest to read. Just go down each column of fund names, and check off those that have a year-to-date performance of 8.35 percent or more. These are the mutual funds that are currently on target to reach the goal for the current year. After you have seen for yourself the large number of mutual funds which are currently on target, you will then begin to relate emotionally to the idea that 20 percent annualized compounded growth is a realistic and achievable goal. (Also look at random on other dates in prior years.)

With the thousands of mutual funds that are available, with the ease with which they can be traded, and with the simplicity of our trend-following plan to move you into and out of the market (described in Part 4), the ability to aim for the goal we describe is there for everyone to pursue.

Let me ask you again: Do you agree that by attaining 20 percent compounded growth using only your own individual investment portfolio it is possible for everyone to become a self-made millionaire? For instance, how about a white-collar worker who is in middle management of a large corporation? Does she not probably believe that unless she becomes president of the company, there is no way for her to become wealthy? Now we all know that is not true.

Or how about a blue-collar worker. He knows he will never be president of the company he is working for and therefore believes he does not have any chance of becoming wealthy. Again, that is not so. All he has to do is become fully invested and work to attain 20 percent annualized compounded growth.

And how about all of the employees in the secretarial pools of large corporations? The majority of them believe it is absolutely not within their power to become wealthy unassisted. But again, all of us now know this is not true.

FORMULA FOR WEALTH

Before we leave the 20 percent Annualized Compounded Growth Table (Figure 4-2), let us review the formula to attain wealth:

$$\text{Compounding} + \text{Time} + \text{Money} = \text{Wealth}$$

I know that most people feel that the most important component in the formula is money. However, that is not true. In reality, the most important ingredient is time. Sure, compounding is important, but it takes *time* to get the maximum benefits from compounding. Let me share with you why time is more important than money. Refer to the Mary and John scenario at the bottom of Figure 4-4.

At the top of the figure, there is a table that shows the amount of money needed to be saved and invested each year at different ages, in order to grow to $1 million with 20 percent annualized compounded growth. If you want to get the younger members of your family excited about the potential gains of compounding, show them that starting at age 25 and only saving and investing $113 each year (until age 65) and attaining the Fabian Investment Goal, their investment account would grow to $1,000,000.

Over the years I have always stressed the importance of compounded growth. In fact, in the June 1986 issue of the *Fabian Newsletter* I made this statement: "One of my objectives is to make all of my readers so keenly aware of the tremendous power of compounded growth that any time in their lives, they consciously know that if they do not have compounding working for them, they will feel cheated." My reasoning is this: If you wake up each morning and feel you are being cheated because you do not have compounding working for you, sooner or later you will do something about it.

Once again, compounding is the cornerstone . . . the very essence . . . that makes it possible for everyone to become wealthy and, if given enough time, to become a self-made millionaire. With the potential rewards that compounding can produce, isn't it unrealistic not to have compounding working for you every day of your life? Isn't it also unrealistic when you have this tremendous power available to only invest a small portion of your potential investment dollars to help you accumulate wealth and therefore enhance your quality of life?

Whenever I look at a 20 percent compounded growth table, I am reminded of something that a speaker said at a motivational seminar I attended some years ago. The speaker suggested that everyone find an inspirational saying and tape it to his or her bathroom mirror so that each morning it would be seen and would help to get one's day off to a good start. I recommend you do the same. For your inspiration, make a copy of the 20 percent compounded growth table and put it up where you will see it daily. In this way, you can remind yourself of the growth that can be

FIGURE 4-4

Yearly Savings To Accumulate $1 Million By Age 65 With 20% Compounded Growth.

**Yearly Investment
To Reach Goal of
$1,000,000
With 20% Compounded Growth**

Age Now		
25	$	113
30		283
35		705
40		1,766
45		4,464
50		11,568
55		32,102
60		111,983
65		1,000,000

Mary -Age 40

Contributed $2,000 to her IRA for 5 years.
After 5 years the value of her IRA is $17,800 compounding at 20%.
She stops contributing to her IRA and lets it continue to compound at 20%.
After 20 years, at the age of 65, her IRA Value is $684,710.
Her principal investment is $10,000.

John – Age 45

Contributed $2,000 to his IRA.
Compounding at 20%, until he reaches the age of 65.
When he reaches the age of 65, his IRA value is $448,051.
His principal investment is $40,000.

yours in the future (the language of the subconscious). This is also the positive input your "success mechanism" needs to help you stay on target for your financial goals.

THE IMPORTANCE OF ACCUMULATING WEALTH

As a result of what has been said so far, it is my hope that everybody will set their goal at 20 percent compounded growth. Then, after doing that, they will search for an investment they can live with over the long term and thereby maximize the power of compounded growth.

I say this because the vast majority of the population is so busy striving to get ahead and working to make enough money to sustain their ongoing lifestyle, they have not bothered to set the required financial goals that could enable them to become wealthy. They are so engrossed in working day to day that they give little time or thought to effectively putting money to work. Why does this happen? It is because people do not believe putting money to work is as beneficial to them as the daily work they perform on the job. In fact, many may argue that they would not want to risk interfering with their daily obligations to spend time trying to become a money speculator.

Further, they believe it is impossible for them, today, to get returns on money greater than 6 percent or 8 percent. This is obvious because there are trillions of dollars in CDs and savings passbook accounts. Over and over again we see evidence that our behavior is based on what we believe, and it makes no difference whether or not what we believe is true.

OUR SELF-IMAGE

Here is another idea from *Psycho-Cybernetics* that pertains directly to what we believe about ourselves and gives us the opportunity to see how we form our self-image. Beliefs about ourselves have been unconsciously formed from our past experience, our successes and failures, our humiliations, our triumphs, and the way others have reacted to us. From all of this we mentally construct a self—that is, a picture of ourselves. Once an idea or belief goes into this picture, it becomes true, as far as we are personally concerned. We do not question its validity but proceed to act upon it just as if it were true. In short, we will always act like the sort of person we conceive ourselves to be.

The principles outlined in *Psycho-Cybernetics* are not just theory; they are reality. Thus, you can see how important it is for you to become a

believer in the ability to accumulate wealth—in fact, to begin to see yourself as a wealthy person. Once you believe something is possible, you have
taken the first step to making it happen.

DEVELOP A FINANCIAL LIFESTYLE

If you stop and think about how you spend your time each day, you will
quickly realize that the biggest portion of your time—as well as most of
your mental and physical energy—goes into making a living. Just surviving is expensive. You have to buy food, clothing, and shelter.

Clearly, the biggest part of your day is spent in the pursuit of money.
Any way you look at it, you've got to make a living. You work, you earn,
you pay. Most likely what you earn is not usually enough. Most people just
survive. But perhaps you've decided to get ahead, to break away from the
herd. You've decided there is something better for you and your family.
Because you're not lazy, you may have taken a second job, maybe even a
third. But is this really the answer? It may provide a temporary fix, but face
it, there is only one of you. You only have two hands. You only have so
much mental and physical energy for the day, and as hard as you try, it still
may not be enough to set you financially free.

If working harder isn't the answer, what is? The answer is working
smarter. Remember what George Clason said in his book *The Richest Man
in Babylon?* Here it is again:

> *Every gold piece you save is a slave to work for you. Every copper it
> earns is its child that also can earn for you.*

Working smarter is putting the power of compounding to work for
you. Follow the advice from *The Richest Man in Babylon,* where it is recommended that everyone save at least one tenth of what they earn. Put this
money to work, earning and growing for you. And then put the earnings to
work for you too. If you truly want to become wealthy, then pay yourself
first—before you pay anybody else. Each month, when you sit down with
your checkbook and face a pile of bills, make a point of paying yourself
first—a full 10 percent of your earnings, or more if you can. This is easier
to do than you think. And it's fun! After all, who is more important than
you and your family?

I am talking about developing a financial lifestyle. In the morning you
rise, shower, dress, eat breakfast, and go to work. Just add one more item to

your routine—think about your financial future. Simply concentrate on the wealth you expect to attain (the language of the subconscious), and pay yourself one tenth of what you earn. No big deal. You'd be surprised how readily you can adjust to living on 90 percent of your earnings. You've probably heard how many people of various faiths give 10 percent to their church.

When you consider how much time and effort you put into the pursuit of money, it makes sense to give it the importance and priority it deserves. One thing is for sure: It makes no sense to work hard all day, all week, all year long, and have nothing to show for it. Remember that your entire life can be outstanding or mediocre to the extent that you have money to pay for necessities and luxuries. Your finances affect virtually every aspect of your life. Obviously, then, it makes good sense to get your financial affairs in order.

BECOME A FINANCIAL ARCHITECT-BUILDER AND CREATE THE WEALTH YOU DESIRE

Thus far, you have seen only a few examples of the tremendous sums of money you can accumulate by attaining my investment goal. Although one or more of these scenarios may be applicable, none has been tailored specifically for you. In the pages that follow, you will find data tables and worksheets designed specifically to help you create your personal Blueprint for Wealth.

Think of yourself as a financial architect-builder, following your personal Blueprint for Wealth. Just as any architect refers to standard data tables for building requirements, so will you refer to the 20 percent compounded growth data tables for your personal wealth requirements. These tables will help you determine how much wealth you can build into your future, year by year, up to 30 years. To compute beyond 30 years, remember that your money doubles every 4 years at 20 percent compounded annually. Be sure that your blueprint goal is at least $300,000, in liquid cash, the amount we have established as the minimum goal to attain by age 65 or at retirement.

All the data tables—lump sum, monthly, and yearly—are based on the investment goal of 20 percent annualized compounded long-term growth. This is the investment goal you will use to work for your personal Blueprint for Wealth, for the rest of your life.

The Compounded Growth Data Table, shown in Figure 4-5, is based on lump-sum contributions and shows the future values from 1 through 30 years at the 20 percent annualized rate. Note that the table is constructed so that the number of years appears in a vertical column at the left. Note also that the various lump-sum amounts appear as headings, from $1,000 to $100,000, in a horizontal line at the top.

Let us see how it works. By selecting a specific lump sum such as $1,000 (top left), you can determine its future value from 1 to 30 years by simply moving down the column. Note that an original $1,000 investment grows to $2,488 in 5 years. Continuing down the column, you can see how this same $1,000 increases to $6,192 in 10 years and to $15,407 in 15 years. See if you can find the future values of a lump-sum investment of $20,000 for 13 and 19 years. You'll need to find the $20,000 heading and move down the column to the thirteenth and nineteenth lines. The answers are $213,986 and $638,960, respectively. Now consider how much investment money you currently have available, and check its potential value for any future date. Once you realize what is possible with long-term compounding, do not be surprised if you suddenly find more money to put to work for your future wealth. Building wealth is exciting!

The Compounded Growth Data Table in Figure 4-6 is based on yearly contributions and shows the future values from 1 through 30 years at the 20 percent annualized rate. Note that the table is constructed so that the number of years appears in a vertical column at the left. Note also that the yearly contribution amounts appear as headings, from $500 to $25,000, in a horizontal line at the top.

For example, let's say you have decided to place $2,000 per year in your Roth IRA and your current age is 40. Now check the table to see what the value of your IRA account will be in 21 years, when you have reached age 61 and intend to retire. Locate the $2,000 heading on the top line and move down the column until you reach the twenty-first year. The future value is $540,061. If you stop making contributions after age 61 and just let your investment compound at the 20 percent rate, your Roth IRA will double in four more years, making you a millionaire at age 65 with tax-free withdrawals available.

Now see how much money you can accumulate when you contribute $3,000 per year and it compounds at the 20 percent annualized rate. Find the $3,000 heading, then move down the column to see the future values in 15 and 20 years. The results are $259,326 and $672,077, respectively. Now check the future value of a $10,000 yearly contribution after 15 years. The result is $864,421.

FIGURE 4 - 5

Lump Sum 20% Compounded-Growth Data Table

Year	$1,000	$2,000	$5,000	$10,000	$20,000	$30,000	$40,000	$50,000	$100,000
1	1,200	2,400	6,000	12,000	24,000	36,000	48,000	60,000	120,000
2	1,440	2,880	7,200	14,400	28,800	43,200	57,600	72,000	144,000
3	1,728	3,456	8,640	17,280	34,560	51,840	69,120	86,400	172,800
4	2,074	4,147	10,368	20,736	41,472	62,208	82,944	103,680	207,360
5	2,488	4,977	12,442	24,883	49,766	74,650	99,533	124,416	248,832
6	2,986	5,972	14,930	29,860	59,720	89,580	119,439	149,299	298,598
7	3,583	7,166	17,916	35,832	71,644	107,495	143,327	179,159	358,318
8	4,300	8,600	21,499	42,998	85,996	128,995	171,993	214,991	429,982
9	5,160	10,320	25,799	51,598	103,196	154,793	206,391	257,989	515,978
10	6,192	12,383	30,959	61,917	123,835	185,752	247,669	309,587	619,174
11	7,430	14,860	37,150	74,301	148,602	222,903	297,203	371,504	743,008
12	8,916	17,832	44,581	89,161	178,322	267,483	356,644	445,805	891,610
13	10,699	21,399	53,497	106,993	213,986	320,980	427,973	534,966	1,069,932
14	12,839	25,678	64,196	128,392	256,784	385,176	513,567	641,959	1,283,918
15	15,407	30,814	77,035	154,070	308,140	462,211	616,281	770,351	1,540,702
16	18,488	36,977	92,442	184,884	369,769	554,653	739,537	924,421	1,848,843
17	22,186	44,372	110,931	221,861	443,722	665,583	887,444	1,109,306	2,218,611
18	26,623	53,247	133,117	266,233	532,467	798,700	1,064,933	1,331,167	2,662,333
19	31,948	63,896	159,740	319,480	638,960	958,440	1,277,920	1,597,400	3,194,800
20	38,338	76,675	191,688	383,376	766,752	1,150,128	1,533,504	1,916,880	3,833,760
21	46,005	92,010	230,026	460,051	920,102	1,380,154	1,840,205	2,300,256	4,600,512
22	55,206	110,412	276,031	552,061	1,104,123	1,656,184	2,208,246	2,760,307	5,520,614
23	66,247	132,495	331,237	662,474	1,324,947	1,987,421	2,649,895	3,312,369	6,624,737
24	79,497	158,994	397,484	794,968	1,589,937	2,384,905	3,179,874	3,974,842	7,949,685
25	95,396	190,792	476,981	953,962	1,907,924	2,861,886	3,815,849	4,769,811	9,539,622
26	114,475	228,951	572,377	1,144,755	2,289,509	3,434,264	4,579,018	5,723,773	11,447,546
27	137,371	274,741	686,853	1,373,706	2,747,411	4,121,117	5,494,822	6,868,528	13,737,055
28	164,845	329,689	824,223	1,648,447	3,296,893	4,945,340	6,593,786	8,242,233	16,484,466
29	197,814	395,627	989,068	1,978,136	3,956,272	5,934,408	7,912,544	9,890,680	19,781,359
30	237,376	474,753	1,186,882	2,373,763	4,747,526	7,121,289	9,495,053	11,868,816	23,737,631

Yearly Contribution 20% Compounded-Growth Data Table

Year	$500	$1,000	$2,000	$3,000	$4,000	$5,000	$10,000	$15,000	$25,000
1	600	1,200	2,400	3,600	4,800	6,000	12,000	18,000	30,000
2	1,320	2,640	5,280	7,920	10,560	13,200	26,400	39,600	66,000
3	2,184	4,368	8,736	13,104	17,472	21,840	43,680	65,520	109,200
4	3,221	6,442	12,883	19,325	25,766	32,208	64,416	96,624	161,040
5	4,465	8,930	17,860	26,790	35,720	44,650	89,299	133,949	223,248
6	5,958	11,916	23,832	35,748	47,664	59,580	119,159	178,739	297,898
7	7,750	15,499	30,998	46,497	61,996	77,495	154,991	232,486	387,477
8	9,899	19,799	39,598	59,397	79,196	98,995	197,989	296,984	494,973
9	12,479	24,959	49,917	74,876	99,835	124,793	249,587	374,380	623,967
10	15,575	31,150	62,301	93,451	124,602	155,752	311,504	467,256	778,760
11	19,290	38,581	77,161	115,742	154,322	192,903	385,805	578,708	964,513
12	23,748	47,497	94,993	142,490	189,986	237,483	474,966	712,449	1,187,415
13	29,098	58,196	116,392	174,588	232,784	290,980	581,959	872,939	1,454,898
14	35,518	71,035	142,070	213,105	284,140	355,176	710,351	1,065,527	1,775,878
15	43,221	86,442	172,884	259,326	345,769	432,211	864,421	1,296,632	2,161,053
16	52,465	104,931	209,861	314,792	419,722	524,653	1,049,306	1,573,958	2,623,264
17	63,558	127,117	254,233	381,350	508,467	635,583	1,271,167	1,906,750	3,177,917
18	76,870	153,740	307,480	461,220	614,960	768,700	1,537,400	2,306,100	3,843,500
19	92,844	185,688	371,376	557,064	742,752	928,440	1,856,880	2,785,320	4,642,200
20	112,013	224,026	448,051	672,077	896,102	1,120,128	2,240,256	3,360,384	5,600,640
21	135,015	270,031	540,061	810,092	1,080,123	1,350,154	2,700,307	4,050,461	6,750,768
22	162,618	325,237	650,474	975,711	1,300,947	1,626,184	3,252,369	4,878,553	8,130,922
23	195,742	391,484	782,968	1,174,453	1,565,937	1,957,421	3,914,842	5,872,264	9,787,106
24	235,491	470,981	941,962	1,412,943	1,883,924	2,354,905	4,709,811	7,064,716	11,774,527
25	283,189	566,377	1,132,755	1,699,132	2,265,509	2,831,886	5,663,773	8,495,659	14,159,432
26	340,426	680,853	1,361,706	2,042,558	2,723,411	3,404,264	6,808,528	10,212,791	17,021,319
27	409,112	818,223	1,636,447	2,454,670	3,272,893	4,091,117	8,182,233	12,273,350	20,455,583
28	491,534	983,068	1,966,136	2,949,204	3,932,272	4,915,340	9,830,680	14,746,020	24,576,699
29	590,441	1,180,882	2,361,763	3,542,645	4,723,526	5,904,408	11,808,816	17,713,224	29,522,039
30	709,129	1,418,258	2,836,516	4,254,774	5,673,032	7,091,289	14,182,579	21,273,868	35,456,447

Accumulating wealth is not difficult once you have a goal and a blueprint. By setting aside a portion of your earnings and working toward my investment goal, you can expect to convert even small sums of money into enormous sums in the years ahead.

The Compounded Growth Data Table shown in Figure 4-7 is based on monthly contributions and shows the future values from 1 through 30 years at the 20 percent annualized rate. Note that the table is constructed so that the number of years appears in a vertical column at the left. Note also that the monthly contribution amounts appear as headings, from $25 to $2,000 in a horizontal line at the top.

Let's look at a few examples. Check the value of a $425 monthly contribution after 17 years. For this exercise, you'll have to check two columns—$25 and $400—and add the future values from each. In 17 years, a monthly contribution of $25 grows to $35,124. In the same period, a monthly contribution of $400 grows to $461,978. All together, we see that a $425 monthly contribution grows to $597,102 in 17 years.

Take a few moments now to consider how much you can contribute monthly. Remember, even trifling amounts, when set aside regularly, can grow into enormous sums at the 20 percent annualized compounded growth rate. Make a commitment to set aside a regular portion of your monthly earnings for your future wealth, and you will be rewarded handsomely in the years to come.

BLUEPRINT FOR WEALTH

You are now ready to draw up your personal Blueprint for Wealth. Use the blank certificate provided in Figure 4-8, and refer to the 20 percent compounded growth data tables for the future values. Consider how much serious money you have in a lump sum that you can contribute now. Also consider how much you can contribute monthly and/or yearly. Be generous. After all, you are paying yourself. Finally, determine how many years you will be making these contributions to your future desired wealth.

On your certificate, write the future values for your lump-sum, yearly, and monthly contributions, and add them up. The total is your desired future wealth. Make sure this total is at least $300,000 (the amount we have established as the minimum goal to attain by age 65, or at retirement). If you wish, you can project your desired wealth for one or more future dates, such as 5, 10, 15, 20 years, or more. Follow the same procedure for each period. If your contributions change in the years to come,

FIGURE 4-7

Monthly Contribution 20% Compounded-Growth Data Table

Year	$25	$50	$100	$200	$300	$400	$500	$1,000	$2,000
1	332	663	1,326	2,653	3,979	5,306	6,632	13,264	26,528
2	730	1,459	2,918	5,836	8,754	11,672	14,590	29,180	58,360
3	1,207	2,414	4,828	9,656	14,484	19,312	24,140	48,280	96,560
4	1,780	3,560	7,120	14,240	21,360	28,480	35,600	71,199	142,398
5	**2,468**	**4,935**	**9,870**	**19,740**	**29,611**	**39,481**	**49,351**	**98,702**	**197,405**
6	3,293	6,585	13,171	26,341	39,512	52,682	65,853	131,706	263,412
7	4,283	8,566	17,131	34,262	51,393	68,524	85,655	171,310	342,620
8	5,471	10,942	21,883	43,767	65,650	87,534	109,417	218,835	437,669
9	6,897	13,793	27,586	55,173	82,759	110,346	137,932	275,864	551,728
10	**8,607**	**17,215**	**34,430**	**68,860**	**103,290**	**137,719**	**172,149**	**344,299**	**688,597**
11	10,660	21,321	42,642	85,284	127,926	170,568	213,210	426,420	852,840
12	13,124	26,248	52,496	104,993	157,489	209,986	262,482	524,965	1,049,929
13	16,080	32,161	64,322	128,644	192,965	257,287	321,609	643,218	1,286,436
14	19,628	39,256	78,512	157,024	235,536	314,048	392,560	785,121	1,570,242
15	**23,885**	**47,770**	**95,540**	**191,081**	**286,621**	**382,161**	**477,702**	**955,404**	**1,910,807**
16	28,994	57,987	115,974	231,948	347,923	463,897	579,871	1,159,742	2,319,483
17	35,124	70,247	140,495	280,989	421,484	561,978	702,473	1,404,946	2,809,892
18	42,480	84,959	169,919	339,838	509,757	679,676	849,595	1,699,190	3,398,379
19	51,307	102,614	205,228	410,456	615,684	820,912	1,026,140	2,052,280	4,104,560
20	**61,900**	**123,799**	**247,599**	**495,197**	**742,796**	**990,394**	**1,237,993**	**2,475,986**	**4,951,972**
21	74,611	149,222	298,443	596,886	895,329	1,193,772	1,492,215	2,984,431	5,968,861
22	89,864	179,728	359,456	718,912	1,078,368	1,437,824	1,797,280	3,594,561	7,189,121
23	108,168	216,336	432,671	865,343	1,298,014	1,730,685	2,163,356	4,326,713	8,653,425
24	130,132	260,264	520,529	1,041,058	1,561,587	2,082,116	2,602,645	5,205,290	10,410,580
25	**156,489**	**312,979**	**625,958**	**1,251,915**	**1,877,873**	**2,503,831**	**3,129,788**	**6,259,577**	**12,519,154**
26	188,118	376,236	752,471	1,504,943	2,257,414	3,009,886	3,762,357	7,524,714	15,049,429
27	226,072	452,144	904,287	1,808,574	2,712,861	3,617,148	4,521,435	9,042,871	18,085,742
28	271,616	543,232	1,086,465	2,172,930	3,259,395	4,345,859	5,432,324	10,864,648	21,729,297
29	326,269	652,538	1,305,077	2,610,154	3,915,231	5,220,308	6,525,385	13,050,769	26,101,539
30	**391,852**	**783,705**	**1,567,410**	**3,134,820**	**4,702,230**	**6,269,640**	**7,837,050**	**15,674,100**	**31,348,200**

FIGURE 4-8

**Blueprint for Wealth
Certificate**

Personal Blueprint for Wealth for: _____

Lump Sum Available: _____

Yearly Contribution:_____

Monthly Contribution: _____

Number of Years Contributing: _____

Refer to the 20% Compounded-Growth Data Tables and locate your specific contributions for the number of years you'll be investing. Write these future values below and add them together to obtain your desired future wealth.

(add)

Lump Sum Future Value: _____

Yearly Contribution Future Value: + _____

Monthly Contribution Future Value: + _____

Amount of Future Wealth in _____ Years: $ _____

Beginning Date:_____   Future Date:_____

Display your Personal Blueprint for Wealth in a prominent place so that you will see it daily. Concentrate on the wealth that is coming to you; this is the language of the subconscious, providing positive input for your "success mechanism" which will steadily guide you to the attainment of your financial goal.

simply take your accumulated wealth at the time of the change and make this your new lump sum; then, draw up a new blueprint based on your new contributions.

Drawing up your personal Blueprint for Wealth is as exciting as it is practical. You'll be surprised and delighted with the results you can achieve when you have a goal and work to attain it. The 20 percent Compounded Growth Table (Figure 4-2) is your financial roadmap. As you proceed on the road to riches, you'll have evidence of your progress, and this will prove to be very rewarding indeed.

Resolve now to make compounded growth the cornerstone of your new financial lifestyle. There is no better time to start than today. Do not be surprised if suddenly your life improves dramatically. Knowing that you have a goal and a plan for a financially secure future will lift a great burden from your shoulders, bring you peace of mind, and allow you to more fully enjoy your life right now. Once again, that's the power of compounding!

> *"Start thy purse to fattening."*
>
> —*George Clason, from* The Richest Man in Babylon

CHAPTER 5

Creating Spendable Income

All through our discussions thus far, the aim has been to accumulate wealth in order to enhance your future quality of life. Underneath all of this, however, is the idea that one day you are going to spend part of the money you have accumulated. You will need spendable income.

Talking about spending the money at retirement is a lot of fun. It also is very important because today we all are living longer, staying healthier, and may live as much as one third of our lives in retirement. Are you aware that the fastest-growing age group in America today are people attaining the age of 85? This could result in a lot of people long on life but short on money.

The Spendable Income Table, Figure 5-1, shows a hypothetical example of how the spendable income plan might work. Keep in mind that this is a hypothetical example. The results of the investment on the spendable income worksheet were based on the actual investment results attained by the *Maverick Advisor* newsletter for the years shown (second column). Also be aware that past performance is no guarantee of future results. I felt, however, that telling the story this way provides a better understanding of the concept rather than simply using made-up performance figures.

When I talk with individual investors, I recommend working for a minimum nest egg of $300,000 in liquid assets by age 65 or at retirement. Of course, I encourage much larger retirement goals, but this is the

FIGURE 5-1

A Plan to Generate Spendable Income

This table shows theoretical year-by-year results of the Spendable Income Plan. At the end of each year, 12% of the principal was withdrawn for income (far right column). Note, in this theoretical plan that, by the end of the period, the account still has a value of $486,422.

Spendable Income Plan with 12% Annual Withdrawals
$300,000 to begin

Year	Annual Gain	Value before Withdrawal	Value after 12% Withdrawal	Amount Withdrawn
Apr-Dec 77	20.07%	$360,210	$316,985	$43,225
1978	26.02%	399,464	351,529	47,936
1979	18.10%	415,155	365,337	49,819
1980	37.55%	502,520	442,218	60,302
1981	7.58%	475,738	418,650	57,089
1982	43.13%	599,213	527,308	71,906
1983	19.62%	630,765	555,073	75,692
1984	-6.79%	517,384	455,298	62,086
1985	18.97%	541,668	476,668	65,000
1986	10.49%	526,670	463,470	63,200
1987	22.91%	569,651	501,293	68,358
1988	.05%	501,543	441,358	60,185
1989	27.47%	562,599	495,087	67,512
1990	-5.05%	470,085	413,675	56,410
1991	38.02%	570,954	502,440	68,515
1992	4.08%	522,939	460,187	62,753
1993	17.16%	539,155	474,456	64,699
1994	-5.64%	447,697	393,973	53,724
1995	32.04%	520,202	457,778	62,424
1996	5.10%	481,125	423,390	57,735
1997	23.61%	523,352	460,550	62,802
1998	20.02%	552,752	486,422	66,330

Total Income Withdrawals : $1,347,701

Summary:
Starting Capital: $300,000
Ending Capital: $486,422 (62.14% Increase)
Total Withdrawals: $1,347,701

This model represents a hypothetical example. The rates of return shown above have been calculated by applying historic information provided by reputable sources. It is assumed that all dividends are reinvested. These results do not reflect the effect of taxes, management fees, and charges. Past hypothetical performance is not indicative of future earning expectations.

absolute minimum. For generating spendable income, continue using our simple trend-following plan (See Part 4), starting with an investment of at least $300,000 and taking annual income withdrawals of 12 percent of the principal at the end of each year.

Looking at Figure 5-1, you see the example started with an initial investment of $300,000. Further, you see the performance for the first period was 20.07 percent (second column). This means that at the end of the period, the $300,000 had grown to $360,210. Taking 12 percent of that figure produces $43,225, as shown in the last column, leaving a balance in the account of $316,985 after the withdrawal.

This amount is then invested for the next year where the example shows that in 1978 the performance was 26.02 percent. At the end of that year, the account had a value of $399,464. Taking 12 percent of this total works out to be $47,936. This left a balance, after the withdrawal, of $351,529 to be invested the next year. This same process continues for the remaining periods.

At the end of the last period, you see that the total amount of money that was withdrawn and used for spendable income was $1,347,701. This was four times the amount of money that the example started with. Further, it worked out that the average annual withdrawal was over $70,000.

We also see that at the end of the final year there was still $486,422 left for investing the following year. This figure is $186,422 more than the initial investment of $300,000 that the example started with in 1977. With this spendable income example, you see the formula for wealth in actual practice: Compounding + Time + Money = Wealth.

The example we just reviewed used the absolute minimum, $300,000, you should have at retirement. However, with this potential, shouldn't you strive for $400,000, $500,000, or even $600,000? With $600,000, all of the numbers in our example would double and your quality of life would be enhanced even further. After all, isn't the primary reason for investing to enhance our quality of life?

MERRILL LYNCH ANNUAL SURVEY

Before we proceed to Part 3, let's take a realistic look at the problem for accumulating wealth as reported by the media. Each year since 1993, Merrill Lynch has sponsored a yearly survey on the adequacy of baby boomers' savings rates. As you review their observations, you must keep in mind that Merrill Lynch does not believe it is possible for the majority of baby boomers to get 20 percent annualized compounded growth on their personal stock market investments. In addition, they also believe everyone should "buy and hold," "asset allocate," and "dollar cost average." In Part 3 I will show that if you follow any of these three investment styles, you will not become wealthy, let alone become a self-made millionaire.

Here are some of the results taken from their past surveys. Since the series began in 1993, the findings consistently have shown that the 76 million boomers born between 1946 and 1964 are saving roughly a third of what they'll need to retire in comfort.

They further say that households earning $60,000 to $100,000 a year are doing the best job of saving, but even they are saving only 50 percent to 60 percent of what they will need. They go on to point out that more people believe in UFOs (46 percent) than believe Social Security will exist at their retirement (20 percent). In the worst-case scenario, with Social Security eliminated, the baby boomers are saving only 12 percent of what they will eventually need.

As an observer of people, I know that telling people to make financial sacrifices in order to save more, even for a worthwhile goal, just won't cut it. It's like telling everyone who wants to lose weight, "Just eat less." It doesn't serve any meaningful purpose to recommend things to people when you know that most of them will not do it. Instead, what is needed, as far as accumulating sufficient money for retirement, is to educate them on the power of compounding and then show them a path to follow to maximize its benefits.

Before I describe the path I follow to maximize the power of compounding, I must first point out to you many of the things that you, as an investor, will encounter that will be stumbling blocks in your endeavor to become a self-made millionaire. We'll look at these in the next section.

Now, let's move on to Part 3. To become a self-made millionaire, understanding the investor is even more important than understanding the investment.

PART 3
Understanding the Investor

CHAPTER 6

Investor Observations

Here are a few "investor observations" I have collected over the years:

> "Wall Street is the only place that people ride in a Rolls Royce to get advice from someone who took the subway."
>
> "Human nature is always in conflict with successful investing."
>
> "Everyone has the brain power to make money in the stock market—not everyone has the stomach."
>
> "An investor's worst enemy is not the stock market, but oneself."
>
> "You can't control the market, but you can control your reaction to it."
>
> "There is no security in this life—there is only opportunity."
>
> "You can't win any game unless you are ready to win."
>
> "Money doesn't buy happiness, but that's not the reason so many people are poor."
>
> "Money is not important—but it is right up there with oxygen."
>
> "Turn dollars into wealth."
>
> "There's one thing money can't buy—poverty."

PART OF THE LIFE CYCLE

One day in everybody's life, usually when in their late 40s or early 50s, they wake up one morning, and while sitting on the side of the bed, they take a look down the "tunnel of life." On this particular day, they realize for the first time that they can actually see the light at the end of the tunnel. This is the day they consciously acknowledge their mortality. They know then the probabilities are high they have already lived through the first half of their life. These thoughts make them think deeply about many aspects of living. One aspect is their finances.

They mentally review their past investment successes and failures. They ask themselves: "If I continue to handle my financial affairs in the future the same as I have handled them in the past—with the same poor results—will I ever become wealthy, let alone become a millionaire?" Their answer is no.

I discussed this point several years ago in my first appearance on Louis Rukeyser's *Wall Street Week*. During the second part of his TV program, the format calls for the guest to be questioned by the four regular members of the *Wall Street Week* staff.

One of the questions asked of me, in a humorous vein, was this: "Dick, we understand you manage other people's money, but you will not accept any management client who is under 40 years of age. That seems like reverse age discrimination. Why is that?"

I responded, "My experience shows that until people are at least 40 years of age, they have not lost enough money yet." I went on to say, "Everyone goes through an investing learning curve. When young, we all simply have to try out many of the 'get rich quick' schemes that are always being offered. In addition, the young follow extremely aggressive investment strategies. Only after much money has been lost, only after many years have gone by with very little, if any, monetary gain from their financial attempts—only then are people willing to listen. Only then will they open their minds and seriously consider the benefits of a simple and conservative path to follow for their long-term future."

YOUR SERIOUS MONEY DETERMINES YOUR FUTURE WEALTH

Participating in investment seminars all over the world has been a normal function in my capacity as a newsletter writer and personal money manager. These investment conferences usually offer 40 to 50 different speakers. Keep in mind, those who attend have to make rather large personal expenditures. In addition to the cost of the conferences, they have traveling and hotel expenses. As a result, the attendees are usually people of some financial substance.

One of my side benefits of participating has been the opportunity these conferences have given me to talk with hundreds of individual investors. As a result of the things I have learned, I have formulated a portrait of the typical investment conference investor/attendee.

The typical investor is 50 years of age, has $100,000 available for investment, and anticipates retiring in 15 years. At this time in life, the investor has lived long enough to know that if he or she continues to invest in the future as in the past, and gets the same results, the outcome will be unsatisfactory. The investor's retirement years could become a financial struggle rather than a time of enjoyment. He or she therefore decides to be prudent and separates his or her money into two categories. The investor takes $20,000, which he or she is willing to risk, and calls this "investment money." (I call it "play money"). The remaining $80,000 the investor is not willing to risk. This is the investor's serious money.

It is this serious money that enables the investor to comfortably sleep at night. He or she puts the serious money in a CD at the bank or under the mattress and does not want anyone to even know he or she has it. Here is an interesting phenomenon: For many people, even if CDs were paying zero interest, they would still use them because they really are not concerned if this money grows. They are only concerned that they do not lose it.

Obviously, such people do not have confidence or a strong belief in the investment strategy that they are following with their play money. This explains why they only "invest" a small portion of all of the money they could make available. However, it is my belief, if they found a different investment path to follow in which they believed there was minimal risk *plus* had the potential to attain 20 percent annualized compounded growth, they would dip into their serious money. Our actions are based on what we believe.

Most often our typical investor subscribes to a number of financial newsletters in addition to attending many investment conferences. Through this process, the investor hopes to learn "something" from "someone" that will enable him or her to take the $20,000 and hit a home run. Of course, this seldom happens, but nevertheless the investor keeps trying. However, when all is said and done, it really doesn't matter what happens to the play money, because the investor is wise enough not to use his or her serious money in speculative games. The investor knows the importance of his or her serious money. This is the money that will impact the investor's long-term quality of life.

There is another interesting thing about this group of investors who are only working with their play money. They are also the most speculative. Think about it. Since they are only using their play money, they find it easy to take extra risks.

It is unfortunate that our typical investor is not aware that if he or she just took $80,000 of serious money and used it to work for 20 percent annualized compounded growth, his or her nest egg could grow to $1,232,000 by retirement at age 65. You see, making significant amounts of money is really very simple. All that is needed is to successfully attain, over time, the investor investment goal of 20 percent.

At age 65 the investor could conceivably withdraw up to $125,000 per year without invading his or her principal. In fact, even with such substantial withdrawals, it is possible that his or her principal could continue to grow each year to provide additional future spendable income. We discussed this concept in Chapter 4 of Part 2.

MOST INDIVIDUAL INVESTORS FAIL

You may find this statement hard to believe. In my long financial career, I have discovered that most individual investors over a 10-year period—investing in anything—make little or no money. Oh sure, they may have a good year or two, but then they usually give it all back in a subsequent bad year or two. Most investors are constantly searching for a way to hit that home run in the market—always trying to make a big gain in one year. In attempting to do this, they often put their capital at unnecessary risk. Again, most of these unsuccessful investors already know this. That is why they only use their play money. As I said above, if they could just find an investment strategy that they believed would work profitably for them over the long term, their commitment would increase.

At the workshops I present during investment conferences, after I make this statement about the number of people who fail, I always purposely wait for about five or six seconds and just look at the audience. Then I continue: "As usual, I see people in the audience who are under 40 years of age; they have their mouths and eyes open wide wondering why people would invest at all if most of them fail. At the same time, I see those in the audience who are over 40 years of age, moving their heads up and down and saying, 'My God, he's talking about me.' "

Your present age and the number of years that you have been involved in investing will determine in which of these categories you will find yourself. These same two factors will have an influence on how readily you will accept our Guiding Principles in the next chapter.

CHAPTER 7

Fabian's Guiding Principles

FABIAN AXIOMS

As I have repeated many times, I consider myself first a student of people and then a student of the market. I do not know how to predict what the market will do; however, it is easy to predict what people will do, because we all behave the same way for the same reasons.

One of the questions that has been asked of me at investment seminars during the years while I was writing my newsletter is this: "Dick, you have explained to us how the investment plan that you recommend is simple to understand and easy to follow. Therefore, isn't there a significant impact on the overall market when your thousands of subscribers receive a sell signal?"

My response to that question comes as quite a surprise to the audience. I answer, "Don't worry about it, because most of the subscribers do not sell on that day. The reason being, their emotions, plus the predictions they are hearing from others, get in the way." The important and significant point I want to make is, *knowing what to do and then actually doing it are two completely different things.*

My primary investment management objective has always been to assist individual investors to accumulate wealth from the growth of their personal investment portfolios. When they are successful, it goes a long way toward enhancing their long-term quality of life. While working to fulfill this goal for others, I am always on the lookout to identify those factors which assist people to be successful and also those factors which can be stumbling blocks on their road to success.

Based on my observations, over the past 30-plus years, I have identified many of these factors and have grouped them under a set of Axioms that I want to share with you.

AXIOM #1: SET AS YOUR INVESTMENT GOAL A SPECIFIC COMPOUNDED GROWTH RATE.

I recommend that you make your goal the same as mine. Strive to attain 20 percent annualized compounded growth on your personal investments over the long term—that is, the rest of your life.

I have always believed that setting a personal financial goal is very important. As a result, I want to be as helpful as possible to assist people in setting their goal. Therefore, years ago, early in my career, I went to the library to search out available textbooks which outlined the process for constructing long-term financial goals. After going through several books, it didn't take very long, however, to understand why people never bother to even try to set long-range financial goals.

In the real world, the procedures outlined in the textbooks are not only long and cumbersome, but they just don't work. For example, to properly project for the future, one of the questions to be answered is to predict what the rate of inflation will be 10 and 20 years from now. Most people do not recall that in the 1980s the U.S. inflation rate was 21 percent. Can you imagine anyone 10 to 20 years prior to that date predicting what the inflation rate would have been in the 1980s? Further, the textbook procedures ask you to predict what the value of your house will be when the time comes for you to retire. You are then informed that if you do not predict correctly on the questions asked, any projections you may make will be meaningless.

I have even heard of computer software programs that follow the same process as outlined in the textbooks. They ask the same predicting questions, and in addition, they even ask you to predict how long you are going to live.

I have been told that my middle name should be "Simple," because I reduce everything I recommend to a simple process. My reason is that if what is recommended is not simple, people simply will not do it.

Here is the simple process I followed in setting my own personal long-term financial goal. The process requires answering only four questions. I refer to these questions as the "4 Hows." It is important that the questions be answered in the sequence in which they are presented.

How #1—How Much Money Do You Want to Accumulate?   Many times when I am in a one-on-one discussion with an individual and I ask this question, some people answer, "All the money I can get." I tell them that is not a specific goal. For example, you would not consider going to the finest architect in the world, tell the architect to build you a house, and then leave town. When you came back, you would not expect the house to be exactly the one that you wanted. You did not design it even though it might be a great house. That is why the architect requires the client to sign off on the blueprints before beginning construction.

Getting back to my question about how much do you want to accumulate. When someone answers, "Okay, Dick, I want to accumulate $1,000,000." I say, "Great. Now we can put together a specific plan to follow to work toward reaching that goal."

How #2—How Much Time Do You Have?   Do you want to attain your goal next week? Do you want it in 5 years, 10 years, or 20 years? The path you will follow to reach your goal depends on the amount of time you have to get there.

How #3—How Much Money Do You Have Available to Work With? How much do you have now and how much more will you have over various periods of time in the future? It has always been fascinating to me how people, if they seriously think about a meaningful goal and believe they can conceivably reach it, will eventually find they have much more money to use for investments than they originally were willing to admit.

I keep reminding you we all have two kinds of money: investment money (play money) and serious money. Think about it. What if somebody stopped you on the street and asked, "How much money do you have available for investing?" Your immediate response would be the amount of play money you have invested. All of the other money you keep hidden in a CD or under the mattress, and you don't even think about. After all, that is your security blanket.

Here is the point: Eventually, I want you to feel comfortable enough to put all of your serious money to work in your long-term investment plan. It is my intention, because of the benefits of compounded growth, to get you so motivated about becoming a self-made millionaire, you will gladly put that serious money to work.

How #4—How Are You Going to Put Your Investment Money to Work?   I believe this How is the least important of the four, because it puts the cart before the horse. In fact, for many it is the only question they ask when setting goals. Most likely you are reading this book because you were looking for the answer to this fourth How.

Before we go on, think about this: What difference does it make how or where you are going to put your investment money to work if you have not decided in advance what you want it to accomplish for you?

I was riding on the Hollywood Freeway one day and saw a sign posted on a billboard in front of a small manufacturing plant. It read: "If you don't know where you're going, any road will do." Isn't this another way of saying "If you don't know what you are trying to achieve with your investment dollars, any investment will do"?

Understanding the Goal-Setting Process

With the answers to the first three Hows, answering the fourth How for anyone would be easy to me. Here is what I mean:

Suppose you tell me you want to accumulate $100,000 (How #1) in a 12-year period (How #2), with a $10,000 initial investment (How #3). Where would you invest (How #4)?

Before coming up with a specific investment, the first thing I would do is refer to a *compounded growth* table. I would use the table to determine what rate of return would be needed to get $10,000 in 12 years to grow to $100,000. The compounded growth table will show that 20 percent compounded growth over 12 years will reach your goal. (Refer to the compounding tables in Part 2.)

For the purposes of our discussion right now, do not concern yourself about where you are going to get 20 percent compound growth. We will cover that in Part 4. Just be aware that you now have the most valuable piece of investment information that you have ever had in your entire investment lifetime.

The reason I say this is because the next time someone calls you on the phone and tells you about some great investment he has for you in commodities or oil or Arabian horses, and so on, you can ask yourself this question: "Do I believe that I can get 20 percent compounded growth from that investment?" If the answer is yes, then do it—no problem. But if the answer is no, then you can say, "Sir, I'm sorry I cannot become involved in the investment you are recommending because I have a goal. I really and truly want to reach it. I cannot take your advice because I do not believe it has the potential to give me 20 percent compounded growth. Therefore, if I followed your recommendation, I would have to change my goal. I will not change my goal, and I cannot follow your recommendation."

The same response would be appropriate if someone were to suggest that you invest in municipal bonds. It makes no difference what tax bracket you are in; municipal bonds are not going to give you 20 percent compounded growth over the long term. They are just not structured to attain it. Because the interest earned on municipal bonds is free of all taxes, the interest they pay is less than what you would earn in a money fund. Therefore, anyone who puts money in municipal bonds has to have a goal other than 20 percent annualized compounded growth.

Here is a very interesting thing about goals that Dr. Maltz points out in *Psycho-Cybernetics*. He says that the instant—the millisecond—you set a meaningful goal, the very next thoughts that enter your mind are the 50 or more reasons why you will not be able to reach it. So, I suggest that you follow Dr. Maltz's approach. He says we should not blindly accept, at that particular moment, that you absolutely and positively will be able to reach your goal. Just kind of massage the idea for a couple of days in your mind. Say to yourself, *Well, maybe I can, and if I can, what will it mean to me over time?* Dr. Maltz further points out that the more you fantasize about it, the more you seriously consider it. And the more you become aware of the end results that could be yours as a result of attaining the goal, the more you are going to want it. Consequently, the more you want it—the more your mouth waters and your adrenaline runs—the higher the probabilities are that you will attain it.

Knowledge Is Power?

The Investor Protection Trust of Arlington, Virginia, commissioned a study of 1,001 investors to determine the level of their skills and habits in buying financial products. They found that the vast majority of them are "reckless, financially illiterate, and sitting ducks for investment fraud and abuse." The study goes on to say:

> *Their appalling lack of basic financial knowledge revealed by this survey calls into serious question the ability of most Americans to make the sound, informed financial decisions that would allow them to achieve their goals. Two-thirds of investors have never prepared a specific financial plan, even though having one is considered the cornerstone of wise investing. One of their conclusions was that these findings are particularly troubling because investing is no longer*

optional. The safety-net of pension plans of the past are no longer available to the younger generations.

There have been many surveys taken over the years, like the one quoted above, telling us that individual investors admit to their lack of investing knowledge. It is interesting that individuals cite their lack of investment knowledge as their reason why they are not more successful. In my opinion, however, it is not the lack of knowledge of the many facets of investing that is keeping them from being successful. What is lacking is a definable and meaningful objective or goal that is important to them and that they believe is attainable. This is the missing ingredient for success, and it ties in with the conclusions of those associated with the survey mentioned above.

Another point that I have repeated often: *Attaining your goal is what is of utmost importance; the path you follow to get there is secondary.* During discussions with hundreds of individual investors, however, many of them would say, "What is most important to me is to know that I am following the most sophisticated and clever investment strategy I can find, and the eventual financial results are secondary."

During the past three decades, while listening to many different investment strategies, I have always been searching for the answer to only one question. Since my goal right from the start has been to maximize the benefits of compounded growth, I am *not* looking for the most sophisticated or clever way to get there. The question I am continually asking is this: "What is the simplest path that I would be able to follow over the long term that offers the probability for me to reach my goal?"

Simplicity is important to maximize the benefits of compounding, because compounding only produces its miraculous benefits over time. If the path is simple, it enhances the probabilities that you will stick with the plan over the long term. To realize a high compounded return over just three or four years will not have a lasting impact on your long-term quality of life—for the rest of your life. However, realizing 20 percent compounded growth over 10 or 15 or 20 years will surely impact your long-term quality of life.

AXIOM #2: ALWAYS HAVE ALL OF YOUR AVAILABLE INVESTMENT DOLLARS WORKING

I use the examples of the extraordinary results from compounded growth as the motivating force to get people's attention and then get them to follow through with an investment plan. Human nature being what it is, after the introduction of a new concept the passage of time is required before one can accept the concept fully. For this reason, I stress compounding examples using small amounts of money. This will make it easier for readers to become comfortable with the idea.

I encourage everyone in the beginning to put to work at least a small amount of money so they can personally experience the impact of compounding on their lives. Actually seeing your own money growing at a high compounded growth rate will be the inspiration to make you a serious investor. Once that time comes, it is necessary for you to take an inventory of *all* of your available potential liquid assets. To help you to identify the many sources for these assets, use the Personal Financial Snapshot shown in Figure 7-1. The totals from this table would be a lump-sum amount that you could commit to your investment plan. In addition, determine all of the future periodic investments you would be able to make over time.

Once you are aware of the many benefits that can be yours from compounding, wouldn't it then make sense that you should have as much money as possible working for you?

What Others Do

When you talk with people about investing, you find out that everyone falls into one of three categories. First are those who are not invested at all. They hear about and read about all of the excitement in the investment world. These people are inundated with advice from all sources telling them that they have to become responsible for their own retirement. (Remember the statistic from Chapter 5 that said more people believe in the existence of flying saucers than believe that Social Security will be there for those who retire 30 years from now?)

These noninvestors are particularly upset if they are one of the baby boomers. They know they are out of step. They read almost every day about the billions of dollars that are being put into mutual funds by others in their generation who are actively investing for their retirement.

The next group of people are those who call themselves investors but are working with less than 20 percent of the total amount of the money that they could make available for investing. It is unfortunate, but members of this group account for the largest number of individual investors.

You may be wondering whether you are presently using a large enough percentage of all of your available investment dollars working for

FIGURE 7-1

Liquid Assets	Husband	Wife	Combined
Cash			
Savings			
Money Market & CD's			
Other			
Investments			
Stocks			
Bonds			
Mutual Funds			
Other			
Retirement Assets			
Life Insurance – Cash Value			
Annuities			
IRA's			
Retirement Plans			
Other			
Real Estate			
Residences – Current:Equity			
Undeveloped Land			
Rental Property – Current:Equity			
Other			
Other Assets			
Collectibles			
Receivables			
Partnership			
Closely Held Business			
Other			
TOTAL			
Periodic Future Investments			
Weekly			
Monthly			
Quarterly			
Annually			

long-term growth. One way to answer this question is to remind yourself of one of the critical points you learned during our detailed discussion on the power of compounding. As you'll recall, 20 percent compounded growth over a 10-year period is the same as getting 52 percent growth, each and every year, for 10 years, on your original investment. Therefore, if you truly believed you would get a growth of 52 percent each year for the next 10 years on the total amount of money that you put to work today,

how much money would you have invested? How does your answer compare with the actual amount of money you do have invested today? As I
said before, for people who invest only a small portion of their available
investment dollars, it means they believe that whatever investment they are
using with their play money, it is not appropriate for their serious money.

Also, as mentioned, the people who make up this "play money"
group are also the most speculative. They are looking to hit home runs
every 90 days. They are willing to take extra risks. Why? Because even if
they were to lose a large portion of their play money, they are not seriously
hurt. Their serious money is being hidden and is not subject to risk.

I said there were three groups of investors. The third group, to which
I belong, are those investors who commit 90 percent or more of the total
amount of money that they have available for investing. Keep in mind, this
third group is also conscious of risk—but instead of hiding the major portion of their total available investment dollars, they follow investment
strategies which they believe will protect their current nest egg.

When you think about it, whether you are an investment manager of
other people's money or whether you are managing your own money, there
are two functions you need to fulfill. The first, and most important, is not
to lose the money you already have. Then and only then do you strive to
get the money to grow.

Investing Should Be a Family Affair

A great many of the investors working for long-term growth are married.
However, taking into account the number of people who attend investment
seminars and observing those who do most of the talking, you would
almost naturally come to the conclusion that in investing, it is a man's
world. This is not so.

In fact, if the truth were known, it is the woman in the household who
carries a great deal of the influence as to how investments will be made.

It has been my experience in talking to investors that women have a
major influence in investment decisions. Usually, unless there is a level of
comfort by both parties, no decision is made. The most successful families, in the investment realm, are in harmony.

Further, in my opinion, investing couples should be sure that both are
comfortable with the investment approach they are using to fulfill their
family's long-term financial objectives. When this happens, their probability for success is greatly enhanced.

AXIOM #3: NEVER FOLLOW INVESTMENT RECOMMENDATIONS UNLESS YOU KNOW THAT THE PERSON MAKING THE RECOMMENDATION HAS HIS OR HER MONEY IN THE SAME INVESTMENTS BEING RECOMMENDED

I have always wished there was a rule requiring all financial advisors to tell listeners where they have the majority of their own money working. Also, they should be required to let listeners know whether or not they personally even have any investment money.

I am not saying that those who do not have money to invest should not be giving financial advice. However, if you knew that the person giving you advice had no investment money of his or her own, or was not using the investment he or she was recommending to you, wouldn't you view differently what the person had to say?

Well, for me, that rule is already in place. *All* of the dollars that I have are invested in mutual funds following a plan that I will be describing, in detail, in Part 4.

There have been occasions when new clients join us in our money management company. They ask me where I put my personal money. My answer is this: "If I did not put my own money in exactly the same place where I put your money, that would mean I had two plans. The truth is, I am not smart enough to have two plans; therefore, we are all invested together."

AXIOM #4: NEVER TRY TO PREDICT THE FUTURE DIRECTION OF THE MARKET

Every day at my office I watch CNBC, the TV financial news channel. All through the day you hear new predictions about what the market is going to do or not do. Even though these predictions are seldom right, no one ever seems to worry about it or recognize the predictions that were given yesterday did not come true. They just go ahead and give you another one for today, and then they will give you another one tomorrow.

For you and me, it really shouldn't matter if these predictions are usually wrong. However, a potential problem could develop if you accept one of these predictions. Doing that creates an emotional block. If you accept a particular prediction, either your own or from someone else, it can stand in your way and hold you back when the time comes for you to take some investment action.

I once participated on a TV investment panel in Chicago. As the program was coming to an end, the moderator went around the table and asked each participant what his prediction was for where the Dow Jones Industrials would close at the end of the current year. Other participants gave their predictions. When my turn came, I told the moderator that I did not know. He became annoyed and said that I must at least have an opinion. I then told him, "I cannot afford the luxury of an opinion." He did not understand what I was saying and just went on to the next person on the panel.

Having an opinion, just like making a prediction, can prove to be an expensive luxury. Whenever your opinion interferes with your ability to follow the rules of the investment plan you are following, you can pay a dear price indeed.

Instead of relying on predictions, let me tell you what I do. Believe it or not, everyday I talk to the market. In my talk, I never tell it what I want it to do, because the market does not care what I want. For those people with an open mind, the market will answer any question you ask of it. So everyday I ask, "Market, I have been invested now for quite some time and I have stayed in the market because it has been in an uptrend. Is the uptrend still in place?" If the market answers yes, I say, "Thank you, Market." And then I simply leave my investments untouched because I have all of the information I need.

I know that one day I will ask the market my usual question: "Market, I have been invested for a long time. I have made a lot of money because I have been participating in an uptrend. Is the uptrend still in place?" And one day the Market will say "No!" On that day, I will again say, "Thank you, Market." However, now I am going to move out of my invested positions, because now the uptrend line has been penetrated.

I want you to notice something that is very important. Whenever I asked the market where we were, either in an uptrend or in a downtrend, and it gave me an answer, I never asked why. They do not pay extra dollars for knowing why the market is going up or why it is going down. If it is going up and you are fully invested, you are making money. If it is going down and you are still in, you are losing money. That's really all there is to it. Therefore, you have to know when to be in and when to be out. It doesn't matter why the trend is up or why the trend is down. When the time comes to take action, you must follow through. Don't let an opinion get in your way.

To reach my goal, there is no need to predict what the market is going to do. Further, because I do not predict, I never think about interest rates, the deficit, the balance of payments, who is going to be elected president, or anything else. None of these things have anything to do with making money. There are other people, however, who believe they have to understand these things in order to make money in the market. From my perspective, they are just complicating their lives with no extra reward.

Once again: Never try to predict what the market is going to do. Remind yourself, over and over again, that you cannot afford the luxury of having an opinion.

Let me share with you an extreme example of predicting having to do with the future price of gold. A few years ago I received a copy of Howard Ruff's newsletter, *The Ruff Times,* and in it he said, without any question, gold was going to go to $3,000 an ounce. In the same week I received a copy of a newsletter from Bob Prector, who writes *The Elliott Wave Theorist.* Bob said, without question, gold was going to drop to $150 an ounce in the next year or two. So, my only reaction was *I don't have an opinion.* I was only sure of one thing. One of them was wrong. I did not know which one, but it did not matter because regardless of which way the gold market went (at that time gold was $300 an ounce), our trend line (39-week moving average) would have to be penetrated. Therefore, I knew mechanically that there was no way for gold to get from $300 to $3,000 without developing an uptrend, thereby going above the trend line. There was no way gold could go from $300 to $150 without developing a downtrend, also going through the trend line. What else do you need to know? Do not anticipate market moves. Do not feel it is important to be on board before the action takes place.

During this same time period, there was an ongoing TV commercial in which a young spokesman was advocating, "This could be the buying opportunity of a lifetime to participate in gold." Remember, he said it *could* be. It also could not be. And he said, "The majority of people wait until it gets to the top, and then they buy. So, therefore, if you buy now, you will be sure to ride it to the top." You will also be sure to be in at the bottom if you buy too soon. He did not say that. There is simply no advantage to anticipating or predicting, unless you have an emotional hang-up or you are just trying to prove to yourself or someone else how smart you are. Proving how smart you are is one game; making money is another game. You have to decide which game you want to play. You can't have it both ways.

AXIOM #5: THE FINANCIAL MEDIA ARE NOT YOUR FRIENDS

If you want confusing, conflicting, dangerous, and near-unusable advice, follow the financial media. They continually do investors more harm than good and are particularly loathsome because they come disguised as your friends, with presumably sound financial advice.

The media's interests and your interests are not compatible. You're trying to build wealth, to outpace inflation, to increase your spendable income. They want only to sell more newspapers, magazines, and television shows to increase their circulation and audience share. They know you want financial advice, and advice is cheap, so they give it to you.

Here is an example of the media "trying" to help you make investing decisions. February of each year is the month for the Annual Mutual Fund Edition of *Money* magazine. An acquaintance of mine reviewed and compiled data reviewing the cover stories for the February issues of *Money* magazine over a five-year period. This is what *Money* magazine touted in their headlines about what specific mutual funds to buy:

> *February 1992: "20 Great Mutual Funds to Buy Now."*
>
> *February 1993: "The 12 Funds to Buy Now." Of this list of 12 funds, only one fund name was repeated from the previous year. As a result, you would now own 31 funds (20+11).*
>
> *February 1994: "The Nine Best Funds to Buy Now." None of these nine funds were repeats from the previous years. Now you own 40 funds (20+11+9).*
>
> *February 1995: "Eight Most Dependable Mutual Funds." None of the 40 previously mentioned funds were mentioned in this year's list. You now own 48 different mutual funds (20+11+9+8).*
>
> *December 1995: "The One That Beats Them All!" This fund had not been mentioned once in the prior four years. Now you would have owned 49 different funds (20+11+9+8+1).*

My personal observation: *Have you ever noticed that* Money *magazine never tells you when to sell anything they previously told you to buy?*

AXIOM #6: AVOID THESE INVESTMENT MYTHS—BUY-AND-HOLD, DOLLAR COST AVERAGING, AND ASSET ALLOCATION

The Tragedy of Buy-and-Hold

The following section on buy-and-hold is taken from a report I prepared in the spring of 1991 and updated through 1999.

Introduction

Mutual fund companies, brokers, financial planners, and the financial press always put forth a barrage of statistics showing buy-and-hold as a wise and profitable strategy. However, statistics can be selectively chosen to prove or disprove anything. For this reason, I decided to examine a broad spectrum of stock market data, covering the better part of the twentieth century. I was convinced that the bigger picture would flush out the truth.

In this review you will find the fruits of my efforts. I endeavored to examine every aspect of the buy-and-hold strategy: the historical view, the psychological factor, variations on the theme, money made during bull markets, money lost during bear markets, and whether the strategy is practical, prudent, profitable, or, as my experience told me, potentially tragic.

Those who promote buy-and-hold and its close cousin dollar cost averaging often have ulterior motives. They have prepared clever and persuasive sales pitches. These sales pitches can be very effective. And so as an advocate for individual investors, I feel a responsibility to help prevent the tragedy of buy-and-hold in the 1990s, to protect wealth, and to let the truth be known.

Historical Perspective

One of the most common investment forms of advice today is this: "Invest for the long term. Do not try to time the market. Use a buy-and-hold strategy with dollar cost averaging." You can get this advice free from mutual fund companies, stock brokers, financial planners, the financial press, even from your brother-in-law. But is this a wise and profitable strategy for the future? Or is it a financial disaster waiting to happen? Let's review historical stock market data and you decide.

Historically, the stock market has yielded higher returns over the long term than most other investments. Conventional wisdom says that even though the market has periodic declines, by investing for the long term, you can overcome occasional losses and achieve higher yields. Short-term investing, on the other hand, is impractical because the time periods in which you choose to invest may coincide with market declines. The stock market does have a way of humbling even the most brilliant market forecasters.

Thus, by using a long-term buy-and-hold strategy, you will make money during market uptrends and lose some money during market downtrends. But over the long term, you will achieve greater returns than CDs, treasuries, corporate bonds, money markets, real estate, precious metals, and most other investments. Furthermore, you can expect to do better with this strategy than with any other market strategy. After all, the S&P 500 Index grew nearly 534 percent during the 1980s, returning an annualized rate of 17.55 percent to buy-and-hold investors. This performance record beats almost all money managers, market timers, and forecaster for the same period.

Sounds logical, doesn't it? There's just one problem. The great bull market of the 1980s was the longest in the experience of everyone's investing memory. In fact, most of the investors in the 1990s had not lived through a serious bear market. They do not know what can happen—just how serious their losses can be!

Obviously, you cannot miss with a buy-and-hold strategy in a strong bull market. But in the years to come, do you really expect a repeat of the great bull market of the 1980s and 1990s? Even the most optimistic investors hedge on this question. And for good reasons: the budget deficit, the Middle East War, the drug crisis, the inner-cities crisis, higher taxes, skyrocketing healthcare costs, possible recessions, possible rises in inflation . . . the list goes on.

What's more, while the S&P 500 Index compounded at 17.55 percent during the 1980s, it only compounded at 7.81 percent in the 1960s, and 5.86 percent in the 1970s (source: Ibbotson Associates, Chicago). This brings the average compounded growth for the past 30 years to 10.41 percent. That is not a bad rate of return, but remember, it was achieved after 30 years of steady, steel-nerved, buy-and-hold investing. Thus, if you were planning to use a buy-and-hold strategy—and believe you are capable of sticking to it—you would be wiser to expect a 10 percent compounded rate of return after 30 years, rather than a 17 percent return in the next 10 years.

While I do not predict the market, I do expect to see a mix of some good years and some bad years in the future. The bad years are the problem. If a serious bear market develops anytime during the next 10 or 15 years—and historical data suggests one will—you could easily lose 30 percent, 40 percent, 50 percent, and more of your investment capital. Losses of this severity would certainly render buy-and-hold a financial disaster.

Since most investors do not take the time to do market research, they are unaware of the enormously destructive power of bear markets. They are also unaware of the precious time and earning power lost on bear markets—time that only the very youngest investors can afford to lose.

Riding bear markets to the bottom—as every buy-and-hold investor must do—is in fact a double tragedy. The first tragedy is ending up with a lot less money when you finally hit the bottom. The second tragedy is wasting future market advances just making up your prior losses. Smart investors know that market advances are for getting your money to grow, not for simply making up past losses. And this combination of lost money and lost time makes bear markets double trouble for every buy-and-hold investor.

Let us look at bear markets since 1929 and see the damage they caused, in terms of time and money lost. See Figure 7-2. I have done the research for you, so you can quickly digest the facts. The S&P 500 statistics show that, on average, a new bear market begins every 5 years, lasts 18 months, causes losses of 39 percent, and requires 5½ years to break even, if you are using a buy-and-hold strategy.

Use a calculator. Determine how much money you will have left after a 39 percent decline. Also determine what you could earn in a money fund over 18 months. Consider also what you might make over 5½ years if you were *not* just making up losses.

After you have made these calculations, decide if you can afford to use a buy-and-hold strategy for your long-term investment lifetime.

Buy-and-Hold Is Not as Profitable as Switching

People often ask, "Can you sidestep bear markets to achieve high profits, or is a long-term buy-and-hold strategy ultimately more profitable?" There are many opinions on this question, but opinions do not mean anything unless they correspond to the truth. So, to find the correct answer to this question, I turned to historical stock market data.* First, I charted a hypothetical $10,000 investment in the Dow Jones Industrials, from October 1, 1926, through December 31, 1990 (over 64 years). Next, I charted the same investment, for the same period, using the Dow Jones Transportations. Finally, I charted a hypothetical $10,000 investment in the Standard & Poor's 500 Index from September 26, 1930, through December 31, 1990 (over 60 years).

For each major indicator, I tracked the buy-and-hold strategy along with my trend-following plan. My plan uses a 39-week moving average of indicators' prices to generate buy signals during market uptrends and sell signals during market downtrends. During the downtrends, my plan calls for switching to the protection of money market funds. For the study period, this plan averaged no more than two moves in and out of the mar-

---

* The readings shown in the daily newspapers for the Dow Jones Industrials, the Dow Jones Transportations, and the S&P 500 do not include the reinvestment of dividends. Both the "buy-and-hold" statistics and the "switching" statistics are based on the same newspaper data.

FIGURE 7-2

S&P 500 Bear Market Study

Bear Market	Duration	% Decline	Time needed to break even
Jul '33 – Mar '35	20 months	33.93	2.25 years
Mar '37 – Mar '38	12 months	54.47	8.83 years
Nov '38 – Apr '42	41 months	45.80	6.42 years
May '46 – Mar '48	22 months	28.10	4.08 years
Aug '56 – Oct '57	14 months	21.63	2.08 years
Dec '61 – Jun '62	6 months	27.97	1.75 years
Feb '66 – Oct '66	8 months	22.18	1.42 years
Nov '68 – May '70	18 months	36.06	3.33 years
Jan '73 – Oct '74	21 months	48.20	7.58 years
Nov '80 – Aug '82	21 months	27.11	2.08 years
Aug '87 – Dec '87	4 months	33.51	1.92 years
Jul '90 – Oct '90	3 months	19.92	.58 years
Jul '98 – Aug '98	1.5 months	19.34	.25 years

BEAR MARKET FACTS:

Definition of a bear market: 20% decline or more

Average frequency of bear markets: Every 5 years

Average duration of a bear market: 16 months

Average decline during a bear market: -33.24%

Average time needed to break even: 3.5 years

Profit needed to break even: 50% gain

ket per year. While out of the market, I assumed a money fund yield of 6 percent.

The Results

A $10,000 buy-and-hold investment in the Dow Jones Industrials from October 1, 1926, through December 31, 1990, grew to just $164,922. But the trend-following plan increased the $10,000 to $1,588,382—over nine times more.

For the same period, a buy-and-hold investment in the Dow Jones Transportations resulted in the $10,000 growing to just $74,713. But the plan increased the $10,000 to $1,991,041—over twenty-six times more.

A $10,000 buy-and-hold investment in the S&P's 500 Index, from September 26, 1930, through December 31, 1990, grew to $169,954. But the plan boosted the $10,000 to $970,147—nearly six times more. See Figure 7-3.

I urge you to verify these findings for yourself. For this study I consulted the following sources: *Dow Jones Averages,* Centennial Edition, Dow Jones-Irwin, Illinois: *Standard & Poor's Security Price Index Record,* Standard & Poor's Corporation, New York.

While past performance is not a guarantee of future results, we can learn from history. Certainly, next year will not be exactly like last year, or the next five years exactly like the past five years. Still, there are only seven types of stock market activity: (1) the market can rise sharply; (2) it can rise slowly; (3) the market can decline sharply; (4) it can decline slowly; (5) the market can move sideways in a narrow range; (6) it can move sideways in a somewhat broader range; or (7) the market can crash.

My research shows, over the past 64 years, each of the seven types of market activity occurred many times. Through this entire period the compounding plan worked very well, avoiding crashes and bear markets.

What's more, 64 years of stock market price data prove conclusively that the market does move in trends, either up or down, over a period of months or years. Occasionally, the market moves sideways, but this motion is always temporary.

Sooner or later, the market reestablishes itself in an upward or downward trend. Investors following my compounding plan have a distinct advantage over buy-and-hold investors, because they know the trend and thus can switch, during meaningful market declines, to the safe and steady earnings of money funds during bear markets.

Buy What? Hold What?

The idea behind buy-and-hold is that you will buy something and hold it over the long term for a good profit. But no one bothers to ever ask the critical questions: Buy what? Hold what? Obviously, you have to choose something to buy and hold. What if you choose the wrong stock or mutual fund? Not every mutual fund or stock will be good over the long term. The idea that you can simply buy something and forget it is foolish!

FIGURE 7-3

60+ YEAR STUDY
PERFORMANCE RESULTS

BUY & HOLD VS. SWITCHING

Buy & Hold		39WAR Trading Rules	
$10,000 Starting Value		**$10,000 Starting Value**	
	Ending Value		**Ending Value**
DJI 1926 – 1990	$164,992	DJI 1926 – 1990	$1,588,382
DJT 1926 – 1990	$74,713	DJT 1926 – 1990	$1,991,041
S&P Oct. 1930 – 1990	$169,954	S&P Oct. 1930 – 1990	$970,147
Dollar Cost Averaging		**Periodic Investment Plan**	
(Buy & Hold)		**(Switching)**	
$100 Monthly Investment		**$100 Monthly Investment**	
DJI 1926 – 1990	$559,042	DJI 1926 – 1990	$1,521,167

This model represents a hypothetical example. The rates of return shown above have been calculated by applying historic information provided by reputable sources. These results do not reflect reinvestment of dividends, the effect of taxes, management fees, and charges. Past hypothetical performance is not indicative of future earning expectations.

For example, in 1914, there was a buggy-whip manufacturer traded on the stock exchange called McCrary & Sons. This company had made quality buggy whips since 1826 with great success. Many people bought shares of McCrary & Sons in 1914, convinced the company would continue to be successful. For a while they were. But after the World War I, automobiles replaced horses and carriages, and the demand for McCrary whips dried up. McCrary tried to switch to manufacturing leather accessories for automobiles, but they were too late; they were never really competitive. After the stock market crash of 1929, they closed up shop for good.

Also consider the case of 44 Wall Street, one of the best-performing mutual funds in the early 1970s. Excited over this fund's stellar track record, hordes of investors bought 44 Wall Street in early 1973. Tragically, they invested just in time for the 1973-to-1974 bear market, when this former favorite lost 75 percent of its value.

My point is that you cannot afford to use a buy-and-hold strategy without careful selection and diligent monitoring. No stock or mutual fund is good forever. Like it or not, you will have to do some trading—some pruning in your portfolio from time to time. It is odd, but many investors seem to want an easy way out, a free lunch when it comes to their investing. Buy-and-hold has such an appeal because it appears to be easy. But I am here to tell you that in investing as in life there is no free lunch.

Imagine buying and holding 44 Wall Street and riding the 1973-to-1974 bear market to the bottom. Imagine if you had invested $50,000 in this fund, and at the bottom of the bear your statement read $12,500. How would you feel then? With a loss like that, you would need a 300 percent gain to break even. How easy do you think that feat is?

As far as I am concerned, a buy-and-hold strategy is akin to sticking your head in the sand. Once you understand that you will have to do some trading to protect your wealth, you will also understand that your trading must include avoiding bear markets. Just as stocks and mutual funds are not perennially good, markets are not endlessly bullish.

The Fallacy of Dollar Cost Averaging

Those who insist you cannot profitably move in and out of the market base their opinions on the uncertainty of market forecasting. And they are right. Investors who attempt to time the market on predictions usually end up doing worse than those who follow a straight buy-and-hold strategy.

Still, as we've seen, buy-and-hold has its drawbacks, especially if you buy in at market highs, which many investors often seem to do. So, in order to improve the profitability of buy-and-hold, promoters recommend dollar cost averaging—the practice of making consistent periodic investments over the long term. The idea is that if you make steady purchases ($500 per month, $1,000 per quarter, etc.), you will buy some shares at a high price, some at a low price, and some at an average price, and thus do better than if you make a lump-sum purchase or make random purchases at your own discretion.

All of this sounds logical, but dollar cost averaging is essentially a sales gimmick. It was most likely invented by a stockbroker seeking a way to make sales commissions in a declining market. One day, as the story goes, this broker called his client and recommended XYZ Company, and so his client bought 1000 shares. Then a few days later, the price of XYZ fell 10 points, and the broker was worried sick about what his client would say. So, he took the offensive. He called his client and said. "I've got great news! XYZ has dropped 10 points! Now we can buy more shares at a bargain price!" Most likely, that is how dollar cost averaging was born. It has been refined and promoted in more clever ways ever since.

People do not have the stomach for buying stocks or mutual funds in a declining market, and that is why dollar cost averaging does not work. For example, suppose you have been following a $500-a-month dollar cost averaging program, and the market has continued to climb over several months or even years. So far so good. But then suddenly the market turns down, the following month it drops lower, and the next month lower yet. You are still investing $500 per month, but now you are beginning to worry. You watch the market decline again the following month and again the month after that. How long can you keep this up? Maybe you will watch your account value shrink for six or seven months, but sooner or later, you will think twice before throwing good money after bad. And that is why dollar cost averaging does not work. Emotionally, you cannot see it through.

Although in theory buy-and-hold and dollar cost averaging work well during bull markets, they are certainly impractical during bear markets. Perhaps you have noticed that buy-and-hold promoters conveniently use 1980 and 1990 statistics to back up their arguments. But remember, we experienced the longest bull market in the experience of investors at that time.

Now those years are behind us. What are the chances of an encore performance in the next two decades? In fact, sometime during the next decade, we will probably see a serious bear market. If so, buy-and-hold investors will lose 30 percent, 40 percent, 50 percent, and more of the investment capital. While dollar cost averaging may be an improvement over a straight buy-and-hold strategy (provided you are capable of following it faithfully), it is no match for a strategy that successfully avoids bear markets.

Here's proof: We tracked a $100-a-month investment in the Dow Jones Industrials, from February 1926 through December 1989, using the dollar-cost-averaging strategy and the trend-following compounding plan.* The compounding plan generated buy signals during market

---

* The readings shown in the daily newspapers for the Dow Jones Industrials do not include the reinvestment of dividends.

uptrends and sell signals during market downtrends. Sell signals call for a switch out of equities and into money funds, thereby enabling followers to avoid bear markets.

The results of this comparison study show that the trend-following compounding plan is nearly three times more profitable than dollar cost averaging. In conclusion, the idea that dollar cost averaging is a valid investment approach is a fallacy. Refer back to Figure 7-3.

Big Advances Follow Bear Markets

We have talked about the tragedy of riding bear markets to the bottom and losing a substantial portion of investment capital. And we have touched on the tragedy of wasting future market advances just getting even again. But there is an even greater tragedy than either of these: Missing out on the advances that follow bear markets.

When we discuss buy-and-hold, we talk about it theoretically. We assume that an investor following this strategy actually buys and holds a stock or mutual fund over several years. But the psychology of buy-and-hold investing forces another, more common scenario—that of selling at the bottom and missing out entirely on the big advance that follows every bear market.

Arguments for buy-and-hold are always structured on hindsight— that is, if you would have bought this mutual fund 10 years ago, you would now have X dollars. The problem is that in the real world of investing, nobody has the advantage of hindsight. In actual practice, it is emotionally very difficult to hold on to a stock or mutual fund in a declining market. If you are an experienced investor, you know this is true. Most often, investors buy high and sell low. The reason for this is that investors act emotionally rather than rationally. When the market is going up, investors become optimistic and buy. When the market is going down, investors become pessimistic and sell.

Fed up with the market and sick with losses, many investors sell at or near the bottom. Some leave the market for good. Others quit the market for several months or a year. The problem with this latter group is that by the time they jump back in, they could have missed the biggest part of a new advance. Usually, the biggest portion of the advance occurs within the first nine months following a bear market low.

Investors who have suffered bear market losses seek greater safety, so they put their money in CDs, treasuries—even in tin cans which they bury in their backyards. Ironically, they desperately need the larger stock market gains to get even again. If they earn just 5 or 6 or 7 percent in a CD, they cannot begin to make up their losses, and that is why this tragedy is the worst one of all.

In Figure 7-4, you can see the dramatic advances that followed the 12 bear markets since 1929—on average, a gain of 124 percent each. If you are serious about accumulating wealth, you must use these special opportunities for getting your money to grow. It is tragic to waste them making up bear market losses and even more tragic to miss them entirely. The solution is not to leave the market and the high profits it can yield, but instead to avoid bear markets in the first place.

Asset Allocation

The asset allocation concept became popular following the 1987 market crash. According to proponents of the approach, the main benefit of asset allocation is that it provides added investment flexibility that you do not have when using just one investment segment.

To back up this claim, advocates point to studies of various market segments over time. For instance, if you look at international stocks, precious metals stocks, corporate bonds, and domestic U.S. stocks over a 10-year period (source: Morningstar, 10-year data range from 12/31/83 to 12/31/93), you find that U.S. stocks outperformed the other market segments during 3 of the 10 years. International stocks outperformed the other sectors 4 out of 10 years. And precious metal stocks and corporate bonds each outperformed the other sectors 2 years out of 10.

Since no single market segment is always the top performer, proponents advocate spreading your money out among various market segments. In this way, they say, you will be able to adapt to any and all economic and investment climates.

In theory, no one can argue with this logic. However, the actual method followed by many advocates of asset allocation leaves obvious drawbacks which seem to be in direct opposition to the logic. The concept is to select a number of asset classes. For example, 50 percent to equities, 25 percent to bonds, 10 percent to precious metals, and 15 percent to others. The idea is to select asset classes that are not closely correlated, so that while one asset class is declining, another will be moving up. Ideally, this will provide positive rates of return in all markets, but not as high a return as from a trend-following plan covering all investment areas of the world.

FIGURE 7-4

S&P 500 Index
Advances Following Bear Markets

Bear Market	Total %Advance
Sep '29 – Jun '32	+ 177.27
Jul '33 – Mar '35	+ 131.64
Mar '37 – Mar '38	+ 62.24
Nov '38 – Apr '42	+ 157.70
May '46 – Mar '48	+ 259.39
Aug '56 – Oct '57	+ 86.35
Dec '61 – Jun '62	+ 79.78
Feb '66 – Oct '66	+ 48.05
Nov '68 – May '70	+ 73.53
Jan '73 – Oct '74	+ 125.63
Nov '80 – Aug '82	+ 228.81
Aug '87 – Dec '87	+ 64.77*

* Through 7/16/90

There is an investment approach known as Modern Portfolio Theory (MPT) that defines exactly how a portfolio should be allocated among various asset classes so as to maximize return for any particular level of risk. These allocators "rebalance" portfolios periodically to conform to the formulas of MPT, but there are seldom dramatic shifts between asset classes. Typically, the portion of capital invested in any particular asset class will change no more than a few percentage points at each rebalancing.

Most investors following the traditional asset allocation approach (either in a specific asset allocation fund or as an investment strategy) always have some money invested across all market segments, regardless of which individual sector is the current high performer. This means that gains in certain segments could be negated by losses in others. In the end, this equals flat performance.

In addition, investment recommendations in traditional asset allocation strategies are primarily based on forecasts—in other words, predictions on how different market segments *might* perform in the future, rather than analysis of their current trends. Wouldn't it make more sense to be primarily invested where the current evidence points to the highest potential for gain? This way you can avoid the need to be invested, at least with some money, in all segments at all times. Instead, doesn't it make more sense that at any one time you may be holding more than only one particular type of fund? For instance, if the domestic equity market were the only market segment showing a strong uptrend, your portfolio could consist of only domestic equity funds. At other times you could be 100 percent invested in money market funds. This is a protective measure that helps you to reduce risk in the event that no market segment is in a distinct uptrend.

AXIOM #7: THE VALUE OF TREND FOLLOWING

The success of my compounding plan can be credited to a simple trend-following approach to investing. Before proceeding any further there is one very relevant factor that everyone must absolutely recognize:

**The Fabian Compounding Plan does not use
market timing!
It is built on trend following.**

In the future, during the years while you will be following the compounding plan, you must keep reminding yourself of this truism.

There is a significant difference between market timing and trend following. Market timing is predicated on predicting the future direction of the market. Its objective is to be positioned in an investment *before* a new trend develops. We all know how unreliable predictions have been in the past.

Trend following, on the other hand, depends only on discipline. Without exception, everyone has the capacity to be a disciplinarian and follow simple rules.

My trend-following plan was adopted to help investors preserve capital during declining markets. It has always been my belief that the only people who can ever be wiped out by a severe and long-lasting market crash are those who participate in such declines. Trend following enables us to stand aside.

Because it enables investors to step aside during meaningful market declines, this trend-following strategy increases their comfort level. As a result, followers of this plan are willing to commit a larger percentage of their total available investment dollars than they would be willing to commit to other more complicated and therefore risky plans.

I developed the trend-following investment approach to avoid bear markets like the one I participated in during 1969. My approach adopts what might be called a buy-and-hold approach during bull markets and then moves to money funds or other safe vehicles during bear markets. To the extent that an investor successfully follows this approach, principal is preserved while the market is falling and then one participates again once a new bull market (up-trend) is recognized.

At the beginning our trading strategy focused on equity-based domestic mutual funds nearly exclusively. Over the years, when many new and different types of mutual funds became available, we expanded the areas of the world and sectors of the market that we use in our trend-following process. With so many choices now available, our strategy is to buy whichever asset class is moving up most rapidly (i.e., which has the highest momentum). As you will see in Part 4, after we are invested, we monitor each position against the performance of a performance yardstick. If an existing position falls appreciably below the performance of the yardstick, we "rotate up" to a new invested position with a higher momentum.

Does Trend Following Work?

The financial media do not approve of anyone who advocates "trading" mutual funds. Because of this, I felt you would find the following article interesting. Entitled "Is the Time Right for Market Timing?," it appeared in the *New York Times* on October 4, 1998. It was written by Mark Hulbert following the severe market decline that took place during August and September 1998. Here is an excerpt from that article:

> *What a difference two months can make. As recently as this summer, the debate between market timers and buy-and-hold investors was all but dead. Buy-and-hold investors had declared victory, and few were disagreeing. But now, with the broad market down 20 percent from its midsummer highs, the faith of buy-and-hold investors is being tested. . . .*

How should you decide whether to try timing the market? Begin by acquainting yourself with the compelling statistical case against it: Fewer than 20 percent of market timers are able to beat a buy-and-hold strategy on a risk-adjusted basis. Buy-and-holders, however, mistakenly consider the matter to be solely about statistics. Investors don't give up on a buy-and-hold strategy because they are ignorant of the data. They do so because they can't take the psychological pain of an extended market decline. . . .

The lesson, of course, is that you shouldn't wait until the bottom of the next bear market to discover that you're a closet market timer. After all, investors who try to execute a buy-and-hold strategy but lose nerve at the bottom of the next bear market will likely be worse off than investors who pursue a thoughtful market-timing strategy that looks inferior on statistical grounds. Latter-day converts to the buy-and-hold strategy assure me that they won't be foolish and throw in the towel in a bear market. But I don't believe them. . . .

Why is it so psychologically difficult to stay fully invested, when it's statistically clear that most investors would be better off in the long run if they did? The long run is much longer than the typical investor's attention span. Nevertheless, the psychological strain of buying and holding shouldn't seduce you into thinking that following just any market-timing system will do better. Not all market timers are created equal. There are a select few market-timing newsletters—just five among all those that I have tracked over the last 15 years—that have shown that they can immunize investors, relatively speaking, from more risk than the performance they may forfeit in the process. [See Figure 7-5.]

In the table in Figure 7-5, look at the column on the right to see the average number of switches made per year. My first observation is that we are proud to find ourselves in this group and next we are even more proud that we accomplished it with an average of only 1.7 annual switches. The low number of annual switches is one of the prime reasons why our recommended investment approach makes it easier for people to be willing to commit a larger portion of their investment dollars into the Fabian Compounding Plan than into other plans.

AXIOM #8: MONITORING—THE KEY TO LONG-TERM SUCCESS

You should know if the investment plan you are considering has the potential to attain your goal and at the same time provide you with a high degree

FIGURE 7-5

Switch-Hitters

The best-performing market timing strategies of the investment newsletters monitored by the *Hulbert Financial Digest*. Returns are those for the Wilshire 5000 index when the newsletter recommends investing in stocks and for the 90-day Treasury bill when it is out of the market.

Newsletter	Annualized Return Dec. 31, 1982, to Aug. 31, 1998	Risk* vs. Market (Market = 100)	Avg. Number of Switches† a Year
Systems and Forecasts	+17.0%	73.7	16.6
Wilshire 5000 value-weighted total return	+15.6%	100.0	0
Market logic	+15.1%	52.4	31.4
Fabian Premium Investment Resource	+14.8%	78.7	1.7
The Elliott Wave Theorist	+12.0%	50.1	1.2

*Risk calculation is based on standard deviation.
†"Switches" refers to strategy switches into or out of the market
Source: Hulbert Financial Digest, October 1998.

of comfort. To assure yourself of attaining both of these objectives, you must first examine the past history of the investment you may be considering. To make it easier for you to accomplish this with the compounding plan, I am supplying you with a great deal of historical data, covering more than 30 years.

Reviewing the past is important. You must decide if you *believe* your investment plan has the potential of attaining your goal. You wouldn't want to waste your time on a plan that can't meet the goal, nor do you want to waste your time with a complicated or stress-producing plan that you would more than likely abandon later.

There is another big advantage to following a plan that you are comfortable with *before* committing your serious money. It means you will able to monitor the plan *after* your serious money has been put to work. *Monitoring* means checking the progress of the plan while your money is working to see whether it is meeting the goal. This process lets you know you are on target, keeping your comfort level high and, even more important, keeping you motivated to remain committed. Eventually, it helps you to find more money to put to work.

I will spell out specific monitoring steps in Part 4.

AXIOM #9: PRACTICE PATIENCE

Putting first things first, the primary reason you are investing all of your serious money is to strive to reach the goal of 20 percent annualized compounded growth. Furthermore, to keep your comfort level high, you always want to know that you are continually on target to attain that goal. You accomplish both of these objectives by monitoring. What I have just described is the development of "a state of mind." You will see in Part 4, when we go thoroughly into the details of the investment plan together, that very little actual time is required to ensure your success.

Even though this is true, human nature dictates that many investors will feel they have to be making money all the time—every single day. I wish it were so, but that is not the way it works.

In the big picture, the market can do only three things. It can go up, it can go down, or it can move sideways. When the market is clearly moving either up or down, it is easy to be in tune as to what you and your investments should be doing. It is the side-trading range that will prove emotionally difficult. Often these "trading range" periods take place during a transition, from an up market to a down market or vice versa. At other times, they take place while the market takes a breather, a *pause to refresh*. These gray areas can cause extra trading. Such times as these may make one more susceptible to listening to the predictions of others regarding the future direction of the market. During these times, you are frustrated while trying to recognize the current market trend. See Figure 7-6. This is when patience will pay a big dividend.

A successful compounding plan investor does not allow an investor to be concerned whether the market is going up or down, as long as the investor is along for the ride on the right side of the market (in or out). At times it is wise to take to heart the old sayings such as "go with the flow," "never fight the tape," or "don't ever say the market is wrong."

AXIOM #10: MAKE TAX-DEFERRED INVESTING A TOP PRIORITY

One of the best ways to maximize the power of compounding (and minimize the effects of taxation) is to use tax-deferred investment vehicles.

These enable your accounts to grow free of current taxation and thereby compound at a faster rate.

The compounding plan, using mutual funds, is ideal for use with tax-deferred vehicles. That is why everyone is encouraged to take maximum advantage of those that are available to them. Tax-deferred investments include Individual Retirement Accounts (IRAs), Roth IRAs, Simplified Employee Pensions (SEPs), Keoghs, 401(k) and 403(b) plans, and variable annuities.

FIGURE 7-6

"HE JUST SITS THERE AND WAITS FOR STOCK MARKET RALLIES."

Source: Copyright ©1999 by *Barron's* magazine. Used by permission of Roy Delgado and the publisher.

The IRA is the simplest vehicle to use, but it permits only modest annual contributions. The SEP and Keogh are primarily for self-employed persons, but they allow much larger contributions. The 401(k) and 403(b) are used by corporate employees and also allow generous contributions. The variable annuity can be used by anyone and allows very large contributions, although, unlike the other vehicles, contributions must be funded with after-tax dollars.

The basic difference between qualified and nonqualified investments is that qualified vehicles—for example, the IRA or 401(k)—are funded with pre-tax money, and non-qualified vehicles—for example, variable annuities—are funded with after-tax dollars.

Remember that while qualified plans can help alleviate your tax burden every year, they will not eliminate it altogether (the exception, at retirement, being the Roth IRA). At some point after you retire, taxes will come back into the picture again. In the meantime, you just cannot beat tax-deferred compounded investing for building wealth.

The decisions you make in choosing a specific tax-deferred vehicle to use will have a long-term impact on your financial future. You should seek out adequate counsel in selecting a plan. On the Internet, you can find general information on each of the available tax-deferred plans. One such site can be reached at http://quicken.com/retirement/articles.

Observations

401(k)

In 1999 there were 27 million Americans participating in their employers' 401(k) plans. Collectively, this group's investments were worth more than $1 trillion. At least 10 percent of these accounts were worth more than $100,000, but half of them were worth less than $10,000. This would indicate that many participants are not investing their full eligible amount.

Each passing year, more trading choices are being made available for 401(k) participants. These additional options have caused confusion. Many participants feel they are not capable of making the "proper" investment decisions. Hopefully the goal-oriented strategy in Part 4 will assist them.

Variable Annuities

Variable annuities offer the potential for tax-deferred growth over the long term with virtually no limit to the amount of money that can be invested.

Other qualified plans usually offer many more investment options than can be found with variable annuities. Therefore, everyone should first maximize their investments in whatever qualified plans that are available to them and then consider using variable annuities with "excess" long-term investment dollars.

To maximize your potential for a high compounded growth from your investment, consider only variable annuity products that offer at least 15 different mutual funds to choose from. In addition, never consider putting a qualified retirement plan into a variable annuity.

LET'S MOVE ON TO PART 4

When you visit your doctor's office, just before he gives you an injection, which you know will be good for you, he says, "This is going to hurt just a little." Likewise, Part 4 is going to hurt, just a little. Up until now we have talked about ideas, concepts, philosophy, psychology, and so on. Except for those instances where I pointed out some things you may have done wrong while investing your money in the past, it has been a comfortable, informative, and entertaining process.

You are now going to discover my answer to the fourth "How": How are you going to put your investment money to work to strive for 20 percent annualized compounded growth for the rest of your life? In order to answer this all-important question, I have to get specific. In the process, I am going to make you feel like you are back in a classroom at school.

The effort on your part will be well worth it, however. At the conclusion of Part 4 you will say: "The recommended plan I will be using with my investment dollars is easy to understand and simple to follow. I know it has the potential to make me a self-made millionaire."

The Foundation of the Compounding Plan

PART 4 - 1

Implementing the Fabian Compounding Plan: The Basics

CHAPTER 8

Long-Term Investing

Before writing a commentary or preparing the text for my seminar talks, I always visualize my audience. From the very beginning it has been my mission to help as many people as possible to reach their long-term financial goals and to become self-made millionaires. So, here in Part 4, the investment section of the book, I asked myself: Who will be my audience?

My answer: Everyone who wants to improve his or her long-term financial future, but particularly everyone among the 63 percent of American households who have an annual income under $50,000. The people in this income group typically do not believe it is possible for them to become wealthy, let alone become self-made millionaires. And yet I know that they can, simply by following my compounding plan. And so I intend to provide the appropriate material to prove it.

It stands to reason, for the people who do not believe that investing can have an important impact on their lives, there would be no reason for them to become knowledgeable about putting money to work. I kept this in mind as I prepared both the investment background information for the compounding plan and the investment steps to follow to successfully implement it.

HISTORICAL BACKGROUND OF MUTUAL FUNDS

Because I use only mutual funds with my compounding plan—and when you adopt it, you will too—I want to review some basic information on mutual funds.

Mutual funds were originally called investment trusts. The first to appear was Foreign & Colonial Government Trust. It originated in London in 1868. Its stated purpose was to provide the small investor with the same advantages used by wealthy individuals. The idea was to diminish some of the risk of investing through diversification.

Later, in Boston a large number of wealthy sea captains, who spent long periods of time away from home, sought out individuals with financial backgrounds to look after their assets. As the number of these original trustees grew, a Massachusetts judge introduced the "prudent man rule." It provided that a trustee could invest the money of his client as he saw fit, provided he conducted himself faithfully, exercised sound discretion, and patterned himself after the manner in which prudent men managed their own affairs. The implementation of this rule is the foundation on which the mutual fund portfolio managers continue to function today.

The first American mutual fund, named the Massachusetts Investors Trust, was introduced in 1924. Once introduced, mutual funds grew and had enormous acceptance. Because of this, in 1936 Congress had the Securities and Exchange Commission undertake a special study of these new financial instruments. The result of the study was the Investment Company Act of 1940, which established industry regulations that are used for investor safety.

MUTUAL FUND BASICS

A *mutual fund* is a company that makes investments for individuals and institutions according to its stated investment objectives. When you purchase shares in a mutual fund, your money is pooled with the money of other investors who have similar investment objectives. The fund's professional portfolio manager then uses this pooled money to buy liquid investments, such as stocks, bonds, and other types of securities, that fall within the scope of the fund's objectives. The objectives for each mutual fund are spelled out in its prospectus.

The share price of a mutual fund, called the *net asset value,* or NAV, rises and falls according to the fluctuations of the value of the individual securities held in its portfolio. Every fund is required by law to pass on its profits to investors through dividends and annual capital-gains distributions. These gains result when the portfolio manager sells the fund's securities for a profit.

A mutual fund can be classified in a number of different ways. First, a fund may be singular or a member of a *fund family*. A fund family is a mutual fund organization that offers several funds of different types and objectives, so that you can transfer or allocate your investment dollars as you see fit.

For an even wider choice, you can purchase funds through discount brokerage firms, which offer funds from a number of different fund families. This enables you to choose from hundreds, even thousands, of funds from many fund families. And you can usually buy or exchange shares in these funds with little or no transaction fees.

Mutual funds are either open-ended or closed-ended. The shares of an open-ended fund increase or decrease based on the number sold to investors, while closed-end funds have a fixed number of shares. In the latter case, the fund itself trades on the stock exchange, and before you can buy shares, another shareholder must be willing to sell them.

Mutual funds can be either load or no-load. Load funds are typically sold by stockbrokers and financial planners who charge a commission called a *load*. This commission can range from 3 percent up to 8.5 percent of your total investment. No-load funds, which I prefer and recommend, are sold by fund families and through discount brokers. They are commission-free. The discount brokers receive their compensation for handling the transactions directly from the mutual fund companies. All funds, load and no-load, have advisory or management fees which cover operating expenses. Most companies charge from 0.5 percent up to 1.5 percent annually, which is assessed on your total investment. This small fee is deducted from your account periodically.

MUTUAL FUND ADVANTAGES

Mutual funds offer a combination of important features that, together, are not found in other investments. These features include the following:

- *Diversification*   The old saying "Never put all of your eggs in one basket" is especially true for stock market investing. With a large amount of pooled capital, mutual fund portfolio managers are able to diversify among dozens of securities, thereby reducing your risk.
- *Instant liquidity*   At any time, you can sell your mutual fund shares and have the money wired to your bank account or simply transferred to a liquid money market fund.

- *Large or small investments*   With mutual funds, you are never priced out of the market, since most companies will accept investments as low as $250. Of course, you can invest as much as you wish.

- *No sales commissions*   With hundreds of top-performing no-load funds available today, you can direct your account yourself and put the money you would have spent on sales commissions to work for your future.

- *Professional portfolio management*   Backed by their company's resources, fund managers have the time, experience, and information that is needed to make profitable investment decisions. Many of the best-managed funds consistently outperform the market as a whole.

- *Tax-deferred investing*   There are a wide range of tax-deferred investment vehicles available, including IRAs, Roth IRAs, SEPs, Keoghs, and variable annuities. These vehicles allow you to build your fortune faster, free of current income taxes. (Of course, you will pay taxes later, when you make withdrawals, except for money invested in a Roth IRA.)

- *Telephone exchange privilege*   Most mutual fund companies and discount brokers let you transfer your money between funds as your investment strategy dictates. You can make these exchanges with a simple phone call (called *telephone switching*).

- *Invest through discount brokers*   There are thousands of mutual funds available through discount stockbrokers. With just a single phone call (or online access), you can choose from hundreds of funds at dozens of fund families. Most of these funds can be traded without paying a transaction fee.

Now let's review my recommendations for using mutual funds as your investment tool to help you to become a self-made millionaire.

THE CREATION OF THE FABIAN COMPOUNDING PLAN

When evaluating investments, I feel it is more important to understand why a particular investment strategy was created rather than just trying to understand the strategy itself. As you will soon see, my compounding plan was created to solve certain problems inherent in the market—and human nature—which typically cause investors to fail. In fact, one way to describe the my plan is to say it is an effective investment plan that enables the average person to succeed and thus go on to become a self-made millionaire.

When I began my financial career in the late 1960s, a very impressive bull market was in progress. With the market rising steadily, the small investor "discovered" mutual funds as the surefire way to get rich. Unprecedented amounts of new money poured into mutual funds and, to meet demand, the mutual fund companies created new funds in unbelievable numbers. It was during this time that I became a stockbroker. Armed with the knowledge of the power of compounding, I sold mutual funds, advocating a long-term buy-and-hold strategy. Unfortunately, that bull market came to an end in 1968.

After I experienced the bear market of 1969 to 1970 and saw many of the mutual funds I owned, and had sold to others, decline by 30 percent or more, I realized I had to reevaluate my investment approach. I was not alone because, immediately following this period—and for the next 10 years—more money was taken out of mutual funds than was added. This was the first time in the history of mutual funds that this had happened.

In early 1970 I came to the conclusion, based on my own personal bear market experience, that buy-and-hold was not the path to follow. I knew I wanted to use compounding, and I was still convinced that mutual funds were the most appropriate investment tool to use. But I had a dilemma. I needed an investment strategy that would not lead to devastating losses, which seriously hamper the powerful effects of compounding.

To solve my dilemma, I started on a search for an alternative approach to the buy-and-hold strategy. As a result of this search, it was apparent that the market moves in trends, up or down, for periods ranging from a few months up to several years. I then discovered the value of using a 39-week moving average to identify the trend of the market. (I'll explain this in more detail further on.)

So, in 1970 I gave up my stockbroker license and obtained from the Securities and Exchange Commission a license to be a Registered Financial Advisor. In this new capacity, I could then manage investment dollars for others, using my new trend-following trading plan with mutual funds.

Once I completed the research on this new trading approach and had my new license, I went back to all of the people to whom I had sold mutual funds and told them they had three choices: (1) they could accept their recent losses and abandon the stock market; (2) they could continue to invest, following a buy-and-hold strategy and run the risk of losing money again; or (3) they could join me and follow my new trend-following plan that would give them the gains they wanted while also protecting them from devastating losses. The majority of them choose to adopt my new trend-following approach.

BEAR MARKET PROBLEM

Because of the devastation of bear markets, and also the negative emotional responses investors have to them, I have observed that most people believe there is no safe and consistent investment plan available that they could follow comfortably over the long term. Unfortunately, without such a plan, they won't be able to become wealthy.

What's more, most people, because of their aversion to risk, are unwilling to place more than 12 percent, 15 percent, or occasionally 20 percent of their investment capital to work. They shield the remainder of their money from loss in savings passbook accounts and/or treasury bills. This is the sad dilemma most investors face, because if they can't find an investment plan that is safe, simple, and effective, they can't attain a high enough compounded growth rate to become wealthy in a reasonable amount of time. Fortunately, this is the dilemma I overcame with my compounding plan and will be sharing with you.

CREATION OF MONEY MARKET FUNDS

Money market funds were created in 1971. But to keep everything in perspective, let me remind you that in 1973 to 1974, the market experienced the most severe bear market since 1929, with most investors suffering losses of 40 to 50 percent and even more. So, in 1975, as a result of this devastating bear market, mutual fund families began offering the telephone-switching feature. This was a great advance because telephone switching enabled investors to move their money between the safe haven of "money funds" and the growth-oriented "stock mutual funds" simply by making a toll-free telephone call.

It was the advent of the telephone-switching feature that made this plan practical. You'll see how we use this feature, both to stay liquid and to keep our money growing, in just a moment.

HOW THE FABIAN PLAN STARTED

In 1976, 10 years after I first entered the securities industry, I wrote my first book on mutual fund investing: *How to Be Your Own Investment*

Counselor. In this book I described my recommended trading rules. In addition, I said that at a later date I would write a mutual fund advisory newsletter, supporting those who followed the Fabian Compounding Plan. I outlined what it would be called, what it would contain, and how much it would cost. A few months after my book was published, I started receiving checks in the mail asking for subscriptions to this newsletter. To meet this enthusiastic response, I wrote the first issue of the *Fabian Telephone Switch Newsletter* and began publishing it in April of 1977.

MY INVESTMENT PHILOSOPHY

What I had learned during my first 10 years working with individual investors has been confirmed over and over again since then. So, based on my experiences and insights into human nature, I have developed an investment philosophy that serves as the foundation of this compounding plan.

You see, in every investment transaction there are two components. One component is the investment itself; the second component is the investor. Have you ever thought about this? Everyone knows that the world is deluged with information about every conceivable type of investment. But *virtually no one pays much attention to the second component, the investor.* Well, that is what makes my plan different. With my plan, the investor comes first, the investment second.

I have long believed that it is necessary to meet people's emotional needs first, before trying to encourage them to use any particular investment vehicle or strategy. Isn't it true that any investment approach, no matter how profitable, has absolutely no value for those who can't or won't follow it? It is a mistake to think that just because a particular investment has been profitable for some people in the past, others will use it, and that this fact alone will encourage people to invest their serious money in it. Well, that's not how real-life investing works.

Over the years, I have observed that there are some things people will do and some things they will not do. One of the things they won't do is invest a large percentage of their money (their serious money) in complex and time-consuming investments. They just do not have the time, patience, understanding, or temperament to implement and monitor such strategies. It does not matter how potentially profitable these complicated investments may be. They won't do it, and I don't blame them.

My philosophy, therefore, is to put people first, offering an investment approach that is easy to understand and simple to follow. It has pleased me immensely that, over the years, hundreds of investors who have used my plan have written to me (and also approached me at investment conferences) to tell me what a positive impact this plan has had, and continues to have, on their lives. Many have told me they tried numerous investments and investment strategies over the years, but none worked for them until they found this compounding plan.

Why is simplicity so important? Because if the investment plan is simple, you will be able to follow it. If you can follow it, and it is also effective, then you can reap the power of compounded growth at 20 percent. And if you can reap the power of compounded growth at 20 percent, in time you will become a self-made millionaire. It's just that simple.

CHAPTER 9

The Basics of the Plan

HISTORY OF THE FABIAN COMPOUNDING PLAN

My plan was launched in 1976 based on backtesting. In other words, the plan was verified to be effective using historical share price data. But since then, the plan has proven enormously successful in a quarter century of actual operation being followed by tens of thousands of investors. When you understand that this plan is both simple and effective, and that you can easily adopt it for yourself, you will believe you can become a self-made millionaire.

Some of the information regarding my plan was first published in 1976 in my book *How to Be Your Own Investment Counselor.* The essence of the plan, as described in 1976, is still valid today. But over the years, I have made minor modifications to keep up with changes in the mutual fund industry and the investment markets. For example, in 1976 there were only 450 mutual funds. Since then, that number has grown to over 11,000. Let's see how it works.

THE COMPOUNDING PLAN OBJECTIVE

The objective of the Fabian Compounding Plan is to accumulate wealth through the power of compounding. To realize the full potential of compounding, however, we must make a commitment to persistently work the plan. Therefore, the plan must be easy to understand and simple to follow. If it is, then we can make it a routine part of our lives, allowing it to grow our investment dollars into the fortune we desire.

We use mutual funds for our investment vehicle. The biggest advantage of using them is their simplicity. The only decision one has to make regarding their use is to determine whether the general market is going up or going down. *All* mutual funds will move *in the same direction* as the general market. This is really the only premise you must accept regarding this method of investing, and it is easily proved.

Look at the mutual fund listing page in your newspaper for any day that the Dow Jones Industrials are up. A glance down the change column will show you that virtually all of the domestic growth funds are up for that trading day. Look at the same mutual fund listing on any day the Dow Jones Industrials are down, and you'll see that virtually all of the domestic growth funds are down.

The only unknown is how much each fund will go up or how much each will go down. But once you see that you can consistently identify the direction of the general market, then you will agree that you can consistently be right using mutual funds. The only problem, then, is to identify and use one or more of the better-performing funds (more on this further on). But even if a mediocre fund is used, a profit will still be realized.

Trading Strategy
The Aggressive/Growth Part of the Plan

When the technical indicators I will be explaining in a moment tell us the direction of the general market is in an *uptrend,* we will "switch" our investment dollars into *growth-oriented mutual funds.*

The Conservative/Holding Part of the Plan

When the technical indicators I will explain shortly tell us the direction of the general market is in a *downtrend,* we will "switch" our investment dollars to the safety of *money market funds.*

All mutual fund companies offering the telephone-switch feature also offer a money market fund. A money fund, as it is called for short, is essentially a safe haven for your money, offering a rate of return consistent with passbook savings. During severe short-term market corrections and, most important, during long-term market declines, we do not want our investment dollars subjected to market losses. So, switching to money funds makes for a safe and effective way to keep our money growing, while the general market is unproductive.

See the sidebar for an overview of trading strategy.

FUND SELECTION AT BEGINNING OF THE MARKET BUY CYCLE

In selecting the specific mutual fund or funds to use, we need only observe and compare the actual performance results of funds over the recent past. This is important: It is a phenomenon of growth-oriented mutual funds that the ones that perform best at the beginning of an upward market cycle usually continue to perform best for the entire cycle. Don't ignore or erase from your mind any of the other available funds. Different market climates, at different periods of time, will produce different market leaders.

TWO TECHNICAL INDICATORS

There are only two indicators that you will need to maintain and observe in order to operate the trend-following compounding plan. These two indicators give *all* of the signals necessary to properly position your investment dollars. Remember, while the market trend is up, you will be positioned in growth-oriented mutual funds, and while the market trend is down, you will be positioned in money funds.

The two indicator tables to be maintained are as follows:

1. *Dow Jones Composite Index*   Lists week-ending closing readings, plus a 39-week moving average reading of this index (a good source for this index is your daily newspaper). See Figure 9-1. We use the Dow Jones Composite Index because this index is made up of 65 large companies, industrials, and transportations that accurately reflect the general domestic market.

2. *Domestic Fund Composite* (DFC)   Lists week-ending closing prices, plus a 39-week moving average reading of this index. See Figure 9-2. We use the Domestic Fund Composite because this index is made up of five growth-oriented mutual funds that accurately reflect the trend of the investment vehicles we use with the compounding plan. The average mutual fund in the DFC is composed of 200 common stocks. The performance of an individual

fund is, of course, the net performance of the stocks it holds. Since the DFC is made up of five funds, it represents roughly up to 1,000 stocks—again, a good reflection of the general domestic market.

As you've already seen, you only need to know the trend of the market, either up or down, to know exactly how to position your investment dollars. Remember that all domestic growth-oriented mutual funds will move in the same direction as the domestic general market. So once you know the direction of the general domestic market, you will know what to do.

But why do we take a 39-week average reading of our indicators to determine the trend of the market? Obviously, we could use other time periods. However, a shorter time frame, say, 20 weeks, will generate more frequent switch signals. And a longer time frame, say, 52 weeks, will result in waiting too long for the switch signals to develop. Both could result in less profits.

The problem with the use of most technical indicators is that they give too many false signals, or *whipsaws,* as they are called. In other words, a sell signal is given followed almost immediately by a new buy signal, and at other times the reverse. When this happens too often, most investors lose faith in their indicators and, as a result, give up their investment plan. The same is true when an investor tries to use too many indicators, often finding them contradictory to one another. In practice, I have found that the two indicators, with their 39-week average readings, give the greatest number of accurate signals, while also keeping the investor on target to reach his or her goal.

HOW THE MARKET TREND IS IDENTIFIED

The way we determine the market trend is to watch the relationship between the most recent weekly reading of the two technical indicators and their 39-week moving average readings (39WAR). The 39WAR is simply the closing readings for the past 39 weeks divided by 39 (the average for this period).

Essentially, we want to know, for each indicator, whether its current reading is above or below its 39WAR. In other words, is the "current reading" higher or lower than the "average reading" for the past 39 weeks? This tells us whether the current market action is stronger or weaker than the past market action.

The 39-week moving average is primarily a momentum index. It smooths out the widely oscillating weekly price movements so that the

FIGURE 9-1

	W/E DATE	CLOSING READING	39 WEEK AVG.	WD	W/E DATE	CLOSING READING	39 WEEK AVG.	WD
1	1/ 2/98	2611.15	2415.61	8.09	10/ 2	2498.09	2750.72	-9.18
2	1/ 9	2518.42	2427.46	3.75	10/ 9	2484.70	2749.85	-9.64
3	1/16	2575.10	2441.59	5.47	10/16	2650.09	2751.77	-3.70
4	1/23	2556.85	2452.98	4.23	10/23	2642.76	2753.98	-4.04
5	1/30	2604.30	2465.45	5.63	10/30	2692.28	2756.23	-2.32
6	2/ 6	2684.80	2477.47	8.37	11/ 6	2789.11	2758.91	1.09
7	2/13	2750.58	2490.65	10.44	11/13	2758.71	2759.12	-0.01
8	2/20	2740.39	2503.36	9.47	11/20	2829.95	2761.41	2.48
9	2/27	2746.25	2515.14	9.19	11/27	2882.39	2764.90	4.25
10	3/ 6	2775.95	2527.75	9.82	12/ 4			
11	3/13	2804.45	2540.38	10.39	12/11			
12	3/20	2884.77	2553.24	12.98	12/18			
13	3/27	2842.60	2564.80	10.83	12/25			
14	4/ 3	2918.21	2578.97	13.15	1/ 4/99			
15	4/10	2891.25	2590.59	11.61	1/ 8			
16	4/17	2960.79	2604.09	13.70	1/15			
17	4/24	2897.25	2614.45	10.82	1/22			
18	5/ 1	2900.07	2624.18	10.51	1/29			
19	5/ 8	2867.43	2634.04	8.86	2/ 5			
20	5/15	2870.85	2646.01	8.50	2/12			
21	5/22	2866.19	2656.43	7.90	2/19			
22	5/29	2824.59	2667.39	5.89	2/26			
23	6/ 5	2856.09	2677.54	6.67	3/ 5			
24	6/12	2833.82	2686.83	5.47	3/12			
25	6/19	2810.28	2693.59	4.33	3/19			
26	6/26	2855.59	2701.86	5.69	3/26			
27	7/ 3	2898.23	2710.29	6.93	4/ 2			
28	7/10	2920.23	2718.99	7.40	4/ 9			
29	7/17	2947.40	2729.26	7.99	4/16			
30	7/24	2831.48	2727.06	3.45	4/23			
31	7/31	2786.06	2746.86	1.43	4/30			
32	8/ 7	2702.28	2753.60	-1.86	5/ 7			
33	8/14	2649.21	2758.23	-3.95	5/14			
34	8/21	2674.17	2761.19	-3.15	5/21			
35	8/28	2551.58	2761.09	-7.59	5/28			
36	9/ 4	2411.00	2755.18	-12.49	6/ 4			
37	9/11	2469.12	2752.55	-10.30	6/11			
38	9/18	2536.08	2752.46	-7.86	6/18			
39	9/25	2566.15	2753.62	-6.81	6/25			

WEEKLY SUMMARY TABLE DOW JONES COMPOSITE INDEX

FIGURE 9-2

| | WEEKLY SUMMARY TABLE | | DOMESTIC FUND COMPOSITE INDEX | | | | | |

	W/E DATE	CLOSING READING	39 WEEK AVG.	WD	W/E DATE	CLOSING READING	39 WEEK AVG.	WD
1	1/ 2/98	100092.36	95026.85	5.33	10/ 2	97230.40	108722.83	-10.57
2	1/ 9	95461.53	95476.53	-0.02	10/ 9	93697.55	108677.60	-13.78
3	1/16	98983.84	95977.13	3.13	10/16	100763.46	108723.24	-7.32
4	1/23	90720.11	96486.97	2.31	10/23	103095.84	108835.43	-5.27
5	1/30	100422.09	96910.72	3.62	10/30	106036.13	108979.38	-2.70
6	2/ 6	103404.95	97364.35	6.20	11/ 6	109585.83	109137.87	0.41
7	2/13	104603.70	97840.47	6.91	11/13	108117.28	109227.96	-1.02
8	2/20	105869.56	98299.85	7.70	11/20	112041.51	109386.21	2.43
9	2/27	107491.44	98788.35	8.81	11/27	115071.75	109580.58	5.01
10	3/ 6	108485.44	99280.29	9.27	12/ 4			
11	3/13	110227.77	99750.59	10.50	12/11			
12	3/20	112702.05	100247.58	12.42	12/18			
13	3/27	112691.75	100762.88	11.84	12/25			
14	4/ 3	115111.43	101273.64	13.66	1/ 4/99			
15	4/10	114384.72	101741.20	12.43	1/ 8			
16	4/17	114610.66	102200.19	12.14	1/15			
17	4/24	113039.88	102569.38	10.21	1/22			
18	5/ 1	114764.98	102954.61	11.47	1/29			
19	5/ 8	113425.66	103332.88	9.77	2/ 5			
20	5/15	113199.99	103773.14	9.08	2/12			
21	5/22	113108.06	104159.32	8.59	2/19			
22	5/29	111475.22	104552.41	6.62	2/26			
23	6/ 5	112806.71	104891.03	7.55	3/ 5			
24	6/12	111366.50	105200.41	5.86	3/12			
25	6/19	112039.64	105460.96	6.24	3/19			
26	6/26	115372.72	105820.61	9.03	3/26			
27	7/ 3	117147.35	106171.75	10.34	4/ 2			
28	7/10	119316.61	106564.16	11.97	4/ 9			
29	7/17	120875.41	107077.17	12.89	4/16			
30	7/24	115783.01	107470.57	7.73	4/23			
31	7/31	113663.97	107891.14	5.35	4/30			
32	8/ 7	109881.82	108184.00	1.57	5/ 7			
33	8/14	106674.06	108429.87	-1.62	5/14			
34	8/21	107240.02	108621.82	-1.27	5/21			
35	8/28	100969.14	108688.00	-7.10	5/28			
36	9/ 4	95730.08	108534.74	-11.80	6/ 4			
37	9/11	98813.70	108558.35	-8.98	6/11			
38	9/18	100419.05	108636.56	-7.56	6/18			
39	9/25	102675.52	108796.22	-5.63	6/25			

overall market trend (or momentum either up or down) is readily identified. Thus, if the 39WAR is rising, the market is in an uptrend. If the 39WAR is falling, the market is in a downtrend.

AN UPTREND IS A BUY SIGNAL

When the current readings of our two indicators penetrate up through their 39-week moving averages, the market action is considered positive. We call this a *buy signal.* As long as the current readings remain above their 39WARs, we position our investment dollars in the growth-oriented mutual funds.

A DOWNTREND IS A SELL SIGNAL

When the current readings of our two indicators penetrate down through their 39-week moving averages, the market action is considered negative. We call this a *sell signal,* and during this time, we switch our investment dollars to the protection of money market funds.

That's all there is to it. Simple enough? On the pages that follow, I will provide more details, answer some questions, and provide some helpful tips. But in a nutshell, that's the Fabian Compounding Plan.

SOLVES ALL MARKET AND INVESTOR PROBLEMS

As simple as it seems, the compounding plan solves all of the problems inherent in the stock market and human psychology that can cause investors to fail (remember, this was the reason it was created). My plan is easy to understand and simple to follow. It doesn't take much time to implement. Once in place, it takes just five minutes a week to monitor. The plan captures growth during market uptrends, and protects against losses during market downtrends. It provides discipline with its simple trading rules. It eliminates confusion and worry, since it tells you exactly what to do at all times. And it has the potential to achieve the 20 percent annualized compounded growth goal, so that over time you can become a self-made millionaire.

BEST TIME TO START

Once you have decided to start using this plan, your first question will be "When is the best time to begin?" The answer with this plan is *now!* Since your objective will be accomplished over the long term, the sooner you get started, the better. The two indicators will tell you whether to use the aggressive part of the plan now or to use the conservative part now. That's the beauty of it: It always tells you what to do.

Your frame of mind, along with your attitude about the stock market during each cycle, will influence your probabilities for long-term success. Be easy on yourself by letting the market tell you what it wants to do. And then *go along* with it. *Don't* fight the market and become emotionally upset because it does not behave as you think it should behave. The road to the poorhouse is paved with the wreckage of those who bet on their own predictions and lost.

Most of the time while following the plan, you will feel very confident. After you have switched into a growth-oriented mutual fund and the market continues to move higher, everything will seem right with the world. You'll get this same confident feeling after you switch into a money fund and the market falls apart. You may feel uneasy, however, when the market trend is going through a transition, changing directions from up to down or down to up. At these critical times, your faith in the investment plan, and how strongly you want to accomplish your long-term financial objective, will be tested. To assist you at these times, I have included some ideas you should keep in mind during each phase of the plan.

ATTITUDE DURING MARKET CYCLES

While positioned in a money fund, you will switch into a growth-oriented mutual fund when the current readings of both *the Dow Jones Composite Index and the Domestic Fund Composite Index pass above their 39-week moving average readings.* This is a market uptrend and a buy signal.

During a market uptrend, remind yourself that the stock market moves in cycles. No matter how strong it may appear at any particular time, history has taught us that all growth is cyclical. Remind yourself that growth-oriented mutual funds during up markets usually outperform the market indices such as the Dow Jones Industrial Index. Remind yourself of your reason for investing: the long-term accumulation of wealth. Since your goals are long term, there is no reason to be concerned when the indicators tell you to switch to money funds. When that occurs, you will view this move as assurance that you will have the maximum amount of capital available to switch back into the growth-oriented funds on the next buy signal.

While positioned in a growth-oriented mutual fund, you will switch into a money fund when the current readings of both *the Dow Jones Composite Index and the Domestic Fund Composite fall below their 39-week moving average readings.* This is a market downtrend and a sell signal.

During a downtrend remind yourself that the stock market moves in cycles. No matter how weak it may appear at any particular time, history has taught us that all of the doom and gloom we hear at such times never come to pass. Eventually, the market will make allowances for all of the bad news and will start up again. Remind yourself that the money fund you are using is paying the highest yields available consistent with liquidity and safety of principal. Remind yourself of your reason for investing—the long-term accumulation of wealth. Since your goals are long term, there is no reason to be concerned when the indicators tell you to switch. When that occurs, you will view this move as your next opportunity to add compounded growth to your existing investment dollars.

SELECTING YOUR MUTUAL FUNDS

The easy answer here is to use the fund (or funds) that performed best over the recent past. Earlier I said that a phenomenon of growth-oriented mutual funds is that the ones that perform best at the beginning of an upward market cycle usually continue to perform best for the entire cycle. However, since this cannot be guaranteed, we must monitor their performance. I therefore encourage you to maintain weekly summary tables for at least five mutual funds for your potential future selection.

While your investment dollars are positioned in a growth-oriented mutual fund during market uptrends, make periodic comparisons of the mutual funds you are monitoring to evaluate their performance. For each of these funds, maintain 4-week, 8-week, 12-week, and year-to-date performance tables. A comparison of these results will help you determine if your fund is performing as well as the others, and whether you need to redeem your shares and switch to one or more of the better-performing growth funds.

The Domestic Fund Composite Trading Plan

TECHNICAL INDICATORS

The availability of investment data is important to implementing and monitoring my plan. There are many sources of investment data on the Internet, along with Fabian.com, and new ones are being added almost daily. However, we strive to keep it simple.

As you have already learned, the DFC Plan uses only two technical indicators to generate buy and sell signals—current readings and 39WARs of the Domestic Fund Composite and The Dow Jones 65 Composite. You can find these indicators in the following:

- The 39-week average reading (39WAR) of the Domestic Fund Composite (DFC) can be found monthly in the *FIR Newsletter* and is updated weekly over the FIR 24-hour telephone hotline. (See below for alternative indicators if you don't subscribe to the newsletter.)
- The 39-week average reading (39WAR) of the Dow Jones 65 Composite (DJC) can be found in the *FIR Newsletter*.

Note: For mutual fund investors who do not have access to the *FIR Newsletter*, there are two substitute indicators that may be used:

- Current and 39-week average reading (39WAR) of the S&P 500 Index.

- Current and 39-week average reading (39WAR) of the Dow
  Jones Industrials Index.

Readings for these indicators can be found in all major newspapers. In addition, weekly updated charts for both of these market indicators, along with their current 39WARs, can be found in the Benchmark section of the web page at www.fabianlive.com. There is no charge to access this website and obtain this information.

TREND-LINE CHARTS BRING MARKET MOVES INTO FOCUS

Historically, market trends have lasted for months and sometimes for years. To calculate the 39-week average reading for any market indicator, you simply add up its week-ending prices for the previous 39 weeks and divide by 39. The result is a single reading that represents the average of the past 39 weeks (approximately 10 months). An example of the process is shown in Figure 10-1.

You can obtain a new reading for the 39WAR at the end of each week by adding in the latest week-ending price and subtracting the one from 40 weeks past. The 39WAR smoothes out the widely oscillating daily price movements so that a clear picture of the trend emerges. Plotted on a chart, these readings show a line that is either rising or falling, depending on the prevailing market trend. When the current price is also charted, you can readily see where it is in relation to the 39-week trend line.

Figure 10-1 also plots the daily prices and the 39WAR for the Kaufman Fund. In the chart, the jagged line represents the daily prices, and the smooth line represents the 39WAR. Note that there were times when the daily prices were above the 39WAR, and other times when the daily prices were below the 39WAR.

Figure 10-2 is a five-year chart of the Fidelity Magellan Fund, along with its 39WAR. This shows, from 1982 through 1986, when you would have been invested in the Fidelity Magellan Fund and when you would have been in a money fund, provided you had confirmation from the Dow Jones 65 Composite Index and Domestic Fund Composite Index.

SELLING IS AN IMPORTANT PART OF INVESTING

From my years of experience in working with investors, I know that many of them are reluctant to sell some or all of their existing mutual fund hold-

FIGURE 10-1

Listening To The Market

Week Average Reading

Date of last 39 Fridays	Price	39 Week Average
Mar-28-97	5.22	5.53
Apr-04-97	5.18	5.53
Apr-11-97	5.08	5.53
Apr-18-97	5.09	5.53
Apr-25-97	4.99	5.53
May-02-97	5.33	5.53
May-09-97	5.49	5.53
May-16-97	5.52	5.54
May-23-97	5.69	5.54
May-30-97	5.79	5.55
Jun-06-97	5.82	5.57
Jun-13-97	5.85	5.57
Jun-20-97	5.95	5.58
Jun-27-97	5.90	5.59
Jul-11-97	6.06	5.60
Jul-18-97	6.15	5.61
Jul-25-97	6.20	5.63
Aug-01-97	6.27	5.64
Aug-08-97	6.26	5.66
Aug-15-97	6.17	5.68
Aug-22-97	6.25	5.69
Aug-29-97	6.26	5.71
Sep-05-97	6.44	5.73
Sep-12-97	6.55	5.75
Sep-19-97	6.65	5.78
Sep-26-97	6.65	5.81
Oct-03-97	6.80	5.84
Oct-10-97	6.84	5.87
Oct-17-97	6.58	5.89
Oct-24-97	6.57	5.91
Oct-31-97	6.40	5.92
Nov-07-97	6.42	5.94
Nov-14-97	6.34	5.96
Nov-21-97	6.47	5.98
Nov-28-97	6.37	6.00
Dec-05-97	6.50	6.02
Dec-12-97	6.22	6.04
Dec-19-97	6.17	6.06
Dec-26-97	6.13	6.07

Sum of last 39 Week Ending Prices = 236.62
39 Week Average = 236.62/39 = 6.07

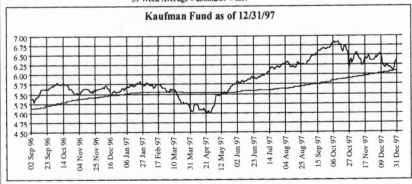

Kaufman Fund as of 12/31/97

Source: Kaufman Fund, 1998.

FIGURE 10-2

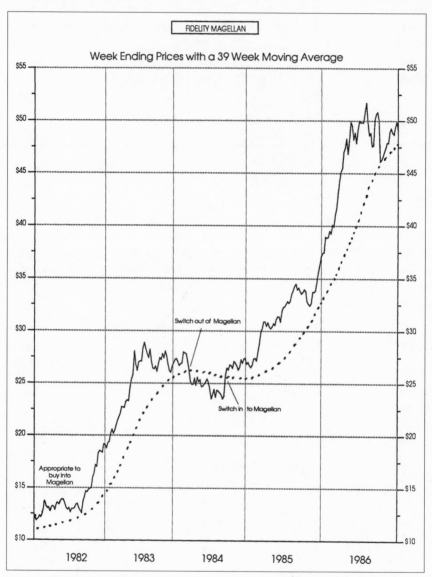

Source: Fidelity Magellan, 1987.

ings even though the trading and monitoring rules of the plan tell them to do so. So, let me offer this advice. To become a self-made millionaire, not only is it important to follow the switch signals but also to make sure your funds are performing well enough to meet the 20 percent annualized compounded growth goal. If your fund is an underperformer, you'll need to redeem your shares and purchase a better-performing fund or funds.

39-WEEK DIFFERENTIAL (39WD)

The 39WD (available on our website) is the percentage that the current reading of a fund or indicator is above or below its 39-week average reading.

For example, when the 39WD of the DFC is +6.26, it is 6.26 percent above its 39-week average reading. Simply put, the 39WD tells us how close we are to a potential buy or sell signal. In the above case, the DFC would have to drop by over 6 percent to penetrate down through its 39WAR for a sell signal (provided the Dow Jones Composite has also crossed down through its 39WAR). All market indicators on the website include their current 39WD. You can tell at a glance whether a buy or sell signal is approaching.

HOW MANY FUNDS TO BUY?

During domestic market uptrends (buy signals), my recommendation is to put 100 percent of the money you have available for investment in the diversified domestic growth-oriented funds. And during market downtrends (sell signals), I recommend putting 100 percent of your investment money into a money market fund. It's just that simple.

So, once you decide to implement the plan, your next step is to decide how many funds to buy. The table below provides general guidelines.

Under $15,000	1 to 2 funds
$15,000 to $30,000	2 to 3 funds
$30,000 to $50,000	3 to 4 funds
$50,000 to $100,000	4 to 5 funds
$100,000 to $200,000	5 to 8 funds

If you need more than two funds, you may want to consider opening an account with a discount broker, such as Charles Schwab & Co., which offers hundreds of no-load funds from which to choose. With an account there, you can cross fund family lines with a single phone call and reduce mail clutter with a single statement.

ORGANIZING FOR SUCCESS

As with most things in life, when investing, organization is an essential element. Careful organization will not only help you monitor your investment performance through the years, but it will also make tax preparation much easier.

Following are three organizational aids you will need:

- *Three-ring binder.* It may seem elementary, but one of the most important tools for investment organization is a simple three-ring binder. Let's call this your investment notebook. Here you will place all the information pertaining to the mutual fund accounts you are using with the plan. See Figure 10-3.

- *General Information Worksheet.* The most important worksheet you will keep in your binder is the General Information form. It provides all of your account and investment information in one easy, at-a-glance format. You will probably want to file this at the very front of your notebook. See Figure 10-4.

- *Telephone and Online Exchange Worksheet.* You should keep a Telephone Exchange worksheet in your binder. Although infrequent, mistakes do happen, and that's why you'll want a written record of any action you have taken on your investments. This information will also help you at tax time. See Figure 10-5.

Let's take a closer look at the Telephone and Online Exchange Worksheet. Each time you purchase or sell a mutual fund, record your transaction by providing the following information:

1. The date and time you called.
2. The full name of the mutual fund or discount broker representative assisting you.
3. The action you are taking.
4. The per share price of the fund(s) you are buying or selling and the total number of shares involved.
5. The total transaction amount.
6. The confirmation or reference number you are given by the representative.

FIGURE 10-3

Your Investment Notebook

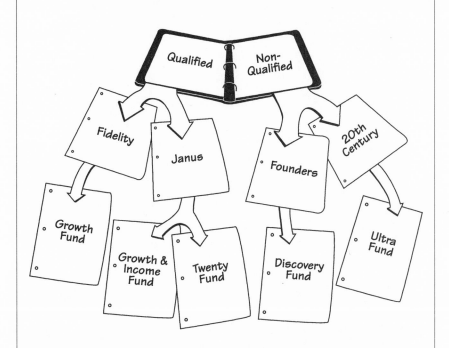

Step 1 Separate your accounts into taxable and tax-deferred categories. Tax-deferred accounts include IRA's, Keoghs, 401(k)s and other tax-favored vehicles such as variable annuities.

Step 2 Make separate sections for each fund family you're using in the two main categories.

Step 3 Under each fund family, make a separate section for each stock fund you own. (Although you may begin the Fabian Plan in a money market account, you'll probably find it easier to organize by stock funds, since you will be invested in them most of the time.)

Step 4 As you receive statements for your stock funds and corresponding money market account, file them in your investment notebook in chronological order with the latest statement on top.

Step 5 If you're using multiple stock funds in a fund family, but switching to just one money market fund for downtrends, make a separate section for the money market accounts as well.

FIGURE 10-4

General Information Worksheet

Name _____Tax I.D./Social Security # _____

Fund Family _____

Telephone Exchange # _____Information #_____

Equity Fund Name	Account #	Money Fund Name	Account #

Fund Family _____

Telephone Exchange # _____Information #_____

Equity Fund Name	Account #	Money Fund Name	Account #

Fund Family _____

Telephone Exchange # _____Information #_____

Equity Fund Name	Account #	Money Fund Name	Account #

FIGURE 10-5

Telephone Exchange Worksheet

Date	Time	Full Name of Cust. Serv.Rep	Reason for Call	Price per Share	No. Of Shares	Total $ Amount	Reference or Confirmation No.

Note: If you are trading online with your computer, print out the pages showing the details of your trade, including the order acknowledgement page and confirmation number.

Later, check the transaction confirmation information you receive from your fund family or discount broker, making sure that their details match your details. If for some reason they do not, call the company to reconcile the problem using the information from your Telephone and Online Exchange Worksheet.

PERFORMANCE HISTORY—DOMESTIC FUND COMPOSITE PLAN

Figure 10-6 shows how the simple DFC switching plan has actually performed over the long term. This table has four headings:

- Column 1 lists the DFC buy dates.
- Column 2 lists the DFC sell dates, which have been generated since April 1977.
- Column 3 shows the performance results for each of the periods of time while the plan was invested in the market.
- Column 4 shows the amount of interest earned while in money funds waiting for the next buy signal.

From time to time, over the years, the individual mutual funds making up the DFC are changed. However, the funds are never changed during a buy cycle. The reason is to keep everything as simple as possible.

DOMESTIC FUND COMPOSITE CHARTS—1966 TO 1999

In 1976, when I was organizing the data for the book *How to Be Your Own Investment Counselor,* I wanted to be able to show as much history as possible on the mechanics of the Domestic Fund Composite Plan. It is hard to believe now, but in 1976 mutual fund data banks with past prices did not exist. So, in order to get week-ending fund prices, I had to go down into the basement of California State University at Long Beach and manually record week-ending mutual fund prices from back issues of *Barron's.* (I have been married for over 50 years, and I can honestly say that the only time that my wife Marie ever seriously considered leaving me was during the many weeks while we worked together in the library basement, gathering this pricing data.)

FIGURE 10-6

Fabian Investment Resources
Domestic Fund Composite
Performance Table

1	2	3	4
			Interest Earned
			While in
Buy Date	**Sell Date**	**Gain (Loss)**	**Money Funds**
4/1/77	10/23/78	48.16	4.21
3/28/79	10/23/79	3.58	0.89
11/16/79	3/18/80	2.11	2.88
5/23/80	7/23/81	45.20	16.52
8/27/82	1/27/84	47.57	5.12
8/6/84	12/7/84	(6.72)	0.94
1/17/85	9/12/86	32.05	0.44
10/30/86	10/16/87	19.56	3.16
4/11/88	4/15/88	(3/16)	0.36
6/2/88	11/14/88	(1.13)	0.45
12/6/88	1/23/90	23.44	0.90
3/19/90	3/22/90	(1.62)	1.18
5/18/90	8/7/90	(4.25)	3.55
1/25/91	8/24/92	33.99	0.56
11/6/92	3/31/94	20.39	1.02
8/30/94	11/23/94	(4.22)	0.58
1/9/95	7/16/96	30.97	1.00
9/16/96	8/12/98	42.42	0.80
11/9/98	9/22/99	16.97	*

GAIN SINCE INCEPTION		345.31	44.56	389.87
Divided by years				22.50
AVERAGE ANNUAL RETURN				17.33

Note (*) As of 9/23/99, the DFC was not invested.

Source: Fabian Investment Resources.

Even though accumulating these prices was a very tedious task, I just felt compelled to make the effort. As I saw it, if I was going to recommend to individual investors that they put all of their serious money into the Domestic Fund Composite Plan, I had to show them at least 10 years of history. I wanted to show enough of a life span so that they could see both up and down markets. The DFC charts covering the period 1966 to 1999 are shown in Figures 10-7a through 10-7e.

Take the time and review these DFC charts. Identify each buy and sell signal from the dates shown on the Past Performance Table in Figure 10-6. Keep in mind, however, the DFC chart represents only one of the two indicators required to generate each signal. First, the DFC must penetrate its 39WAR, and then the DJC (Dow Jones Composite) must also confirm the trend by penetrating its 39WAR. In the real world, very seldom, if ever, do both indicators go through their individual 39WAR on exactly the same day. You will find that since 1977, when the newsletter was first published, the DFC Plan, on average, issued only one buy and sell signal per year.

FIGURE 10-7A

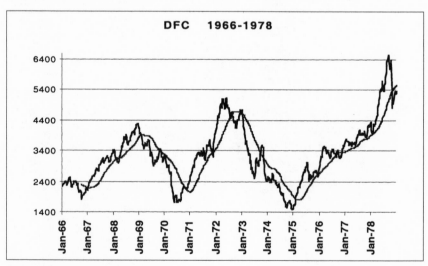

Source: Fabian Investment Resources.

FIGURE 10-7B

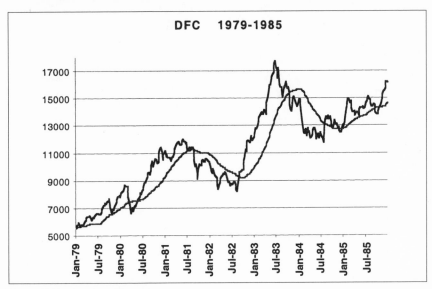

Source: Fabian Investment Resources.

FIGURE 10-7C

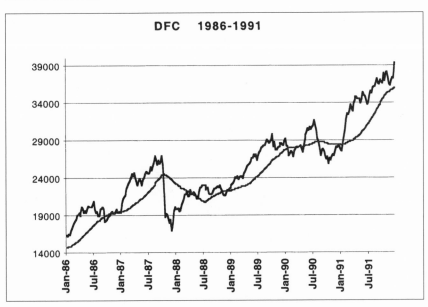

Source: Fabian Investment Resources.

FIGURE 10-7D

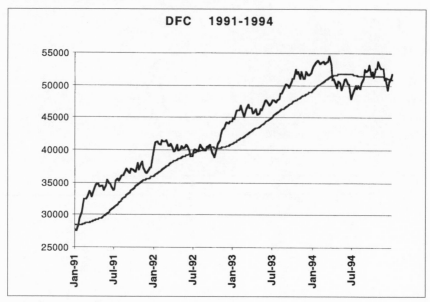

Source: Fabian Investment Resources.

FIGURE 10-7E

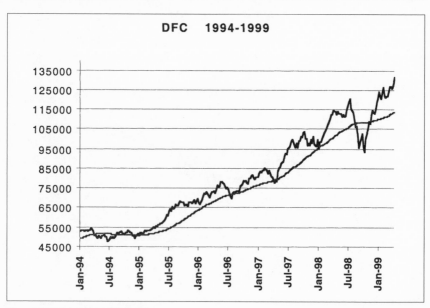

Source: Fabian Investment Resources.

As you examine the charts, you will see that in January 1984, a sell signal was not issued until after the DFC had gone well below its 39WAR. This was because the confirming Dow indicator did not go below its 39WAR until later. Notice that during 1985, the DFC went below its own 39WAR, but a switch signal was never generated during that year, because the confirming Dow indicator did not confirm by going below its 39WAR before the DFC once again moved higher.

CHAPTER 11

Getting Started with the DFC Plan

IMPLEMENTING THE FABIAN COMPOUNDING PLAN

I have emphasized many times that my plan is an investment approach that is easy to understand and simple to follow. In order for you to implement my plan, however, I am assuming you can answer the following questions and understand their significance:

1. What is compounded growth?
2. Why is it important to have a goal of 20 percent annualized compounded growth?
3. What is a mutual fund and what are the benefits of using them in your investment plan?
4. What is the difference between a trend-following investment strategy and a buy-and-hold strategy?
5. What is "telephone switching"?
6. What is the Domestic Fund Composite and why was it created?
7. What is the Dow Jones 65 Composite and where can you find its current reading?
8. What is the significance of the 39-week average reading and how is it used?
9. Which do you believe is more important: the investor or the investment?

After you are comfortable with your answers to the above questions, you "see the entire picture" and are then ready to begin following the specific steps to becoming a self-made millionaire.

MAKE YOUR INITIAL DEPOSIT INTO A MONEY FUND

Always start the my compounding plan by opening your account with your chosen mutual fund company or discount broker and placing your initial investment in a money market fund. After you receive a confirmation statement, you will then determine the current trend of the general market. The trend will tell you whether to remain in the money fund or switch to growth-oriented mutual funds.

THE FIRST STEP FOR INVESTORS
WITH NO MUTUAL FUND HOLDINGS

I will begin by assuming you are starting the implementation of the plan with at least $15,000, and you do not own any mutual funds. Later, I will discuss what to do if you already own some mutual funds or have less than $15,000 to invest when you begin.

At the start you should already have your three-ring binder investment notebook in place. You should list all the sources of data you may need from Fabian.com, Yahoo, Clear Station, etc. You should have a current copy of the *FIR Newsletter* or be prepared to use one of the substitute data sources I will be referencing. As a result, you will know whether you should be buying domestic growth-oriented funds, because a buy signal is in place, or staying in money market funds, because a sell signal is in place.

A substitute for the DFC and DJC indicators are the current readings of the S&P 500 and Dow Jones Industrials (DJI) indexes, along with their individual 39WARs. The trading rules are the same using these substitute indicators.

To determine the specific mutual funds to buy, refer to the "Domestic Funds" pages in the newsletter. Figures 11-1 and 11-2 are replicas of the Domestic Funds pages from the February 1999 issue of the newsletter. Four of the columns are identified with circled numbers.

- Column 1 shows the performance results covering the previous full buy cycle—9/16/96 to 8/12/98.

FIGURE 11-1

© Fabian Premium Investment Resource — February 1999

DOMESTIC FUNDS

Fabian Buy Cycles 9/16/96-8/12/98 (#1)	11/9/98 1/29/99 (#2)	# of cycles better than DFC/ total # cycles	Ticker	Ranking (see notes)		Domestic Indicators (#3)	Price	As of 1/29/99 39WAR	39WD (#4)	4 wk	8 wk	12 wk	Drawdown 7/20/98 8/12/98	Drawdown Avg per 3 cycles
42.42%	16.31%					DFC (16.67% for 21.83 yrs)	126524	111124	13.86%	4.63%	11.18%	15.46%	-9.96%	-9.91%
44.97	4.93					Dow Jones 65 Composite	2899.26	2760.70	5.02	0.99	2.99	3.95	-8.18	-7.11
3.21	0.29					Dow Jones 20 Bond	106.45	105.83	0.58	0.03	-0.49	0.10	-0.30	-0.75
45.23	5.18					Dow Jones Industrials	9358.83	8771.57	6.70	1.93	3.80	4.27	-7.99	-6.88
49.21	10.06					Dow Jones Transportations	3202.37	3086.88	3.74	1.68	4.92	7.88	-11.50	-9.59
12.72	20.06					OTC Industrials	1408.01	1220.67	15.35	7.96	15.28	19.89	-10.59	-12.13
58.52	13.22					Standard & Poor 500	1279.64	1122.49	14.00	4.10	8.74	12.15	-8.44	-6.67
22.15	1.21					Value Line Composite	431.10	433.19	-0.48	-1.38	1.67	0.35	-10.34	-8.72
						Unit Investment Trusts								
*	5.31		DIA			Diamond	93.28	87.32	6.83	2.08	3.41	4.30	-7.99	-7.99
62.13	13.00		SPY			Spider	127.66	111.92	14.06	3.53	8.16	12.19	-8.33	-6.68
38.98	8.06		MDY			Midcap Spider	70.94	64.90	9.31	-2.49	13.69	6.36	-9.95	-10.58
						Aggressive Growth Funds — category average				11.16	19.00	5.31	-11.08	-11.32
54.91	24.14	6/7	TWCUX	4	J S ✪	Amer Century 20th Ultra	$35.77	29.70	20.46	7.06	17.08	23.36	-10.46	-10.32
37.90	-1.39	1/3	BAETX	13	F J S	Babson Enterprise II	21.31	22.33	-4.59	-6.21	-3.10	-2.08	-9.32	-8.07
34.52	17.19	2/5	BARAX	15	◇ F J S	Baron Asset	52.74	46.68	12.99	4.35	16.11	16.11	-12.91	-10.43
11.63	19.18	1/2	BESCX	24	F J S	Berger Small Company Growth	4.02	3.62	11.06	6.35	19.64	18.89	-12.72	-12.07
22.73	7.80	3/6	DNLDX	20 >	J S	Dreyfus New Leaders	42.13	41.47	1.59	1.98	7.36	7.67	-10.09	-9.37
46.88	22.71	3/5	FDCAX	7	F	Fidelity Capital Appreciation	23.79	20.16	18.02	7.94	16.67	21.85	-9.54	-8.20
44.93	27.86	1/2	FFTYX	8	F	Fidelity Fifty	19.09	15.68	21.76	13.29	22.37	27.18	-11.97	-11.65
40.38	3.05	3/4	FLPSX	10 >		Fidelity Low-Priced Stock	22.62	22.69	-0.31	-1.01	2.13	2.63	-9.86	-6.74
16.00	25.36	1/4	FDISX	22	F S	Founders Discovery	25.97	21.29	22.00	6.57	19.23	25.25	-10.55	-14.26
39.50	23.27	4/7	FIDYX	11	F J S	Invesco Dynamics	16.66	14.10	18.18	5.44	16.93	22.85	-10.67	-9.79
11.98	16.05	1/3	FIEGX	23	F J S	Invesco Small Company	11.71	10.23	14.50	1.12	11.87	16.36	-11.62	-13.58
58.56	42.11	1/1	JAOLX	3	F J S	Janus Olympus	31.59	23.03	37.15	14.54	32.84	41.91	-10.16	-12.52
8.99	11.45	4/6	KAUFX	25 >	F J S ✪	Kaufmann Fund	5.70	5.42	5.13	0.35	7.55	11.06	-11.05	-11.47
23.57	9.33	1/2	MGSEX	19	F J S	Managers Special Equity	61.25	58.19	5.26	0.05	7.19	8.73	-10.30	-11.48
36.36	1.47	0/1	OAKSX	14	F J S	Oakmark Small Cap	14.37	14.93	-3.72	-2.71	-0.76	1.19	-11.26	-8.89
-9.98	15.80	1/2	PBEGX	28	F J S	PBHG Emerging Growth	24.03	21.93	9.60	0.33	13.24	15.80	-10.65	-14.29
28.37	4.78	3/5	OTCFX	17		Price Sm Cap Stock (frmly OTC)	20.51	20.30	1.03	-1.35	3.70	4.42	-9.55	-7.81
*	99.85	0/0	UOPIX	*		Profund Ultra OTC	157.18	81.99	91.70	31.81	64.07	101.90	-14.87	-14.87
39.11	49.81	2/5	RSEGX	12	F J S	Rob Stephens Em Growth	27.50	19.76	39.20	19.83	41.74	49.96	-14.32	-14.99
40.49	29.70	1/3	RSVPX	9	F J S	Rob Stephens Value + Gwth	29.03	23.09	25.70	12.00	20.93	28.64	-8.84	-11.37
95.49	45.00	1/2	RYOCX	1		Rydex OTC	48.24	32.86	46.83	16.63	30.52	45.96	-7.46	-7.46
82.93	8.69	3/7	SAFGX	2	F J S	Safeco Growth	23.22	22.49	3.26	2.29	7.67	7.72	-11.68	-11.80
28.17	5.89	0/2	SWSMX	18	S	Schwab Small Cap Index	16.28	15.74	3.45	0.18	6.09	5.44	-10.67	-12.44
5.74	22.54	1/7	SCDVX	26	F J S	Scudder Development	39.49	34.23	15.37	4.86	18.94	21.76	-10.00	-13.43
-3.12	15.30	5/7	SRFCX	27	F J S	SteinRoe Capital Opportunities	29.76	28.44	4.65	1.36	13.07	14.77	-13.46	-12.53
29.73	28.08	1/2	ACBGX	16	F J S	United Services Bonnel Growth	20.96	17.12	22.40	7.16	19.77	27.17	-8.54	-14.76
49.98	27.15	3/6	VALLX	6	F J	Value Line Leveraged Growth	52.44	41.75	25.62	8.30	19.87	26.10	-11.50	-10.18
22.48	15.06	3/5	CUEGX	21	F J S	Warburg Pincus Emerging Grth	40.58	37.06	9.51	1.53	13.89	14.79	-10.55	-11.62
54.84	14.89	1/1	WMICX	5	F J S	Wasatch Micro-cap	4.14	3.75	10.39	3.76	13.03	15.20	-10.09	-11.87
						Growth Funds — category average				5.13	12.32	16.42	-9.20	-8.09
68.56	12.46	2/2	BEOGX	4	J S	Amer Cent Bnhm Eq Gwth	23.30	20.73	12.41	2.60	8.66	11.51	-9.31	-8.45
62.64	15.43	1/2	BRGRX	9	F J S	Bramwell Growth	24.99	21.46	16.46	3.61	12.24	14.68	-8.11	-10.35
58.52	23.59	3/7	CLMBX	17	S	Columbia Growth	45.19	37.76	19.68	6.30	16.14	22.70	-10.13	-9.23
60.78	11.68	5/6	DGAGX	13	F J S	Dreyfus Appreciation	43.28	38.49	12.45	2.88	6.78	10.38	-8.19	-5.15
40.17	5.73	2/7	DCVIX	38	F J	Dreyfus Core Value	29.75	28.25	5.30	1.67	3.37	4.90	-8.91	-6.85
55.79	19.39	2/2	DRTHX	18	F J S	Dreyfus Third Century	13.02	10.87	19.75	6.03	12.28	18.71	-10.55	-8.21
59.36	17.82	4/5	FBGRX	16		Fidelity Blue Chip Growth	52.96	44.82	18.15	5.20	11.87	16.96	-8.14	-6.77
54.63	23.84	5/7	FCNTX	20 >		Fidelity Contrafund (clsd)	60.10	49.59	21.19	6.05	16.21	23.28	-8.73	-6.95
66.88	9.82	2/2	FDGFX	5	F	Fidelity Dividend Growth	29.13	25.95	12.25	1.39	6.95	8.81	-7.47	-8.46
48.41	32.96	2/2	FDEGX	27		Fidelity Emerging Growth	34.45	26.44	30.29	11.15	22.36	32.35	-9.31	-11.12
38.04	18.04	4/7	FDGRX	39	F	Fidelity Growth Company	53.81	45.01	19.55	6.40	13.42	17.34	-9.65	-8.50
53.76	20.54	5/7	FMAGX	22 >	✪	Fidelity Magellan (clsd)	127.16	106.14	19.80	5.58	13.90	19.61	-9.23	-7.50
46.91	38.95	2/2	FMILX	30		Fidelity New Millenium(clsd)	31.74	22.88	38.75	21.11	32.49	38.72	-9.32	-11.64
40.85	26.16	4/7	FOCPX	37		Fidelity OTC	47.52	37.44	26.92	8.92	20.55	28.50	-8.97	-9.23
62.86	13.68	2/2	FSMKX	8	F	Fidelity Spartan Market Index	88.74	77.36	14.71	4.03	9.07	12.62	-8.33	-6.53
49.43	17.04	4/4	FDSSX	26	F	Fidelity Stock Selector	30.16	26.87	12.25	5.05	12.92	15.92	-8.84	-7.92
29.25	-1.65	2/7	FDVLX	41	F	Fidelity Value	45.82	46.43	-1.31	-1.14	0.00	-2.23	-8.09	-7.00
47.91	18.62	5/7	FRGRX	28	F S ✪	Founders Growth	21.83	18.67	16.90	6.96	13.55	17.77	-10.27	-9.52

Source: Maverick Advisor.

FIGURE 11-2

© Fabian Premium Investment Resource   February 1999

DOMESTIC FUNDS

Fabian Buy Cycles 9/16/96- 8/12/98	# of cycles better than DFC/ 11/9/98 1/29/99	total # cycles	Ticker	Ranking (see notes)		Price	As of 1/29/99 39WAR	39WD	Weekly performance as of 1/29/99 4 wk	8 wk	12 wk	Drawdown 7/20/98 8/12/98	Drawdown Avg per 3 cycles
					Growth Funds (continued)								
43.85%	15.30%	2/2	FEQFX	35	F J S	Fremont Growth	$16.06	13.99	14.76%	4.63%	11.15%	14.58%	-9.95%	-8.21%
53.82	18.96	2/7	FLRFX	21	F J S	Invesco Growth	6.79	5.55	22.42	5.11	12.25	18.19	-7.99	-7.70
22.68	28.15	2/3	JAENX	43	F J S	Janus Enterprise	38.74	29.86	29.75	6.96	21.95	28.49	-8.81	-8.60
51.53	31.81	3/7	JANSX	25	F J S	Janus Fund	36.71	28.97	26.72	9.09	22.14	31.21	-8.32	-6.02
45.89	41.62	1/2	JAMRX	32	F J S	Janus Mercury	27.41	19.78	38.60	13.69	31.70	41.49	-9.78	-8.95
89.78	36.75	4/6	JAVLX	2	F J S	Janus Twenty	59.83	43.85	36.45	12.25	27.79	36.90	-9.15	-8.04
55.64	8.97	3/5	LLPFX	19	◊	Longleaf Partners	25.42	23.60	7.73	4.22	7.86	7.91	-8.50	-6.01
28.01	5.75	0/2	MNGFX	42	F J S	Montgomery Growth	20.92	20.20	3.58	1.45	3.43	4.62	-9.36	-8.07
46.13	18.17	2/7	NMANX	31	S	Neuberger & Berman Manhattan	12.10	10.66	13.48	1.26	13.62	17.21	-11.70	-11.60
44.64	5.47	2/7	NPRTX	33	S	Neuberger & Berman Partners	25.95	24.47	6.04	1.76	3.47	4.73	-9.81	-8.44
42.08	-6.64	1/3	OAKMX	36	F J S	Oakmark Fund	34.76	35.40	-1.82	-2.96	-3.50	-7.63	-9.54	-6.89
52.99	12.99	2/7	PRGFX	24		Price Growth Stock	32.56	28.66	13.60	1.53	8.04	11.77	-10.26	-7.41
34.93	14.22	2/3	RPMGX	40		Price Midcap Growth Stock	34.54	30.48	13.33	1.35	10.61	14.22	-10.42	-8.96
81.77	18.29	2/2	RYNVX	3		Rydex Nova	34.80	29.45	18.15	4.72	11.83	16.54	-12.75	-11.56
59.65	13.65	2/2	SNXFX	15	S	Schwab 1000	34.78	30.39	14.46	3.79	9.06	12.63	-8.57	-7.02
62.05	13.46	1/1	SWPIX	11	S	Schwab S&P 500	19.75	17.26	14.45	4.17	8.87	12.37	-8.35	-8.35
47.28	5.32	4/7	SCDUX	29	F J S ◊	Scudder Large Co Value	27.93	26.42	5.70	1.60	2.47	4.16	-9.02	-7.58
63.38	22.59	2/2	SNIGX	7	F J S	SIT Large Cap Growth	52.38	43.86	19.43	7.69	16.35	21.55	-9.94	-7.79
44.51	7.41	3/7	SOPFX	34	F J S	Strong Opportunity	39.63	36.40	8.89	2.62	6.53	6.69	-9.36	-7.78
90.59	24.31	1/1	TEQUX	1	F J S	Transamerica Equity Growth	27.31	22.03	23.99	10.21	20.89	24.19	-10.27	-10.11
53.65	3.34	2/2	TWEBX	23		Tweedy Browne American Value	22.38	21.97	1.88	-1.58	1.09	2.04	-8.68	-6.69
63.53	13.64	2/2	VFINX	6		Vanguard Index Trust 500	118.74	103.53	14.69	4.20	9.00	12.58	-8.33	-6.53
59.93	20.33	3/6	VPMCX	14		Vanguard/Primecap(clsd)	51.13	42.20	21.15	7.28	12.64	19.24	-7.59	-7.97
62.35	19.19	3/6	VWUSX	10		Vanguard US Growth	39.52	32.97	19.88	5.41	12.31	18.16	-7.84	-5.86
61.03	22.73	2/2	CUCAX	12	F J S	Warburg Pincus Capital Apprec	23.36	19.80	17.98	6.38	15.59	21.39	-9.62	-8.26
					Growth and Income Funds		category average		1.45	6.02	8.38	-8.54	-6.62
41.47	-0.86	1/2	TWEIX	19	J S	Amer Cent Eq Income	6.07	5.86	3.63	-3.80	-3.30	-1.41	-2.61	-2.43
36.62	-5.92	1/2	TWVLX	25	J S	American Century Value	5.73	5.89	-2.67	-5.29	-6.18	-6.81	-5.35	-4.11
61.19	12.58	2/4	BIGRX	6	J S	Amer Cent Benhm Incm & Gwth	30.25	26.53	14.02	3.42	8.43	11.62	-8.61	-6.63
37.94	-0.82	3/6	BVALX	24	F J S	Babson Value	44.91	45.20	-0.65	-2.11	-0.34	-2.06	-10.90	-7.28
29.94	17.25	1/2	BGINX	27	◊ F J S	Baron Growth and Income	25.87	23.11	11.95	4.02	15.99	16.30	-13.63	-11.54
38.86	23.08	2/7	BEOOX	23	F J S	Berger Growth and Income	14.30	11.77	21.53	7.04	15.50	22.57	-8.22	-6.67
48.47	18.75	1/3	CMSTX	12	S	Columbia Common Stock	25.52	21.53	18.56	4.59	12.74	17.69	-9.56	-7.36
46.57	5.28	4/7	FEQIX	15	F	Fidelity Equity-Income	55.46	52.74	5.15	-0.07	3.61	4.04	-9.40	-6.37
50.46	10.45	3/4	FEQTX	10	F	Fidelity Equity-Income II	30.18	27.34	10.38	1.32	6.71	9.23	-8.80	-6.57
63.17	16.86	5/7	FFIDX	4	F	Fidelity Fund	37.98	32.91	15.41	3.63	11.15	15.84	-8.02	-6.95
56.78	11.22	6/6	FGRIX	8	F	Fidelity Growth & Income	46.43	41.38	12.21	1.33	6.21	10.31	-8.58	-6.22
36.01	1.13	3/7	FRMUX	26	F S	Founders Blue Chip	7.12	6.91	3.01	-2.73	-1.01	-0.01	-7.83	-6.55
42.24	7.51	3/6	FIIIX	18	F J S	Invesco Ind Income	15.36	14.25	7.78	1.99	3.97	6.57	-6.75	-5.34
57.08	26.56	1/1	JAEIX	7	F J S	Janus Equity Income	20.11	16.05	25.26	7.43	19.43	26.17	-7.63	-7.63
70.41	25.37	2/3	JAGIX	1	F J S	Janus Growth & Income	31.43	25.68	22.41	8.01	18.24	24.90	-8.93	-8.10
40.09	0.57	2/5	LEXCX	20	F J S	Lexington Corporate Leaders	15.47	15.33	0.90	-1.46	0.38	-0.27	-8.19	-6.15
48.57	14.37	2/5	LEXRX	11	F J S	Lexington Gwth & Incm	22.37	19.66	13.80	2.10	9.40	13.49	-10.03	-7.56
39.53	-0.35	1/5	PRFDX	21		Price Equity-Income	25.66	25.20	1.81	-2.51	-1.96	-1.47	-6.00	-4.26
38.94	0.68	1/6	PRGIX	22		Price Growth & Income	25.82	25.20	2.44	-1.64	0.06	-0.55	-7.75	-5.27
29.30	19.95	0/1	RSGIX	28		Rob Stephs Gwth & Incm	14.99	12.96	15.64	6.69	16.99	19.32	-11.49	-12.87
47.65	8.68	4/7	SAFQX	14	F J S	Safeco Equity	23.62	21.24	11.18	1.59	4.17	7.26	-8.25	-6.06
44.02	5.60	3/7	SAFIX	16	F J S	Safeco Income	23.82	22.95	3.79	1.49	3.91	4.81	-9.85	-5.65
43.38	0.75	2/6	SCDGX	17	F J S	Scudder Growth & Income	25.76	25.73	0.13	-2.09	-0.87	-0.70	-9.24	-6.52
61.33	9.81	2/6	SLASX	5	F J S	Selected American Shares	31.74	28.93	9.71	1.86	6.22	8.17	-9.97	-6.59
48.18	3.08	2/3	VEIPX	13		Vanguard Equity-Income	24.34	23.09	5.40	-1.58	-0.08	1.88	-6.24	-4.70
66.43	14.75	2/2	VQNPX	3		Vanguard Growth and Income	32.60	28.45	14.59	5.98	10.19	13.81	-9.06	-7.12
56.45	4.56	3/6	VWNFX	9		Vanguard Windsor II	30.08	28.42	5.83	0.77	3.01	3.29	-8.06	-5.71
68.06	11.99	4/5	WPGFX	2	F J	Weiss Peck and Greer Gw & Incm	40.94	36.59	11.89	0.66	5.89	10.61	-10.30	-7.14

Source: Maverick Advisor.

- Column 2 shows the performance results covering the most recent buy cycle—11/9/98 to 1/29/99.
- Column 3, in the top center of the page, shows the Domestic General Market Indicators. This list starts with the Domestic Fund Composite and ends with the Value Line Composite. Below the Domestic Indicators you'll see an Aggressive Growth Funds heading, followed by a list of 100 top-performing mutual funds.
- Column 4 shows the 39WD for all the Domestic General Market Indicators and all of the listed domestic mutual funds.

PREPARING TO BUY

Before I purchase a mutual fund, whether it is at the beginning of a new buy cycle, or months later, I always ask this question: "Are there any General Market Indicators (GMIs) that are currently on target to reach the goal?" General Market Indicators include the Dow Jones Industrials, the S&P 500, the Value Line Composite, and so on. The reason for my GMIs question is this: As long as there are GMIs on target to reach the goal, I know I can always find individual mutual funds that are also on target.

Let's see which GMIs were on target to meet or exceed the goal in February 1999. Examine Columns 1 and 2 of Figure 11-1.

In Column 1, the heading shows the dates for the previous buy cycle of 9/16/96 to 8/12/98. That was a period of 23 months. By multiplying 23 months by 1.67 percent, our monthly goal, the result is 38.41 percent. This means that any GMI or individual mutual fund that grew by 38.41 percent or more over 23 months attained the goal for that period. For the Domestic GMIs listed at the top of Column 3, five of them exceeded the goal.

In Column 2, the heading shows the dates for the current buy cycle of 11/9/98 to 1/29/99. That was a period of approximately three months. Multiply three months by 1.67 percent; the result is 5.01 percent. Once again, look down the performance list for the Domestic Indicators in Column 2. You see that five of the indicators had performances greater than 5.01 percent.

In both of these market cycles, several GMIs were on target to meet or exceed the goal, which indicates that many growth-oriented mutual funds were available that were also meeting or exceeding the goal.

SELECTING FUNDS TO BUY AT THE BEGINNING OF A NEW MARKET CYCLE

The best time to become fully invested is immediately following a new buy signal—that is, right after both the DFC and DJC (or S&P 500 and DJI) have crossed upward through their respective 39-week averages.

I will now repeat the process followed in evaluating the Domestic General Market Indicators to help you select the individual funds to buy. During this discussion I am assuming we are at the beginning of the new buy cycle that began on 11/9/98.

Look again at Column 1 in Figure 11-1. As I stated earlier, this column represents the performance results from the previous full buy cycle. These performance figures relate to the specific mutual funds shown in Column 3 under the heading of Aggressive Growth Funds. Look down Column 1 on both Figures 11-1 and 11-2 and identify, with a check mark, all performance figures higher than 38.41 percent. This is the performance required to be on target to reach the goal. (During this period the DFC showed a growth of 42.42 percent and the S&P 500 showed a growth of 58.52 percent.) You will find that, out of this group of 100 funds listed on these two pages, over 70 of them exceeded the goal. Any number of these top-performing funds would have been appropriate for your use.

You can obtain a free copy of the current information that we discussed by sending an e-mail to the newsletter or calling their 800 number.

If you are working with less than $15,000, you should be investing within only one fund family, such as Janus, Invesco, or Vanguard. Follow the same performance evaluation process. Note in Column 1 that there were six funds within the Janus family, three funds within the Invesco family, and six funds within the Vanguard family that had performance results greater than 38.41 percent. You could have used any of these funds from any one family and remained on target for your goal.

SELECTING FUNDS TO BUY DURING MID-CYCLE

As a new participant of the this plan, you may come aboard in the middle of a market cycle. This "mid-cycle" period begins 90 days after a buy signal has occurred, or after the composite indicator has risen 10 percent or more above its 39-week average reading. Similarly, if you are a long-time participant, you may find yourself with new money to invest in the middle of a cycle.

For mid-cycle purchases, refer to Figures 11-1 and 11-2 and look down Column 2 on the two FIR mutual fund pages. (The funds on target for the goal in Column 1, the previous cycle, were already identified above.) In Column 2, put a check mark next to each performance figure that exceeded the growth required to meet the goal. Multiply the number of months the current buy signal has been in effect by 1.67 percent. In this instance, it was three months, or 5.01 percent. Out of this group of 100 funds, you would have over 80 funds meeting or exceeding the goal.

As mentioned, investors with less than $15,000 invested should be working within one fund family. At the time of this performance evaluation, there were six funds within the Janus group, four funds within the Invesco group, and four funds within the Vanguard group that had performance greater than 5.01 percent for this three-month period.

The next step is to identify those mutual funds that have check marks in Columns 1 and 2, indicating superior performance for both the past full cycle and the current cycle. The result: There were over 60 mutual funds on target to reach the goal during both of these buy cycles. Any of these would be appropriate for your use. If you are using a single fund family, look for funds within your fund family that have check marks in both columns and choose among those.

MONITORING

While following this plan, your objective is to grow your investment dollars at 20 percent compounded annually. To meet this goal, you'll need to monitor your progress during the year, making sure you're averaging at least 1.67 percent per month. Why 1.67 percent? Because our goal is 20 percent compounded annually, and 20 percent divided by 12 months is 1.67 percent average monthly growth.

Now, as long as you are on target to meet the goal, you are a successful investor on your way to becoming a self-made millionaire. But if you are not on target, you'll need to "rotate up" into a fund (or funds) that is meeting or exceeding the goal (I'll show you how to do this in a moment).

Monitoring the progress of your investments lets you know whether or not you continue to be on target to reach your goal. Knowing you are on target keeps your comfort level high, and even more important, it keeps you motivated not only to remain committed to the plan but also to find more money to add to your investments. Knowing you are on target means that you are on your way to becoming a self-made millionaire.

Remember, as I said in Part 3, even before you start the plan, just believing it is possible to become wealthy from your investments greatly enhances your self-image. It has a positive effect on how you respond to people and events that make up your daily life. Since that is true even before you start the plan, just imagine how you will feel once your plan has been implemented and you have tangible evidence that you are well on your way to becoming a self-made millionaire.

MONITORING PROCEDURES

To make sure your funds remain on target for the goal, at the end of each month, repeat the performance evaluation process outlined for buying funds. Also multiply the number of months that the present buy signal has been in effect by 1.67 percent. The result is the performance your fund or funds need to stay on target.

Look down Column 2 in Figure 11-1 to see how many of the Domestic General Market Indicators and Aggressive Mutual Funds are currently on target to reach the goal, or refer to other past performance sources, which are described in Part 4-3. This is the same process you followed to make your initial purchases. Therefore, during a buy cycle, you want to know at the end of each month if the funds you purchased are still on target to reach the 20 percent annualized compounded growth goal.

ROTATING UP

During your initial selection process, you chose mutual funds with strong momentum, and most of these will continue to be the top performers during the remainder of the buy cycle. On occasion, however, you will have to replace an underperformer. As mentioned, this is called "rotating up."

My experience has shown that only one fifth of your initial purchases will require rotating up prior to the next sell signal. You rotate up to a better-performing mutual fund when the performance of any one of your existing funds for a two-month period falls below the required average monthly performance of your performance yardsticks.

Should the performance for any of the mutual funds you are holding fail to keep up, sell them. With the proceeds, rotate up by buying a mutual fund that is currently showing its current performance to be on target to reach the goal. You'll accomplish this by following the selection process already discussed.

FOR INVESTORS WITH CURRENT MUTUAL FUND HOLDINGS

I have already described the steps involved in initiating the performance evaluation process. Its objective is to identify those specific mutual funds that are currently performing well enough to be on target to reach the goal (1.67 percent times the number of months the current buy cycle has been in place). You can also use this procedure to determine the performance status of the mutual funds you currently own.

Since you want to become a self-made millionaire, and since you need to earn at least 20 percent annualized compounded growth to accomplish this, you'll need to sell any funds that are not on target. It should not matter how long you may have held your existing mutual funds or why you bought them in the first place. Furthermore, it should not matter if your existing broker or financial planner believes you should not change your existing mutual fund holdings. The only thing that should matter to you regarding the mutual funds you presently own is that their performance during the current buy cycle is equal to or greater than the 1.67 percent average monthly growth.

Many investors already own diversified domestic growth-oriented mutual funds when they begin following this plan. This should be obvious, but I will say it anyway. If a sell signal is in effect at the time you decide to begin following the plan, you must sell all of the diversified domestic equity funds you currently own.

The mutual fund listings in the financial section of many newspapers show the current year-to-date growth for each fund in their mutual fund section. This is true for *Barron's* and *USA Today,* to name just two. Some newspapers show the performance for each listed mutual fund for the past 12 months. The *New York Times* follows this procedure. In addition, many individual mutual fund families have their own web page on the Internet, showing past prices to use in your computations. If these sources are not available, a visit to your local library will yield mutual fund pricing and performance statistics from various periodicals.

It is also possible to determine past performance for any individual mutual fund by reviewing its chart. One helpful source is the Big Charts web page at www.bigcharts.com. Here, you can enter the fund's ticker symbol or the name of the fund. After entering the ticker symbol or name, click on *Quick Chart.* The chart will then appear.

Once you have the past performance data, you can determine if your current holdings (or previous holdings) have what it takes to meet your goal (again, 1.67 percent average growth per month). If not, you'll need to rotate up while an uptrend (buy signal) is in place or choose entirely new funds to use once the new buy signal is generated.

REGARDING YOUR EMOTIONS

From an emotional standpoint, in order to be successful following the plan, you must thoroughly understand the goal. Please be patient as I state it one more time. Your goal is 20 percent annualized compounded growth over the long term—that is, for the rest of your life. There is nothing in the goal or the plan to give you instant gratification.

What the plan does for any particular month, two months, six months, or even a year is not relevant to the long-range gratification of becoming a self-made millionaire. The plan has been proven successful in nearly a quarter century of real-life use, and in another 10 years of back-testing before its introduction in 1976. I know it works and so do tens of thousands of happy practitioners, many of whom have already become self-made millionaires.

So, let me offer this advice: To be successful with the compounding plan (or for any other serious endeavor), there is a price to pay. And that price is a thorough understanding of what you are working to accomplish and the patience and discipline to follow through on it. History shows that only a small percentage of the population ever attains wealth. If you have not been successful in the past in attaining this worthwhile goal, then you must decide to henceforth do things differently. And that's why I have gone to great lengths to provide extensive and ongoing documentation of the effectiveness of my plan, along with advice on dealing with the discipline and emotional dilemmas typically associated with investing. You can succeed by diligently following the steps outlined in this book. I'm doing my part to show you the way. The rest is up to you.

CONCLUSION

Now that I have walked you through the steps to implement my plan, do you agree with me that it is easy to understand and simple to follow? Most people find that it is.

The great thing about the plan is that it tells you *at all times* what to do with your mutual fund investments. Therefore, if at some time in the future, because the market is not moving straight up or straight down, or because you are hearing conflicting predictions from the media or so-called investment experts, simply go back and review the long-term charts of the DFC in Figure 10-7. As you review the charts, ask yourself: "If I had strictly followed the plan for the previous 30 years, would the results have been satisfactory?" Once you acknowledge this to be true, you can then ignore all of the predictions, go on with your life, and stop worrying. With patience and diligence, you will achieve your goal of becoming a self-made millionaire.

I will now walk you through the "embellished" version of my plan. We will be using some of these concepts in the final, "personalized" version of the plan, which is detailed in Chapter 14.

Implementing the Fabian Compounding Plan: The Advanced Course

Chapter 12

The Multiple Composite Trading Plan

THE SECOND PERSPECTIVE FOR IMPLEMENTING THE FABIAN COMPOUNDING PLAN

Here in Part 4-2, I show you how I use my compounding plan for my clients. At FFS we have not changed the basic plan, but we have expanded on it. You might refer to this section as the "advanced course."

OPENING COMMENTS

I want to briefly explain why the plan requires more steps at FFS than are needed to implement the Domestic Fund Composite Plan described in Chapters 8 through 11. As a money management company, new money for investment is received almost every day. This requires more monitoring steps than would be required for an individual investor. We need the ability to search the entire world at all times, to look for the best investment opportunities currently available. To accomplish this, I expanded the basic compounding plan without changing the fundamentals and created the Multiple Composite Trading Plan (MCTP). The basic plan monitors two composites. The MCTP monitors 39 composites.

My purpose in sharing these more involved procedures is to provide additional background information for those who want to learn more and also to demonstrate how we use investment yardsticks, Momentum Scores, and rotating up to enhance performance. You can use these performance-enhancing tools as part of the personalized plan as described in Chapter 14.

THE FABIAN TRADITION

Over the years, it has always been the Fabian tradition to share our investment philosophy. We freely tell why we do what we do, as well as exactly how to implement the investment strategies we follow. I have already shared with you how an individual can implement my plan by using mutual fund performance data available in newspapers, at the library, or on the Internet.

My management company continues to be dependent on the original, simple, trend-following plan to determine when to be in the market. But once there, our objective is to maximize the gains the market has to offer.

When I first started my newsletter in 1977, there were approximately 450 mutual funds. When the new millennium began, there were in excess of 11,000 funds, with indications that there will be many more in the future. To take advantage of these new opportunities, I decided to expand my simple trend-following plan to include many more sectors of the market all over the world.

MULTIPLE COMPOSITE TRADING PLAN

It is an accepted principle in the investment arena to group mutual funds based on their stated objectives. A few examples of these groupings are aggressive growth, small company, income, and science and technology. I began the MCTP by combining all of the funds with a similar investment objective which were also available at Charles Schwab (the management company trades through Charles Schwab). This process created 39 groups. Then, for each group, we created a representative composite to gauge the performance of that group. Some composites were generated from groupings with less than 10 funds, while others were formed from groupings of over 100 funds. Some composites were formed from domestic funds, while others were formed from funds representing regions in other parts of the world.

Next, we created what we call the "Multiple Composite Snapshot of the World," or MCSW. This is essentially a table showing the performance data for all 39 composites. World markets move independently of our domestic market, based on their own economic and political situations.

Therefore, the purpose of the MCSW is to tell us where the best investment options exist each day.

To see how the world markets change and how we strive to maximize market gains, turn to Figures 12-1 and 12-2. Here you'll see copies of the MCSW as of December 31, 1997, and as of December 31, 1998. In the top middle section of each snapshot page, you'll see the names of both composites monitored by the *FIR Newsletter*: the Domestic Fund Composite and the International Fund Composite.

Below these you'll see five groupings of the 39 composites that I developed for the MCTP. These include Domestic Diversified, Domestic Sector, International, Bond, and Market Segment. Below that, you'll see the General Market Indicators. These are the expanded tools I use to take advantage of the new opportunities that the mutual fund industry has made available to us.

THE TRUTH, THE WHOLE TRUTH, AND NOTHING BUT THE TRUTH

At the bottom of each snapshot page you'll see the pronouncement "The Truth, the Whole Truth, and Nothing but the Truth." This phrase reminds me every day that I am capable of responding emotionally to market conditions the same as every other investor. I am not always immune from the hype and propaganda from the financial press. I see and hear the opinions of so-called "investment experts" who share their reasons why they believe the market will be going up or down. Even though I know better, sometimes I begin to accept some of this rhetoric and become emotionally involved. When this happens, the phrase brings me back to the world of reality.

The phrase reminds me, in no uncertain terms, that the information shown on the snapshot page is the real story. It is not lying, exaggerating, or giving an opinion or a prediction. It is stating each day exactly what is happening all over the world. Everything presented here can be substantiated. It is simply telling it like it is.

I can't tell you the number of times I have heard on CNBC or read in *Barron's* or the *Wall Street Journal* about some particular segment of the market that was supposedly going to be the next great leader. Again, I'm not immune. Sometimes I get caught up in this hype. However, I do not put my money into any segment until the MCSW page verifies that the trend for it has enough momentum to justify a purchase. I hold back because I remember all of the predictions of the past, when the touted segment failed

FIGURE 12-1

Multiple Composite Snapshot of the World

as of Wednesday 12/31/97

39 WD	% Off High	16-Week		% Dec 97	% Nov 97	% Oct 97	% Sept 97	%Aug 97	1997 YTD	Momentum Score
			FIR Newsletter Composites							
4.68	-4.64	-2.87	Domestic Fund Composite	1.66	1.16	-4.42	5.84	-4.14	30.84	2.27
-3.86	-2.90	-5.68	International Fund Composite	1.69	-2.10	-7.81	6.79	-7.37	8.34	-2.63
		Fabian Financial Services	**Domestic Diversified Composites**							
6.39	-1.75	-0.81	S&P 500	1.63	4.58	-4.05	5.21	-5.62	31.66	5.82
1.11	0.00	-6.19	Aggressive Growth	1.05	0.44	-2.88	5.20	-4.97	18.97	1.10
-1.51	-4.12	-3.43	Balanced	1.05	-1.12	-1.75	3.53	-2.98	14.81	0.11
4.04	-0.68	-0.20	Equity Income	1.95	3.33	-3.22	5.01	-3.54	28.17	5.62
3.79	-1.92	-1.16	Growth & Income	1.99	2.21	-2.10	4.42	-5.05	29.74	5.14
5.49	-1.01	0.14	Growth	3.41	2.69	-2.74	5.12	-4.48	31.15	8.14
2.40	-0.87	-0.57	Income	2.20	0.88	-1.16	4.28	-2.31	22.78	4.70
4.41	-9.73	-10.74	Micro Cap	-1.52	-0.88	-5.41	9.02	3.86	24.78	-6.63
4.89	-6.86	-7.19	Mid Cap	1.33	-0.13	-4.74	7.42	-1.94	9.48	0.16
5.85	-4.90	-5.23	Small Company	1.39	-0.27	-3.58	8.93	2.42	31.33	0.72
		Fabian Financial Services	**Domestic Sector Composites**							
-7.92	-8.07	-21.14	Science & Technology	-4.00	-2.14	-11.05	4.54	0.32	5.71	-15.67
-0.45	-6.69	-5.58	Health & Biotechnology	-0.82	-0.18	-3.02	7.84	-2.94	16.86	-3.33
4.34	-1.88	-0.24	Real Estate	2.02	1.80	-3.41	8.06	-0.09	17.85	4.14
1.69	-7.77	-4.83	Telecommunications	1.73	1.32	-6.71	9.29	-5.12	23.23	1.43
-30.88	-46.79	-27.15	Domestic Gold	5.08	-21.53	-16.99	4.70	0.71	-41.51	-19.87
7.74	0.00	7.84	Utilities	3.37	5.84	-0.44	5.45	-2.85	24.72	12.36
		Fabian Financial Services	**International Composites**							
-28.46	-31.42	-32.77	China	-1.19	-5.71	-26.39	-1.74	-7.39	-23.59	-21.29
-20.28	-19.75	-23.26	Emerging Markets	-0.86	-3.52	-17.75	3.87	-10.23	-7.58	-14.12
1.35	-0.19	-0.28	Europe	3.65	1.20	-4.63	8.96	-6.08	18.71	6.19
-4.05	-3.00	-12.05	Global Small Cap	0.80	-5.44	-5.98	5.83	-0.55	4.60	-6.83
-1.76	-1.25	-3.83	Global	1.72	0.68	-4.77	5.11	-5.16	13.83	1.74
-4.99	-8.25	-7.22	International Small Cap	1.71	-2.64	-6.07	4.98	-4.05	0.95	-2.26
-4.29	-1.24	-7.17	International	1.94	-0.42	-7.50	7.57	-7.24	12.04	-0.29
-18.68	-16.71	-16.99	Japan	-4.30	-5.96	-5.68	0.16	-10.75	-16.13	-17.40
-4.14	-13.00	-14.14	Latin America	6.61	4.05	-19.48	9.25	-9.19	29.16	7.53
-27.45	-33.80	-25.25	Pacific Basin	-5.24	-5.11	-14.73	-1.00	-12.44	-32.28	-22.96
-36.38	-44.34	-36.76	Pacific Excluding Japan	-5.45	-5.61	-27.64	-4.13	-13.99	-42.90	-30.33
		Fabian Financial Services	**Bond Composites**							
-17.77	-14.44	-13.78	Emerging Markets Debt	-4.00	0.77	-9.44	1.98	-0.67	-4.02	-11.95
-1.99	-0.25	0.66	General Corporate Bond	0.66	0.11	-0.03	1.48	-1.68	4.91	1.42
-1.15	-0.06	1.63	General Government Bond	0.72	0.03	1.48	1.27	-1.94	4.55	2.21
-1.77	-0.15	1.70	High Quality Corporate Bond	0.64	-0.10	1.08	1.07	-1.70	4.32	1.72
-0.48	0.00	1.35	High Yield Corporate Bond	2.62	-0.16	-1.04	2.08	-0.51	9.00	4.56
6.98	-0.30	8.80	Long Term Treasury	2.28	1.90	4.28	3.73	-4.53	17.27	8.60
-2.24	-0.11	0.71	Mortgage-Backed Govt. Bond	0.55	-0.27	0.48	0.65	-0.75	3.11	1.07
-1.44	0.00	1.92	Short Term Treasury	0.85	-0.12	1.26	1.12	-1.47	6.39	2.21
		Fabian Financial Services	**Market Segment Composites**							
-2.76	0.00	-15.16	Energy	-1.39	-8.12	-2.42	7.19	4.77	17.09	-12.11
8.88	0.00	3.11	Financial Services	5.80	2.62	-2.14	5.95	-5.18	41.85	13.15
-7.12	-4.29	-17.07	Natural Resources	-1.98	-9.05	-4.33	8.14	2.37	5.19	-15.18
-31.36	-64.96	-24.22	South African Gold	3.53	-18.39	-16.80	0.72	1.06	-45.34	-19.73
			General Market Indicators							
0.00	-2.96	-0.82	Dow Jones Industrials	1.09	5.12	-6.33	4.24	-7.30	22.64	4.14
7.58	-3.32	2.06	Dow Jones Transportation	1.77	2.19	-1.52	10.79	-4.08	44.37	4.97
11.56	0.00	11.69	Dow Jones Utilities	5.58	6.62	1.77	2.85	-1.61	17.43	18.67
4.18	-1.36	2.00	Dow Jones Composite	2.03	6.31	-5.34	5.94	-5.58	28.71	7.70
-2.81	0.00	-12.12	Over The Counter Industrials	-2.35	-1.44	-7.75	7.11	1.85	10.04	-10.02
3.28	-6.06	-4.23	Russell 2000	1.65	-0.77	-4.53	7.18	2.16	19.32	0.27
4.80	-0.61	2.13	NYSE Composite (NYSE)	2.42	3.73	-3.24	5.69	-4.86	30.31	6.95
1.60	-4.76	-3.63	Value Line Composite	0.95	0.81	-4.46	5.48	-0.62	17.73	0.48
-24.87	-29.78	-20.75	Gold Fund Composite	4.76	-19.44	-19.72	10.75	0.97	-34.99	-19.78
0.16	0.00	-8.36	NASDAQ Composite	-1.89	0.44	-5.46	6.20	-0.41	21.64	-6.07
-5.29	-13.71	-13.74	NASDAQ 100	-5.68	3.03	-7.07	2.14	-2.97	21.48	-11.87

THE TRUTH, THE WHOLE TRUTH, AND NOTHING BUT THE TRUTH.

FIGURE 12-2

Multiple Composite Snapshot of the World

as of Thursday 12/31/98

39 WD	% Off High	16-Week		% Dec 98	% Nov 98	% Oct 98	% Sept 98	%Aug 98	1998 YTD	Momentum Score
			FIR Newsletter Composites							
7.47	-0.15	20.80	Domestic Fund Composite	7.28	6.30	6.18	6.06	-17.15	16.93	23.95
0.03	-0.05	11.38	International Fund Composite	4.80	5.37	6.25	-3.63	-15.40	7.62	18.10
			Fabian Financial Services Domestic Diversified Composites							
9.27	-0.96	21.87	S&P 500	5.74	6.04	8.11	6.40	-14.47	23.00	21.58
17.87	0.00	31.32	Aggressive Growth	16.11	7.96	3.50	10.80	-19.06	33.88	41.93
7.59	-0.04	16.42	Balanced	5.41	4.51	4.88	5.17	-10.18	18.47	17.77
7.29	-0.44	19.70	Equity Income	6.83	5.46	6.02	6.00	-14.69	15.44	22.13
8.78	0.00	21.79	Growth & Income	7.54	4.81	7.41	7.33	-16.26	21.60	23.60
8.68	0.00	23.89	Growth	10.95	6.26	6.24	6.67	-18.54	16.12	31.28
4.15	0.00	13.65	Income	4.73	3.91	2.05	6.17	-10.16	12.54	14.40
3.83	0.00	21.41	Micro Cap	7.91	9.45	5.04	7.94	-22.48	4.24	27.79
15.28	0.00	28.58	Mid Cap	14.32	7.16	7.74	9.02	-20.45	26.53	39.67
1.15	0.00	19.06	Small Company	10.45	6.85	3.62	6.42	-23.30	2.76	29.56
			Fabian Financial Services Domestic Sector Composites							
21.81	0.00	35.65	Science & Technology	17.80	10.59	5.69	11.93	-20.33	30.74	49.04
12.83	0.00	18.95	Health & Biotechnology	8.08	5.32	5.46	10.76	-13.12	22.88	24.21
-7.12	-16.04	8.45	Real Estate	0.69	2.60	-1.23	3.88	-11.29	-14.34	3.37
10.70	0.00	26.75	Telecommunications	11.30	6.98	10.08	1.02	-21.73	26.81	34.62
-9.38	-29.37	-1.03	Domestic Gold	-0.25	-3.93	-2.34	43.24	-23.66	-20.10	-5.60
8.39	-0.26	17.76	Utilities	7.00	3.03	3.05	7.33	-8.39	20.59	18.56
			Fabian Financial Services International Composites							
0.48	-3.63	29.42	China	-3.03	3.13	19.73	14.84	-14.04	-21.13	6.94
-13.83	-34.50	22.27	Emerging Markets	-0.11	5.64	8.11	2.34	-31.72	-28.59	9.48
0.25	-0.51	9.16	Europe	4.08	5.14	5.58	-5.85	-14.12	16.36	16.09
-4.95	-14.85	6.16	Global Small Cap	4.75	5.39	0.00	-0.41	-15.94	-5.90	14.89
2.55	0.00	15.68	Global	4.87	6.11	7.22	-1.51	-15.51	9.71	19.46
-4.47	-13.06	5.27	International Small Cap	3.94	4.04	2.99	-5.01	-14.96	5.85	13.42
-2.96	-11.91	7.69	International	4.20	4.48	4.08	-5.30	-13.70	2.49	14.92
5.37	-0.11	9.46	Japan	3.91	6.29	5.70	-2.83	-6.61	0.13	16.96
-18.71	-38.03	35.32	Latin America	-7.33	5.59	10.26	6.94	-36.20	-31.40	-3.94
7.15	-0.27	22.59	Pacific Basin	2.18	8.38	12.91	1.54	-11.94	-4.05	19.20
6.68	-1.63	36.55	Pacific Excluding Japan	1.43	6.09	18.66	11.26	-15.65	-12.36	18.28
			Fabian Financial Services Bond Composites							
-16.17	-31.94	22.09	Emerging Markets Debt	-4.28	8.35	6.66	5.10	-34.59	-27.78	3.12
-0.26	-0.25	2.04	General Corporate Bond	0.48	2.44	-1.44	2.35	-1.71	5.31	2.68
0.86	-1.66	0.25	General Government Bond	0.16	0.39	-0.77	2.67	2.55	8.78	0.33
-0.39	-1.75	-0.10	High Quality Corporate Bond	0.27	0.96	-1.62	1.99	1.29	6.36	0.69
-3.94	-5.73	3.31	High Yield Corporate Bond	-0.29	5.75	-2.24	-1.52	-7.13	-2.62	4.05
0.09	-10.26	-3.64	Long Term Treasury	-2.67	1.51	-2.96	3.99	5.58	11.84	-5.31
-0.68	0.00	0.47	Mortgage-Backed Govt. Bond	0.50	0.67	-0.74	1.02	0.73	5.20	1.30
0.67	-2.20	0.07	Short Term Treasury	0.04	-0.44	-0.44	3.37	2.73	8.26	-0.58
			Fabian Financial Services Market Segment Composites							
-16.66	-29.69	-6.65	Energy	-2.38	-7.16	2.58	17.60	-18.75	-19.90	-10.63
2.51	0.00	18.74	Financial Services	4.02	6.28	8.47	2.05	-19.02	10.64	18.56
-13.87	-27.21	-0.89	Natural Resources	-2.95	-2.13	2.96	11.90	-16.61	-22.34	-6.55
-12.42	-32.64	-4.11	South African Gold	-5.89	-3.37	-0.30	39.63	-19.92	-23.31	-15.30
			General Market Indicators							
0.00	-1.50	16.54	Dow Jones Industrials	0.71	6.10	9.56	4.03	-15.13	12.24	12.30
-4.80	-14.56	14.99	Dow Jones Transportation	3.90	4.82	9.35	-3.92	-14.79	-9.06	17.30
1.18	-2.56	15.32	Dow Jones Utilities	2.89	0.69	-1.72	10.25	-0.16	17.35	5.61
-1.21	-0.41	15.83	Dow Jones Composite	1.75	4.80	7.23	3.22	-12.70	6.53	11.92
1.48	0.00	23.22	Over The Counter Industrials	7.32	8.98	8.09	6.48	-23.04	3.30	27.67
-3.99	0.00	14.51	Russell 2000	6.09	5.18	4.01	7.59	-19.49	-5.66	19.37
1.89	-0.21	17.63	NYSE Composite (NYSE)	4.25	5.18	7.71	4.97	-14.98	13.28	17.54
-6.15	-14.01	10.94	Value Line Composite	3.09	3.83	6.56	4.49	-17.69	-5.48	13.29
-15.68	-30.29	0.14	Gold Fund Composite	-8.44	-5.88	0.53	53.39	-22.30	-16.05	-22.50
14.72	0.00	33.17	NASDAQ Composite	12.47	10.06	4.58	12.98	-19.93	29.71	37.29
29.76	0.00	43.93	NASDAQ 100	17.85	11.24	4.09	17.99	-17.20	63.53	48.99

THE TRUTH, THE WHOLE TRUTH, AND NOTHING BUT THE TRUTH.

to turn into a winner. Of course, the reverse is also true, with doom and gloom predictions also failing to pan out. The snapshot page tells the real story and is my guide.

BUYING TOOLS

Let's examine the December 31, 1997 MCSW, shown in Figure 12-1. I want to point out how we use the MCSW to determine what and when to buy, and equally important, when to sell. Look at the columns to the right of the composite names. These columns show the monthly performance for each composite for each of the past five months (August through December) and the year-to-date (1997), plus the Momentum Score. These serve as our buying tools.

We created the Momentum Score to make it both easier and quicker to identify the best performing composites. The Momentum Score (MS) readings are found in the extreme right-hand column. For each composite, the MS is determined by adding together the weighted performance figures for the previous three months. We have a formula for this, but the important thing to know is the result—the higher the MS number, the greater the upward momentum. The purpose of the Momentum Score is to answer the question "What have you done for me lately?"

Earlier, I used the example of looking at the mutual fund listings in *USA Today* to see the large number of mutual funds on target to reach the goal at any time during the year (you'll recall, those meeting or exceeding 1.67 percent times the number of months). I used this example to prove that you can always find funds on target for the goal. But this is not the best procedure for determining which mutual funds are good candidates for purchase on any particular day. As you will see in a moment, the MS reading is more helpful for this purpose.

Let me give you an example. Suppose at the end of June you find a group of funds with a year-to-date growth of 15 percent. This means that this group is currently exceeding the goal, since 10 percent growth at the end of June is all that is required to be on target (6×1.67 percent = 10.02 percent). Since they are on target, they should be held if you already own any of them. But just because they are on target doesn't mean that all of them are equally good candidates for "money purchase" today. The reason is that some of these funds may have had the bulk of their growth early in the year and may now be substantially off their most recent highs. Other funds may have started the year with flat growth but have had superior performance for the past two or three months. Such funds would be better candidates for purchase now. This is how the MS answers the "What have you done for me lately?" question.

To see how I use the MS, look down the right-hand column of Figure 12-1, for Thursday, December 31, 1997, and check off the highest MS readings for that day. Under the Domestic Diversified Composite, you'll find an MS reading of 8.14 for Growth. Under the Domestic Sector Composite, you'll find an MS reading of 12.36 for Utilities. Under the Bond Composites, you'll find an MS reading of 8.60 for Long-Term Treasury. And under the Market Segment Composites, you'll find an MS reading of 13.15 for Financial Services. Compared to the others, these groups were showing superior upward momentum at that time.

Next, go to Figure 12-2. There you'll find the MCSW for December 31, 1998. This snapshot is a year later, and at that time the market was much stronger. When we review the MS column, we find new market leaders. Under Domestic Diversified Composites, you'll find an MS reading of 41.93 for Aggressive Growth, 31.28 for Growth, and 39.67 for Mid-Cap. Under Domestic Sector Composites, you'll see MS readings for Science & Technology at 49.04 and Telecommunications at 34.62.

In the next chapter, I will go through the process I follow to select the specific mutual funds to purchase, based on the composites with the highest MS readings. But before moving on to that, I want to explain the selling tools we use.

SELLING TOOLS

Selling is the hardest part of the investment process, causing many investors to fail simply because they have no effective procedures in place. Again, this is the value of the plan. It tells you not only what and when to buy, but also exactly when to sell.

Refer again to Figure 12-1, which is the 12/31/97 MCSW. Let's examine the three columns to the left of the composite names. I call these our "safety valves," because this data helps us determine when to sell.

The first column from the left is titled 39WD (39-week differential). As you previously learned, this figure represents how much the current reading is above or below its 39-week average and is represented with positive or negative numbers. Look at the very top line. Note that the 39WD for the Domestic Fund Composite is 4.68. This means the current reading for the DFC is 4.68 percent above its 39-week average. Now, look at the second line. You'll see the 39WD for the International Fund Composite is −3.86. This means that the current reading for the IFC is 3.86 percent below its 39-week average. As you already know, any composite (or individual mutual fund in the group) is a candidate to be sold when its current reading falls below its 39-week average.

The second column from the left is entitled % Off High. No matter which mutual fund you are holding, whenever, on average, it is 10 percent below its most recent high, it becomes a candidate to be sold. You can see on this 12/31/97 snapshot that 9 of the 39 composites were more than 10 percent off their highs. This means these composites would have generated their own sell signals, and any funds in these groups would be sold.

Now, turn back to the 12/31/98 snapshot (Figure 12-2). Look at the third column from the left, entitled 16-Week. The number given for this four-month period is very important because I am constantly on alert to verify whether or not I am on target to reach my compounding goal.

Therefore, during the period of time we are holding any fund, I always want to know whether or not that fund is on target to reach the goal. We use 1.67 percent per month for the 20 percent goal. This means any individual fund in the 16-week column that is showing a growth of 7 percent or more (4 months × 1.67 percent = 87 percent) is currently on target for the goal.

Look again at Figure 12-2. Go down the 16-week column. At that time, 25 of the composites were showing growth in excess of 7 percent for the previous 16 weeks. This meant that almost all areas of the world were in an uptrend and were meeting the goal. The opportunities were abundant at that time. But now go back to the 12/31/97 snapshot (Figure 12-1). The performance of markets around the world was very different then. Only one composite had a growth over 7 percent for the previous 16 weeks. Do you see why it pays to know every day how the world markets are performing? To meet the goal, you must sell the underperformers and rotate up.

PERFORMANCE YARDSTICK

When evaluating a fund's performance, it is valuable to also use a General Market Indicator as a performance yardstick. The yardstick becomes another consideration in the selling process. A performance yardstick comes from a review of the most popular General Market Indicators (GMIs). The question to ask is this: Is my fund doing as well as or better than the General Market Indicator which is on target to reach the goal? If it is underperforming the indicator, it may be necessary to sell and rotate up.

A list of GMIs can be found at the bottom of the snapshot pages shown in Figures 12-1 and 12-2. They can be found on the fabian.com website. They are also usually listed in the financial section of most daily newspapers, as well as in the Major Indexes listing in *Barron's* each week (see Figure 14-2 in Chapter 14). In addition, most online brokerage firms have websites that show the most recent readings of several GMIs.

As you go through the current GMIs, you will be searching to find one or more of them with performance results indicating they are on target to reach your 20 percent compounding goal. Provided one or more of the GMIs are currently on target to reach the 20 percent compounded goal, this is evidence that the existing market environment is favorable enough to find individual mutual funds that are also on target to reach the goal. Reviewing the performance of each GMI for the most recent quarter, for the current year-to-date, and since the beginning of the current buy cycle (assuming the market is in an uptrend) will identify those indicators that are on target for the goal.

MONITORING

An important part of the daily monitoring process at my management company is comparing each fund we are holding to two performance yardsticks. This review shows how our current performance is progressing. Should any individual mutual fund for a two-month period fall below the performance of either yardstick, provided the yardsticks are on target to reach the goal, that mutual fund should be sold and rotated up to a fund with a higher momentum score.

Whenever we sell a mutual fund, I immediately refer back to the new daily MCSW (Figure 12-1). Most of the time a new area of the world can be found showing upward momentum, indicating new buying opportunities. If not, there are areas of the market, such as the more stable bond funds and money market funds, where you can temporarily place money as a substitute for cash until one or more of the market segments resumes an upward trend.

ENHANCED INDEX FUNDS

Here are some highlights regarding the newest type of mutual funds called *enhanced index funds* (EIFs). Introduced in 1997, these new funds can enable mutual fund investors to generate growth whether the market is going *up* or *down*. This should make it even easier to attain our 20 percent annual growth objective.

Prior to 1997, the most common of the long-term index funds had been those that duplicated the movement of the S&P 500. Because the S&P 500 had been one of the primary performance leaders in the 1990s, mutual funds based on this index became very popular. In 1997 enhanced index funds were introduced with the objective to outperform the well-known indices—not only the S&P 500, but also the NASDAQ 100, the Russell 2000, and the Profunds European Index. The EIFs have different strategies to achieve growth whether the index is in an uptrend or in a downtrend.

Figure 12-3 shows a listing of the currently available EIFs. The funds in the left column strive to outperform the indexes they are following during an up market. The funds in the right column strive to produce gains while the indexes they are following decline during a down market. For example, in 1998, the Profunds Ultra OTC produced a gain of 100 percent, well in excess of the NASDAQ 100's performance for that year. If a serious market decline caused the NASDAQ 100 to fall as much in one year as it gained in 1998, the Profunds Ultra-Short OTC has the potential to duplicate the 100 percent gain attained by its cousin. Do you see why I believe it will be even easier to realize 20 percent annual growth in the future now that we have these new tools available to us?

SELLING SHORT

What is selling short? It is selling first and buying second, exactly the reverse of conventional investing. This technique is used when the investor believes the market in general or a particular fund or stock is headed down. For an investor to sell an individual stock short, he or she must borrow shares of that stock from a stock broker and then immediately sell them. At some time in the future, these borrowed shares must be returned. If the market declines, the investor makes money because he or she can buy the shares at a lower price before returning them. If the market rises after an investor sells the borrowed shares, the investor will have to buy the shares at a higher price before returning them and will suffer a loss. Short selling is essentially the principle behind the Profunds Ultra-Short OTC fund.

EIF HISTORICAL PERSPECTIVE

Turn now to Figure 12-4, where you'll see how these enhanced funds actually performed during 1998 while working to meet their objectives. In the illustration, you'll find the following:

FIGURE 12-3

ENHANCED INDEX FUNDS

The objective of an Enhanced Index Fund (EIF) is to outperform its related market index during both up markets and down markets. During down markets they strive to produce gains equal to or greater than the decline of its related index.

During Up Markets

EIFs related to the S&P 500 Index :
The objective of **Ultra Bull Profund** and **Rydex Titan 500 Fund** is to outperform by a factor of 2. The objective of **Rydex Nova** is to outperform by a factor of 1.5. The objective of **Potomac US Plus** is to outperform by a factor of 1.25.

EIFs related to the Nasdaq 100 Index :
The objective of **Ultra OTC Profund** and **Rydex Velocity 100 Fund** is to outperform by a factor of 2. The objective of **Potomac OTC Plus** is to outperform by a factor of 1.25.

EIFs related to the Russell 2000, Dow Industrials and Internet Index:
The objective of **Potomac 2000**, **Potomac Dow 30 Plus Fund** and **Potomac Internet Plus Fund** is to outperform by a factor of 1.25.

During Down Markets

EIFs related to the S&P 500 Index:
The objective of **Ultra Bear Profund** and **Rydex Tempest 500 Fund** is to produce gains twice as great as the decline in the index. The objective of **Potomac US Short** and **Rydex Ursa** is to produce gains equal to the decline of the index.

EIFs related to the Nasdaq 100 Index:
The objective of **Ultra Short OTC Profund** and **Rydex Venture 100 Fund** is to produce gains twice as great as the index decline. The objective of **Potomac OTC Short** is to produce gains with a factor of 1.25 greater than the decline in the index. The objective of **Rydex Arktos** is to produce gains equal to the decline of the index.

- Charts for the S&P 500 and NASDAQ 100 for 1998.
- Monthly performance comparisons between the S&P 500 and the NASDAQ 100 and the associated enhanced index funds.

Under the chart of the S&P 500, look at the performance for February, which was an up month. The S&P 500 was up 7.04 percent. During

FIGURE 12-4

S&P 500 INDEX

Past Monthly Performance Figures *

	Jan-98	Feb-98	Mar-98	Apr-98	May-98	Jun-98	Jul-98	Aug-98	Sep-98	Oct-98	Nov-98	Dec-98
S&P 500	1.02	7.04	4.99	0.91	-1.88	3.94	-1.16	-14.56	6.22	8.03	5.91	5.64
Rydex Nova	1.44	9.96	7.23	1.31		5.57			8.56	11.81	8.08	8.99
Potomac US Plus	N/A	N/A	N/A	N/A		5.57			7.38	11.62	8.07	9.31
Ultra Bull Profund	1.36	13.23	9.57	1.70		7.45			11.96	15.21	11.45	10.12
Rydex Ursa					2.85		1.84	16.80				
Ultra Bear Profund					4.99		3.38	34.10				

NASDAQ 100 INDEX

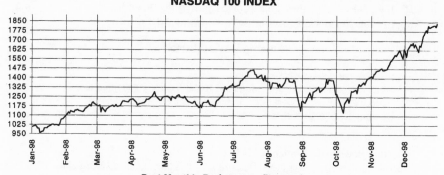

Past Monthly Performance Figures *

	Jan-98	Feb-98	Mar-98	Apr-98	May-98	Jun-98	Jul-98	Aug-98	Sep-98	Oct-98	Nov-98	Dec-98
NASDAQ 100	8.11	11.48	2.22	2.25	-4.49	12.19	2.99	-17.20	17.99	4.09	11.24	17.85
Potomac OTC Plus	N/A	N/A	N/A	N/A		15.22	3.64		7.29	4.58	13.98	20.36
Ultra OTC Profund	16.99	23.42	3.07	3.46		24.98	3.85		38.93	4.42	33.22	24.15
Rydex Arktos					N/A			N/A				
Ultra Short OTC Profund					N/A			40.28				

* There is no guarantee that future performance will be the same as the past.

the same month the enhanced index funds (Rydex Nova and Ultra Bull Profund) were up 9.96 percent and 13.23 percent, respectively. Next, look at the month of August, which was a down month. The S&P 500 was down 14.56 percent. During the same month the enhanced index funds (Rydex Ursa and Ultra Bear Profund) were up 16.80 percent and 34.10 percent. This demonstrates the opportunity you have to make money with enhanced index funds, whether the market is going up or down.

Some of the newest EIFs did not have performance figures for every month in 1998 because they only became available later in the year. In the illustration, during the up months, I show only the performance of the up-market EIFs. During the down months, I show only the performance of the down-market EIFs. This performance comparison shows how the objectives of the enhanced index funds have been met.

SUMMING UP

Up to this point we discussed why the Multiple Composite Trading Plan came into being. We reviewed the Snapshot of the World pages and talked about how the information contained in each column is used. I elaborated on why a "performance yardstick" is important, how and why I use the Momentum Scores, and how you can use enhanced index funds for growth in both up and down markets. Now, in the next chapter, we will review the steps to follow to select the appropriate mutual funds to buy. In addition, I will describe why and how to rotate up.

CHAPTER 13

Implementing the MCTP

HIGHEST MOMENTUM REPORT—SELECTING THE MUTUAL FUNDS TO BUY

You have already seen how the Momentum Scores (MS) shown on the Multiple Composite Snapshot of The World (MCSW) pages identify the composites (fund groups) with the greatest upward momentum—that is, the greatest strength for the most recent period. Once the strongest composites are known, then our focus turns to the specific mutual funds to buy within these composites.

Every day, we conduct a search of 2,500+ funds available to the management company from Charles Schwab & Co. for the purpose of reviewing their MS readings. Next, we prepare a report that lists all of these mutual funds in their MS sequence, from highest to lowest.

Figure 13-1 is an example of this report. In the upper left corner, you'll see the Highest Momentum Report (HMR) for Thursday, December 31, 1998. In the column heading, Composites (top center, just to the left of the fund names), you'll find the names of the composites from the Snapshot page. This is only the first page of a daily multipage report. In actual use, this report usually has at least three to five pages of mutual funds that have a higher momentum score than the investment yardstick we are currently using.

F I G U R E   1 3 - 1

HIGHEST MOMENTUM REPORT - Thursday 12/31/98

Symbol	39WD	% Off High	16-Week	Composites	Fund Name	Dec	Nov	Oct	YTD	Momentum Score
MAKOX	61.26	-0.24	95.10	Pacific Ex-Japan	Matthews Korea	32.47	21.26	25.74	99.07	99.07
TISHX	38.95	-1.29	51.81	Telecommunications	Flag Investors Telephone Income - Class A	21.45	10.38	10.60	64.40	58.58
RSFX	31.58	-0.44	46.71	Technology	Robertson Stephens Information Age	20.86	15.10	1.97	32.84	57.81
TPSCX	35.32	0.00	60.63	Small Company	Transamerica Premier Small Company	17.59	14.86	12.20	54.32	56.14
VWPVX	23.14	0.00	45.26	Growth	Van Wagoner Post-Venture	21.04	11.26	2.16	31.02	54.42
PRSCX	27.96	0.00	44.29	Technology	T. Rowe Price Science & Technology	17.54	12.30	12.05	28.22	53.41
ALTFX	28.96	0.00	38.06	Technology	Alliance Technology - Class A	20.45	8.43	6.32	38.89	52.49
REIGX	18.85	0.00	37.94	Small Company	Robertson Stephens Emerging Growth	16.85	17.39	0.90	19.16	51.54
ATEYX	28.29	0.00	37.52	Technology	Alliance Technology - Advisor Class	19.92	8.45	6.34	38.62	51.46
VWEGX	14.76	0.00	38.07	Small Company	Van Wagoner Emerging Growth	20.04	10.00	2.60	9.27	51.38
TVFQX	20.16	0.00	43.23	Technology	Technology Value	11.79	15.68	24.22	12.61	51.37
IVTAX	25.56	0.00	36.54	Technology	Ivy Global Science & Technology - Class A	16.69	14.93	3.77	25.83	50.20
SLMCX	25.02	0.00	41.63	Technology	Seligman Communications & Information	15.96	10.74	12.98	19.06	49.15
OBMDX	18.63	0.00	26.57	Mid-Cap	Oberweis Mid-Cap	16.59	15.14	1.16	12.41	48.90
TPAGX	32.58	0.00	54.25	Aggressive Growth	Transamerica Premier Aggressive Growth	15.21	13.93	9.07	50.57	48.89
PEMCX	24.23	0.00	35.93	Mid Cap	PBHG Mid-Cap Value	17.86	7.71	10.39	28.09	48.63
PLCPX	28.72	0.00	33.25	Aggressive Growth	PBHG Large-Cap 20 Fund	19.90	7.30	2.18	48.77	48.19
VWMDX	18.27	-0.48	35.90	Mid Cap	Van Wagoner Mid-Cap	17.26	12.41	1.18	18.16	47.52
ISWCX	18.49	0.00	33.23	Telecommunications	INVESCO Worldwide Communications	16.60	8.47	11.13	27.23	47.24
FMCX	13.65	0.00	38.11	Micro Cap	Fremont Institutional U.S. Micro-Cap	13.12	14.49	12.74	2.42	47.10
OBMCX	14.99	0.00	36.00	Micro Cap	Oberweis Micro-Cap	15.27	12.94	6.97	1.07	46.97
KTCAX	25.09	0.00	35.80	Technology	Kemper Technology - Class A	15.59	12.18	6.02	26.88	46.37
JAOLX	25.59	-0.29	31.59	Aggressive Growth	Janus Olympus	18.32	7.42	4.38	43.57	46.25
POGSX	25.74	0.00	41.22	Growth	Pin Oak Aggressive Stock	13.72	11.89	13.20	26.71	45.93
PARNX	14.79	-8.99	46.24	Micro Cap	Parnassus	12.79	12.86	13.61	-5.40	45.25
FUSMX	11.85	0.00	36.65	Micro Cap	Fremont U.S. Micro-Cap	12.70	13.28	12.85	0.19	45.11
JAENX	22.70	0.00	31.69	Mid Cap	Janus Enterprise	17.10	7.62	6.44	28.30	45.04
MPEGX	20.16	0.00	35.22	Mid Cap	MAS Mid-Cap Growth	16.74	7.15	8.66	25.16	44.96
MGCAX	25.81	-0.79	40.09	Aggressive Growth	Managers Capital Appreciation	15.96	12.17	0.89	44.67	44.54
RYOIX	....	0.00	32.54	Healthcare	Rydex Biotechnology Fund	19.01	3.01	6.98	22.08	44.52
JAMFX	25.51	-0.24	33.65	Technology	Janus Mercury	18.01	6.63	3.34	42.07	44.32
ICTEX	24.78	0.00	44.53	Technology	Icon Technology	11.37	13.16	15.82	19.36	43.81
SPECX	24.62	0.00	35.99	Aggressive Growth	Spectra	15.59	9.82	5.36	36.94	43.68
AGFAX	9.54	0.00	44.53	Aggressive Growth	Federated Aggressive Growth - Class A	14.97	8.04	11.12	0.94	43.54
PSTAX	27.17	-0.06	41.64	Growth	Phoenix Strategic Theme - Class A	13.76	11.79	7.56	33.42	43.09
WAEGX	22.96	0.00	32.46	Mid Cap	Citizens Emerging Growth	15.11	8.14	9.25	31.32	42.99
MFMSX	13.06	0.00	24.68	Mid Cap	Marshall Mid-Cap Growth	17.25	5.84	5.22	11.99	42.95
WAMCX	19.96	0.00	42.41	Mid Cap	Wasatch Mid-Cap	13.36	11.15	9.57	14.48	42.66
VWMCX	15.54	0.00	34.91	Micro Cap	Van Wagoner Micro-Cap	14.72	12.06	1.62	13.00	42.31
JAVLX	27.94	-1.35	32.29	Aggressive Growth	Janus Twenty	16.60	7.22	3.72	54.72	42.28
PBTCX	19.90	0.00	26.17	Technology	PBHG Technology & Communications	14.77	12.45	0.42	20.44	42.20
IAMCX	20.29	0.00	26.45	Mid Cap	IAI Mid-Cap Growth	16.07	6.61	6.68	22.78	42.09
ACAAX	19.87	0.00	29.97	Aggressive Growth	Alger Capital Appreciation - Class A	16.56	7.24	3.17	28.81	41.95
PBHEX	11.55	0.00	12.50	Aggressive Growth	PBHG Select Equity	18.73	7.48	-6.02	10.42	41.93
FDISX	14.74	0.00	33.74	Small Company	Founders Discovery	12.82	12.44	7.62	10.07	41.89
CMGIX	15.36	0.00	22.78	Mid Cap	Blackrock Mid-Cap Growth Equity - Institutional	15.65	10.42	-1.62	17.20	40.91
CVGRX	16.05	0.00	30.86	Growth	Calamos Growth - Class A	14.11	10.60	4.01	17.73	40.83
CAGFX	21.96	0.00	32.28	Aggressive Growth	Countrywide Aggressive Growth	14.02	8.20	9.02	17.59	40.75
SHGTX	17.59	0.00	29.90	Technology	Seligman Henderson Global Technology - Class A	12.54	11.27	8.25	13.70	40.48
RBOAX	23.44	-0.05	31.36	Growth	Reserve Blue Chip Growth	15.03	7.24	6.00	32.70	40.30
BTSCX	9.83	0.00	27.63	Small Company	BT Investment Small-Cap	14.55	9.82	2.28	-1.34	40.06
JANSX	19.16	0.00	27.95	Aggressive Growth	Janus	15.56	6.71	4.16	26.36	39.91
CGVFX	23.60	0.00	32.07	Growth	Countrywide Growth/Value	12.90	9.82	8.10	31.09	39.67
FOCTX	20.02	0.00	35.69	Growth	Focus Trust	11.62	10.54	10.95	28.88	39.26
SSGSX	4.18	0.00	29.28	Small Company	Victory Special Growth	12.85	13.18	0.74	-11.46	39.25

Sort order: Momentum Score

Important: It is a big advantage to know at the time you have new money to invest which funds have a higher MS reading than the MS reading for the investment yardstick you are using. History has shown that a fund with strong momentum at the beginning of a buy cycle, or even at mid-cycle, is likely to continue having strong momentum throughout the cycle. So, the funds with the highest MS readings are the best candidates for new purchases.

MONITORING AND ROTATING UP

Once we have made our selections among funds that have MS readings higher than the MS readings of their yardsticks, we proceed to monitoring. At my management company, we do not sit back and wait for the next sell signal. We continually strive to get the entire portfolio working for superior performance.

Each day, we check every fund we are holding to see that its performance, since the day it was purchased, is achieving monthly growth of at least 1.67 percent. In addition, each fund's performance is compared to the performance of its yardstick. Obviously, if an individual fund we are holding is outperforming the current yardstick, and at the same time the yardstick itself is on target to reach the goal, then that fund is giving superior performance and we will keep it in our portfolio. But we continually monitor its performance to make sure.

An example of the management company's daily monitoring report is shown in Figure 13-2. Note that this report shows two investment yardsticks: the Domestic Fund Composite (DFC) and the S&P 500. During the review of our current holdings, if a fund is held for at least 60 days and the fund is underperforming the 1.67 percent monthly growth and/or underperforming the yardstick, it becomes a candidate to be sold. Once sold, it will be replaced with a fund with a higher Momentum Score than the yardstick. This is called "rotating up."

Here is an example of how rotating up works. Look at Figure 13-3. This is a portfolio evaluation that was prepared for a prospective management client on December 31, 1998. The information shown in this report gives examples for selling and monitoring, and how rotating up is used to enhance performance. The three columns to the left of the fund names serve as our monitoring tools to generate sell signals. The column headings are 39WD, % Off High, and 16-Week.

FIGURE 13-2

MONITORING REPORT - 1/1/99

Symbol	Fund Name	Buy Date	Switch Perf	Investment Performance DFC Perf	Yardsticks SP500 perf
FTCHX	INVESCO Strategic Technology	11/2/98	23.07	12.68	9.56
GABGX	Gabelli Growth	11/2/98	16.91	12.68	9.56
JAEIX	Janus Equity Income	11/2/98	17.88	12.68	9.56
JAGIX	Janus Growth & Income	11/2/98	16.35	12.68	9.56
JAWWX	Janus Worldwide	11/2/98	12.07	12.68	9.56
PRGFX	T. Rowe Price Growth Stock	11/2/98	12.53	12.68	9.56
RIMEX	Rainier Core Equity	11/2/98	11.98	12.68	9.56
SRFSX	Stein Roe Growth Stock	11/2/98	14	12.68	9.56
TEQUX	Transamerica Premier Equity	11/2/98	15.36	12.68	9.56
TWCUX	AmCent: 20th Century Ultra	11/2/98	17.1	12.68	9.56
ULPIX	UltraBull Profunds I Shares	11/2/98	19.53	12.68	9.56
UOPIX	Ultra OTC Profunds I Shares	11/2/98	60.82	12.68	9.56
VIGRX	Vanguard Index Trust Growth	11/2/98	13.43	12.68	9.56
CHTIX	Chicago Trust Growth & Income	11/4/98	12.01	12.08	8.87
FLRFX	INVESCO Growth	11/4/98	14.95	12.08	8.87
JAVLX	Janus Twenty	11/4/98	23.49	12.08	8.87
NVLCX	Norwest Advantage large	11/4/98	20	12.08	8.87
PLCVX	PBHG Large-Cap Value	11/4/98	13.65	12.08	8.87
RYMIX	Rydex Telecommunication Fund	11/4/98	17.84	12.08	8.87
RYNVX	Rydex Series Nova	11/4/98	14.74	12.08	8.87
RYSIX	Rydex Electronic Fund	11/4/98	22.78	12.08	8.87
SSTIX	Victory Stock Index	11/4/98	10.05	12.08	8.87
TVFQX	Technology Value	11/4/98	21.16	12.08	8.87
WOGSX	White Oak Growth Stock	11/4/98	19.28	12.08	8.87
PESPX	Dreyfus MidCap Index	11/9/98	12.77	11.17	7.72
TPAGX	Transamerica Premier Aggressiv	11/9/98	24.62	11.17	7.72
WAEGX	Citizens Emerging Growth	11/9/98	16.59	11.17	7.72
WAIDX	Citizens Index	11/9/98	14.41	11.17	7.72
CAGFX	Countrywide Aggressive Growth	11/10/98	18.28	11.28	7.9
POGSX	Pin Oak Aggressive Stock	11/10/98	20.95	11.28	7.9
TPSCX	Transamerica Premier Small	11/10/98	28.52	11.28	7.9
ETHSX	Eaton Vance Traditional	11/19/98	9.24	8.72	5.56
ICTEX	Icon Technology	11/19/98	11.27	8.72	5.56
KTCAX	Kemper Technology - Class A	11/19/98	17.12	8.72	5.56
PBMCX	PBHG Mid-Cap Value	11/19/98	18.4	8.72	5.56
POTCX	Potomac OTC Plus Fund	11/19/98	22.22	8.72	5.56
PSPLX	Potomac US Plus Fund	11/19/98	9.93	8.72	5.56
RYOCX	Rydex OTC	11/19/98	18.71	8.72	5.56
RYTIX	Rydex Technology Fund	12/8/98	8.03	5.4	3.01
JAMRX	Janus Mercury	12/23/98	2.12	1.33	0.07
MGCAX	Managers Capital Appreciation	12/23/98	2.43	1.33	0.07
PLCPX	PBHG Large-Cap 20 Fund	12/23/98	2.94	1.33	0.07
RSIFX	Robertson Stephens Information	12/23/98	1.58	1.33	0.07
SPECX	Spectra	12/23/98	1.82	1.33	0.07
WAMCX	Wasatch Mid-Cap	12/23/98	4.83	1.33	0.07
ISWCX	INVESCO Worldwide	12/30/98	1.43	0.31	-0.23
VWEGX	Van Wagoner Emerging Growth	12/30/98	4.58	0.31	-0.23
VWMDX	Van Wagoner Mid-Cap	12/30/98	1.55	0.31	-0.23

Evaluation as of 12/31/98

	Symbol	3 SWD	% Off High	16-Week	Fund Name	Dec	Nov	Oct	Sep	Aug	YTD	Momentum Score
1	JANSX	19.16	0.00	27.95	Janus	15.56	6.71	4.16	7.03	-17.02	39.86	39.91
2	FTCHX	17.49	0.00	22.63	INVESCO Strategic Technology	14.23	9.12	0.39	10.91	-17.67	36.36	37.78
3	PRWAX	10.83	0.00	24.77	T. Rowe Price New America Growth	12.08	4.77	8.74	3.89	-20.73	21.66	33.30
4	MNGCX	12.51	0.00	28.01	Montgomery Global Communications	8.51	8.71	12.04	-0.98	-23.94	51.09	31.75
5	TWCUX	14.22	-0.33	23.31	AllCENT: 20th Century Ultra	11.37	6.19	4.01	7.22	-18.26	35.81	30.94
6	FMAGX	15.87	-0.68	26.15	Fidelity Magellan	9.27	7.76	7.70	6.05	-15.49	35.49	30.15
7	JAWWX	7.64	-0.11	15.43	Janus Worldwide	7.69	6.33	5.00	-3.19	-14.26	23.43	24.21
8	FRGRX	10.50	-0.44	20.18	Founders Growth	7.76	4.99	7.06	6.18	-17.43	26.14	24.04
9	#MFC	9.91	-0.15	20.80	Domestic Fund Composite	7.28	6.30	6.18	6.06	-17.15	23.06	23.95
10	KAUFX	3.65	0.00	16.07	Kaufmann	6.97	7.06	2.27	6.59	-19.47	3.09	22.14
11	#500IX	11.74	-0.96	21.87	S&P 500	5.74	6.04	8.11	6.40	-14.47	30.03	21.58
12	SLASX	8.42	-0.32	22.64	Selected American Shares	4.77	4.61	11.49	4.55	-17.49	21.67	19.90
13	FPBSX	1.69	0.00	11.50	INVESCO Pacific Basin	1.40	7.38	5.56	-1.72	-11.85	-10.74	12.96
14	SCDUX	3.54	-0.83	16.54	Scudder Large Company Value	0.84	5.62	8.90	4.36	-15.73	12.90	11.75
15	CUIEX	-1.93	-13.50	9.53	Warburg Pincus International Equity	1.54	5.29	5.58	-4.54	-15.16	5.52	11.16
16	VWNDX	-1.58	-14.30	11.84	Vanguard Windsor	+1.76	2.27	9.04	6.44	-20.24	3.18	10.31
17	CSRSX	-5.80	-17.40	8.31	Cohen & Steers Realty Shares	-2.09	2.75	-1.54	5.24	-9.94	-16.64	-2.20
18	SLAFX	-12.10	-32.20	33.06	Scudder Latin America	-5.64	4.45	8.24	9.99	-32.45	-21.72	-2.71
19	FSTEX	-15.60	-32.50	-6.41	INVESCO Strategic Energy	-2.23	-8.50	3.20	19.17	-19.54	-17.75	-11.40
20	LEXMX	-6.48	-13.20	-4.21	Lexington Goldfund, Inc.	-7.06	-2.40	1.21	38.66	-18.77	-9.82	-15.50

The second column from the left is the 39WD. You'll recall that the 39WD is a percentage measurement of how much a fund or composite's current reading is above or below its 39-week average (39WAR). If a fund falls below its 39WAR (negative number), it would be sold. On the date of this report, you'll see that the bottom six funds were below their 39WAR and would definitely be sold.

The third column from the left is % Off High. Any fund that is more than 10 percent off its high is a candidate to be sold. In this column, again, the same six funds that were below their 39WAR were also more than 10 percent off their highs, further indicating they need to be sold.

The fourth column from the left is performance for the past 16 weeks. Each fund's 16-week performance is monitored to ensure that the current holdings are on target with our investment objective. Here the goal is 20 percent annual growth for each individual fund, or 1.67 percent per month. Sixteen weeks is four months, so, for this period, 7 percent is needed to be on target. Thus, any fund under 7 percent growth is a candidate to be sold.

Once this monitoring process is completed, the next question is this: Are the remaining funds in the portfolio still doing their job? In other words, are they meeting the goal, exceeding the performance of the yardstick, and posting high Momentum Scores? Whenever funds are sold, we rotate up to the funds listed on the Highest Momentum Report, which show MS readings higher than the yardstick (Figure 13-1).

After rotating up, the majority of funds in the portfolio should then be outperforming the yardstick. If the funds are doing better than the yardstick, and the yardstick is on target for the goal, then we are ahead of the goal. This is our proactive approach to mutual fund portfolio management, and it ensures superior performance at all times.

IN CONCLUSION

We have now discussed all of the procedures for buying, monitoring, selling, and rotating up. Most importantly, you see how I strive to outperform the yardstick with daily monitoring. The trading strategy that I have reviewed with you is logical and practical for me. It requires daily monitoring, however, as well as the discipline to follow the rules when it's time to take action. The daily monitoring would be too time-consuming for most individuals. Nonetheless, I wanted you to see this entire process so you can understand not only what I do but also why I do it. Now, I will take the best components of the my plan and create a personalized plan for you to follow.

Implementing the Fabian Compounding Plan: A Personalized Program

Checklists and Tools

THE THIRD AND FINAL PERSPECTIVE FOR IMPLEMENTING THE FABIAN COMPOUNDING PLAN

This is it . . . the moment of truth. Everything presented to this point has been in preparation for this section—your personalized plan for becoming a self-made millionaire.

In the beginning of the book, I told you about myself. I told you what I believe and why. In addition, I discussed how the personal life experiences of others explains how they arrive at what they believe. I talked about the lack of appropriate role models and the fact that the financial media is not your friend. I talked about how people have bad experiences with investing and have become very conservative with their money.

Throughout the book I kept reminding you that it is the mathematical power of compounded growth that makes it possible for you (and anyone else) to become a self-made millionaire. I talked about my simple trend-following plan that puts compounded growth to work for you. I talked about following just two rules, one for buying and one for selling, and showed you how I choose funds, monitor their performance, and rotate up to better-performing funds, always striving to meet or exceed the goal.

Although we discussed many ideas, the point is this: *It takes time for any new idea to be accepted.* If you are 30 or 40 or 50 or 60 years old, the beliefs you held prior to reading this book took you 30 or 40 or 50 or 60 years to develop. Many of my ideas may not only be new to you, but they most likely contradict many of the things you have come to believe over the years, or that you know as the conventional wisdom. I have challenged many established ideas. And more than likely, you've never been told that you can become, even with a modest income, a self-made millionaire entirely on your own, using just your investment portfolio.

I believe you can become a self-made millionaire. The question now is, do you believe you can? I hope so, because I have given you the history, the documentation, and the tools you need to believe it yourself.

52 PERCENT GROWTH EACH YEAR FOR 10 YEARS ON YOUR INITIAL INVESTMENT!

During my presentations at investment conferences, the most important segment is when I explain the incredible power of compounded growth. As I pointed out in Part 2 on compounding, 20 percent compounded growth over a 10-year period will produce for you 52 percent growth each year on your initial investment. This is a mathematical truth. So, once I get my audience to accept this very important fact, I ask this question:

Ladies and gentlemen, if you truly believed you could get 52 percent growth each and every year for the next 10 years on the total amount of money you invest today, how much money would you commit?

Without exception, two or three people in the audience will yell out and say "All of it!" Others will say, "All I can find." I have never heard anyone say they are already fully committed and couldn't find any additional money to invest. In pondering these answers, I have come to three conclusions:

1. The investors in the audience presently are not investing all of the money that they could make available.
2. They do not have enough faith in the investment strategy they are presently following to put more of their money into it.
3. The benefits of 20 percent compounded growth over just a 10-year period are so enormous, if they really believed they could attain it, they would be willing to maximize their investment commitment!

For this reason, the most important investment question that serious investors must answer is this: What is the simplest plan that I believe I could follow over the long term which has a high probability of attaining 20 percent annualized compounded growth?

Remember that keeping the plan *simple* is important so that you can easily follow it over the long term, thus ensuring that you will achieve your goal and become a self-made millionaire.

What follows is my answer to this question.

FOUR ASSUMPTIONS

As we get started on your personalized plan, I am making these assumptions:

1. By the time you decide to implement the compounding plan using this personalized program, you have made up your mind that you truly want to become a self-made millionaire.
2. You have at least $15,000 to invest in mutual funds. With at least this amount of money, I recommend that you establish your investment account at a discount broker where you will have access to mutual funds from many different fund families. (For anyone starting with less than $15,000, follow the mutual fund beginners' procedures outlined in Chapters 10 and 11. Later, after your account grows large enough, you can then transfer to a discount broker.)
3. You will have access to the Internet. Daily access is not necessary. Therefore, for the occasional reference, you could rely on the use of a friend's computer, a computer at your place of employment, a library or cyber cafe, or place where they rent computers with access to the Internet.
4. At least for the first year, you will be building your knowledge about the statistical data that is necessary to implement the plan. The newsletter is not required but you may find it simplifies the process of accumulating investment data. There are many other options; therefore, find the source with which you are comfortable.

THE SIX STEPS

Following are the six steps you will follow to implement your personalized investment plan to attain at least 20 percent annualized compounded growth over the long term:

1. Be aware of investment opportunities around the world.
2. Select your current investment yardsticks.
3. Determine which mutual funds to buy.
4. Monitor each of your mutual fund purchases.
5. Determine how and when to rotate up.
6. Know when to sell.

Now let's look at each on in detail.

STEP 1. BE AWARE OF INVESTMENT OPPORTUNITIES AROUND THE WORLD.

Your comfort level will be enhanced when you are always aware of the current mutual fund investment opportunities all over the world. This is particularly important when you are in the process of selecting new mutual funds to buy. You could be making purchases because a new uptrend has begun, because new money has become available to you in mid-cycle, or because investment dollars have become available as a result of rotating up.

You saw in Chapter 12 how my firm uses its Multiple Composite Snapshot of the World (Figures 12-1 and 12-2) to stay aware of investment opportunities around the world. As mentioned, similar information can be found in a weekly table in the Market Laboratory section of *Barron's*. This table is entitled "Lipper Mutual Fund Performance Averages," and Figure 14-1 shows a sample of this report, dated 9/30/99. The Lipper Report includes the performance statistics for 45 different classifications of mutual funds. Immediately preceding each classification name is the number of individual funds that make up that group.

You'll find the two most important items in this report in the first column to the right of the fund names and the fourth column. The first column shows the performance averages for the most recent 12 months. The fourth column shows the performance averages for the most current year-to-date. With this information you can determine which classifications (groups) of funds are on target for the goal for both of these time periods. Again, the measurement to use to determine if you are on target to reach your goal is 1.67 percent growth per month. For example, after nine months of the current year, any classification of funds that shows a growth of 15.00 percent or more in the fourth column is on target for the goal. Obviously, for the prior 12 months, any fund classification showing a growth of 20 percent or more is on target to reach your goal.

FIGURE 14-1

LIPPER MUTUAL FUND PERFORMANCE AVERAGES

Special Quarterly Summary Report:
Thursday, September 30, 1999
Cumulative Total Reinvestment Performance

NAV Mil. $	No. Funds		09/30/89-09/30/99	09/30/94-09/30/99	09/30/98-09/30/99	12/31/98-09/30/99	06/30/99-09/30/99
General Equity Funds							
2,391.2	31	Specialty Dvsfd Eq Funds	+ 57.67	— 14.04	— 6.46	— 5.72	— 2.44
211,632.4	116	S&P 500 Funds	+ 351.90	+ 198.74	+ 27.05	+ 4.84	— 6.35
43,789.6	170	Mid-Cap Core Funds	+ 240.18	+ 104.31	+ 30.78	+ 5.28	— 3.66
28,107.8	208	Mid-Cap Value Funds	+ 183.53	+ 85.55	+ 14.10	— 1.26	— 8.91
19,608.9	202	Small-Cap Core Funds	+ 189.73	+ 84.76	+ 24.96	+ 4.66	— 3.77
146,146.0	228	Equity Income Funds	+ 212.19	+ 108.99	+ 12.29	— 0.54	— 8.60
58,391.7	251	Mid-Cap Growth Funds	+ 288.24	+ 135.88	+ 51.14	+ 17.92	+ 0.61
42,457.2	282	Small-Cap Growth Funds	+ 256.01	+ 105.33	+ 43.76	+ 13.57	+ 0.85
376,173.3	296	Large-Cap Value Funds	+ 275.56	+ 154.41	+ 20.71	+ 2.01	— 8.22
41,815.1	331	Small-Cap Value Funds	+ 174.43	+ 75.64	+ 12.33	— 0.47	— 6.64
327,587.6	402	Large-Cap Core Funds	+ 311.54	+ 167.48	+ 27.74	+ 4.84	— 6.00
333,465.2	381	Large-Cap Growth Funds	+ 379.76	+ 197.21	+ 37.86	+ 8.75	— 3.64
306,600.5	387	Multi-Cap Growth Funds	+ 338.25	+ 161.32	+ 41.88	+ 11.69	— 2.49
158,419.5	449	Multi-Cap Core Funds	+ 270.51	+ 140.60	+ 25.29	+ 4.04	— 6.38
213,857.7	522	Multi-Cap Value Funds	+ 227.09	+ 117.10	+ 16.39	— 0.02	— 9.60
2,310,443.7	4,256	General Equity Funds	+ 264.81	+ 132.71	+ 27.19	+ 5.23	— 5.37
Other Equity Funds							
25,359.6	61	Health/Biotechnology	+ 417.48	+ 122.79	+ 14.39	— 3.24	— 2.29
5,350.7	62	Natural Resources Funds	+ 105.91	+ 48.24	+ 24.36	+ 29.15	+ 1.19
57,922.3	127	Science & Technology	+ 861.85	+ 283.82	+ 101.87	+ 43.36	+ 7.02
4,847.3	12	Telecommunication Funds	+ 465.32	+ 237.15	+ 75.72	+ 25.55	— 1.98
24,739.5	105	Utility Funds	+ 224.49	+ 110.25	+ 14.78	+ 3.47	— 3.36
15,893.1	74	Financial Services Funds	+ 387.23	+ 140.88	+ 10.67	— 5.97	— 12.68
9,090.1	147	Real Estate Funds	+ 86.34	+ 52.01	— 2.28	— 3.17	— 9.12
2,930.5	87	Specialty/Miscellaneous	+ 226.15	+ 89.87	+ 11.35	+ 1.30	— 4.56
2,212.5	47	Gold Oriented Funds	— 23.54	— 44.40	+ 8.38	+ 15.16	+ 19.21
127,831.1	271	Global Funds	+ 164.64	+ 91.68	+ 30.54	+ 9.81	— 1.02
16,500.6	46	Global Small-Cap Funds	+ 121.08	+ 61.98	+ 29.50	+ 12.82	+ 1.00
188,585.2	667	International Funds	+ 132.85	+ 56.11	+ 29.79	+ 11.56	— 3.90
7,008.4	72	International Small-Cap	+ 130.25	+ 72.12	+ 47.20	+ 30.67	+ 9.12
21,062.7	174	European Region Funds	+ 157.15	+ 106.57	+ 15.40	— 0.91	+ 0.95
6,059.9	56	Pacific Region Funds	+ 58.73	— 5.79	+ 78.40	+ 46.14	+ 8.35
6,024.0	51	Japanese Funds	— 7.58	+ 26.87	+ 99.17	+ 71.21	+ 22.78
4,653.4	92	Pacific Ex Japan Funds	+ 46.78	— 18.51	+ 65.99	+ 30.41	— 7.08
682.8	29	China Region Funds	n/a	— 20.40	+ 44.93	+ 22.53	— 7.87
17,124.1	189	Emerging Markets Fund	+ 66.56	— 22.37	+ 42.64	+ 25.42	— 6.73
1,631.1	58	Latin American Funds	n/a	— 23.08	+ 23.49	+ 15.63	— 10.25
51.6	2	Canadian Funds	+ 62.47	+ 21.83	+ 29.62	+ 13.56	— 0.20
399,427.4	1,754	World Equity Funds	+ 97.61	+ 43.39	+ 36.21	+ 16.84	+ 1.68
2,856,004.2	6,685	Equity Funds - EFPA	+ 248.17	+ 110.26	+ 29.41	+ 8.70	— 3.34
Other Funds							
68,189.1	248	Flexible Portfolio Funds	+ 200.17	+ 100.09	+ 15.56	+ 2.42	— 3.66
19,315.5	110	Global Flexible Port	+ 146.14	+ 73.95	+ 18.75	+ 5.96	— 0.64
177,210.4	466	Balanced Funds	+ 192.83	+ 96.54	+ 12.62	+ 1.05	— 4.35
904.7	13	Balanced Target Maturity	+ 103.95	+ 75.33	+ 11.37	+ 3.30	— 1.35
6,536.9	66	Convertible Securities	+ 186.54	+ 84.69	+ 21.00	+ 8.88	— 1.83
27,611.5	98	Income Funds	+ 183.22	+ 81.53	+ 7.67	+ 1.13	— 2.86
299,768.1	1,001	Mixed Equity Funds	+ 188.97	+ 92.78	+ 14.08	+ 2.47	— 3.42
22,085.8	287	World Income Funds	+ 98.22	+ 37.10	+ 4.90	+ 0.04	+ 1.21
472,467.3	2,088	Domestic L-T Fixed Inc	+ 107.94	+ 38.92	+ 0.59	— 0.17	+ 0.11
3,940,159.2	11,998	L-T Equity and Fixed Tax Inc	+ 199.37	+ 86.16	+ 20.92	+ 5.95	— 2.50
		Long-Term Median	+ 175.12	+ 74.61	+ 16.88	+ 2.48	— 2.49
		Funds with a % Change	1,237	3,701	8,935	9,403	9,834

Securities Market Indexes

NAV Mil. $			09/30/89-09/30/99	09/30/94-09/30/99	09/30/98-09/30/99	12/31/98-09/30/99	06/30/99-09/30/99
U.S.Equities							
Value							
10,336.9		Dow Jones Ind. Average P	+ 283.87	+ 168.97	+ 31.80	+ 12.59	— 5.78
1,282.7		S&P 500 Index P	+ 267.38	+ 177.23	+ 26.12	+ 4.35	— 6.56
1,581.3		S&P Industrials P	+ 297.36	+ 188.39	+ 30.07	+ 6.91	— 4.65
592.7		NYSE Composite P	+ 205.61	+ 131.99	+ 17.51	+ 0.51	— 8.54
427.3		Russell 2000 IX P	+ 139.77	+ 66.84	+ 17.52	+ 1.27	— 6.64
International Equities							
Value							
5,149.8		DAX:Dm IX Tr	n/a	+ 155.99	+ 15.01	+ 2.95	— 4.25
6,029.8		FT S-E 100: Pd IX P	+ 162.23	+ 99.25	+ 19.68	+ 2.50	— 4.57
1,760.5		Nikkei 225 Average: Yen P	— 50.60	— 10.01	+ 31.32	+ 27.19	+ 0.43

Cumulative Performance With Dividends Reinvested

NAV Mil. $	No. Funds		09/30/89-09/30/99	09/30/94-09/30/99	09/30/98-09/30/99	12/31/98-09/30/99	06/30/99-09/30/99
Current Value							
10,336.9		Dow Jones Ind Mth Reinv	+ 399.54	+ 198.47	+ 34.04	+ 14.00	— 5.38
3,807.2		S & P 500 Daily Reinv	+ 373.34	+ 205.59	+ 27.80	+ 5.36	— 6.25

S&P 500 calculated by reinvesting daily dividends on a monthly basis.
Dow Jones Ind. is Calculated by reinvesting quarterly dividends paid on a monthly basis.
P-Price only index. Tr-Total Return calculated with reinvestment of dividends. The Nikkei index value is divided by 10 due to space limitation. Source: Lipper, Summit, New Jersey 07901

The lower section of this Lipper Report lists eight different General Market Indicators (GMIs). With this information you can also determine which of the GMIs around the world are currently on target to reach your goal.

STEP 2. SELECT YOUR CURRENT INVESTMENT YARDSTICKS

Next, you'll need to choose your investment yardsticks. You can find them by reviewing the growth of the most popular GMIs. They can be found at the bottom of the Lipper Mutual Fund Performance Averages report. In addition, there is a lengthy list of major indexes each week in the Market Laboratory section of *Barron's* (Figure 14-2). Many of these market indicators can also be found in the financial sections of most daily newspapers.

For each indicator, during a rising market, you want to know which GMIs are currently on target to reach the 20 percent compounded goal for the current year-to-date, for the previous 12 months, and for the current buy cycle. Most of the sources I described do not provide all of this data.

Website Resource General Market Indicators

In the free section of the Fabian Investment Resources website (www .fabian.com) you have access to a list of the major General Market Indicators. Each listed GMI has the following data available:

- Ticker symbol
- Yearly chart including its 39-week average
- The current 39-week average price and 39-week differential
- Performance for:
  Prior buy cycle
  Past 12 months
  Current buy cycle
  Current year-to-date
  Current month-to-date

Isn't it logical, provided there is at least one GMI that shows performance high enough to be on target to reach your goal, that you will have no difficulty finding individual mutual funds from that group that are also

FIGURE 14-2

THE WEEK IN STOCKS

MAJOR INDEXES

12-Month High	12-Month Low		Weekly High	Weekly Low	Friday Close	Chg.	Weekly %Chg.	12-Month Chg.	12-Month %Chg.	Change From 12/31	%Chg.
Dow Jones Averages											
11326.04	7899.52	30 Indus	10649.76	10400.59	10649.76	376.76	3.67	2750.24	34.82	1468.33	15.99
3783.50	2420.60	20 Transp	3081.71	2959.10	3081.71	213.37	7.44	652.19	26.84	(67.60)	(2.15)
333.45	286.44	15 Utilities	305.87	298.36	299.67	(1.87)	(.62)	(11.79)	(3.79)	(12.63)	(4.04)
3366.13	2480.61	65 Comp	3107.88	3048.29	3107.88	109.01	3.64	623.18	25.08	237.05	8.26
1338.32	924.88	Global-US	1256.55	1224.19	1256.55	49.41	4.09	331.67	35.86	87.21	7.46
318.32	62.50	Internet	260.82	233.51	260.82	28.18	12.11	198.32	317.31	110.51	73.52
New York Stock Exchange											
663.12	486.70	Comp	613.51	599.30	613.51	21.03	3.55	126.81	26.06	17.70	2.97
827.71	605.58	Indus	773.19	754.48	773.19	24.86	3.32	167.61	27.68	29.54	3.97
515.70	375.56	Utilities	489.56	481.63	489.56	8.60	1.79	105.86	27.59	43.62	9.78
560.33	365.29	Transp	464.07	457.56	464.07	17.77	3.98	98.78	27.04	(18.31)	(3.80)
584.22	418.75	Finan	500.09	485.57	500.09	26.63	5.62	81.34	19.42	(21.33)	(4.09)
American Stock Exchange											
821.73	574.73	Amex Comp	789.83	781.49	781.49	(5.04)	(.64)	206.76	35.98	92.50	13.43
1165.80	870.19	MajorMkt	1114.26	1088.06	1114.26	40.31	3.75	244.07	28.05	124.11	12.53
Standard & Poor's Indexes											
733.79	483.72	100 Index	698.45	682.60	698.45	28.14	4.20	214.73	44.39	94.42	15.63
1418.78	984.39	500 Index	1336.02	1301.35	1336.02	53.21	4.15	351.63	35.72	106.79	8.69
1724.28	1177.84	Indus	1645.50	1602.14	1645.50	61.00	3.85	467.66	39.70	166.34	11.25
830.12	559.93	Transp	622.28	604.39	622.28	36.49	6.23	62.35	11.14	(46.07)	(6.89)
269.98	232.91	Utilities	248.30	240.18	240.82	(4.09)	(1.67)	(18.26)	(7.05)	(18.80)	(7.24)
151.42	102.04	Finan	129.88	125.16	129.88	8.48	6.99	27.84	27.28	(.29)	(.22)
427.82	283.63	MidCap	389.86	384.82	385.07	6.04	1.59	101.44	35.76	(7.24)	(1.85)
190.15	132.56	SmallCap	177.22	175.58	175.71	1.19	.68	43.15	32.55	(1.66)	(.94)
Nasdaq Stock Market											
2887.06	1492.49	Comp	2886.57	2795.97	2886.57	149.72	5.47	1394.08	93.41	693.88	31.65
2555.36	1197.87	100 Index	2555.36	2467.92	2555.36	150.91	6.28	1357.49	113.33	719.35	39.18
1713.67	913.51	Indus	1662.21	1620.43	1662.19	65.55	4.11	748.68	81.96	357.94	27.44
2372.33	1386.26	Insur	2026.54	1998.67	2016.77	(5.97)	(.30)	630.51	45.48	219.98	12.24
1898.49	1560.82	Banks	1739.97	1705.72	1739.97	63.63	3.80	179.15	11.48	(98.03)	(5.33)
1606.31	736.72	Computer	1569.14	1539.57	1569.14	66.70	4.44	832.42	112.99	434.95	38.35
702.33	323.59	Telecom	692.18	632.44	692.18	75.38	12.22	368.59	113.91	191.27	38.18
1312.76	676.31	NNM Comp	1312.69	1271.21	1312.69	68.50	5.51	636.38	94.10	316.53	31.78
705.42	374.18	NNM Indus	684.93	667.44	684.93	27.34	4.16	310.75	83.05	147.84	27.53
Russell Indexes											
736.69	507.64	1000	690.68	673.59	690.68	27.20	4.10	183.04	36.06	47.81	7.44
465.80	318.40	2000	429.76	426.01	427.71	4.18	.99	109.31	34.33	5.75	1.36
758.94	522.76	3000	710.56	694.00	710.56	26.52	3.88	187.80	35.92	46.29	6.97
615.90	455.58	Value-v	555.35	544.79	555.35	15.56	2.88	99.77	21.90	15.26	2.83
731.41	471.01	Growth-v	707.10	684.43	707.10	34.51	5.13	236.09	50.12	74.11	11.71
564.89	399.74	MidCap	517.02	508.78	515.66	13.93	2.78	115.92	29.00	10.77	2.13
Others											
1067.57	730.83	Value Line-a	969.42	961.42	967.95	10.53	1.10	237.12	32.45	40.11	4.32
472.95	354.28	Value Line-g	420.05	416.84	419.08	3.55	.85	64.80	18.29	(18.07)	(4.13)
12976.99	8850.91	Wilshire 5000	12170.40	11879.10	12170.40	467.10	3.99	3319.49	37.50	852.81	7.54
693.15	430.79	Wilshire SC	658.34	648.09	656.23	16.23	2.54	225.44	52.33	73.38	12.59

a-Arithmetic Index. g-Geometric Index. v-Value 1000 and Growth 1000.

Source: Barron's.

181

on target for your goal? The answer to this question is the essence of our approach to investing.

You can select your current investment yardsticks from those indicators that are on target for the goal in the current market cycle (from the most recent buy signal). During the monitoring process, as you are overseeing the performance of the individual funds you own, you will also monitor the performance of your chosen yardsticks for the same time period.

Should the time come that all or most of the yardsticks are not on target for the goal, this could indicate that the market is either going through a sideways movement or that the trend of the market is changing from up to down. In this case, be on alert that a sell signal, indicating a switch from growth funds to money market funds, may be generated.

STEP 3. DETERMINE WHICH MUTUAL FUNDS TO BUY

As we discussed in Chapter 10, one of the most important tools for investment organization is a simple three-ring binder. Careful organization will not only help you to monitor your investment performance through the years, but it will make tax preparation much easier. In your investment notebook you will maintain both the General Information Worksheet and the Telephone Exchange and Online Worksheet. (Refer back to Figures 10-4 and 10-5.)

Purchasing Enhanced Index Funds

I recommend that enhanced index funds (EIFs) be purchased as a component of your mutual fund portfolio *only* at the beginning of a new market cycle. When a new buy signal is generated by the Domestic Fund Composite, consider for purchase any EIF whose related index is above its 39-week average reading. For example, Ultra OTC Pro Fund could be one of your mutual fund selections, provided the NASDAQ 100, its related index, was above its 39WAR. The EIF purchased should be held until the next DFC sell signal.

When a new sell signal is generated by the Domestic Fund Composite, it would be appropriate to buy, for example, Ultra Short OTC Pro Fund, provided its related index, the NASDAQ 100, was below its 39-week average reading. This fund should then be held until the next DFC buy signal.

Buying at the Beginning of a New Market Cycle in U.S. Equities

Using the information available on the General Market Indicators website and the Top Performing Mutual Funds website, let's look at some examples illustrating how this data can be used.

To start let's go back to November 9, 1998. That was the beginning of a new buy cycle for the Domestic Fund Composite trading plan. In the example shown in Figures 14-3 and 14-4, I selected two performance yardsticks and purchased five mutual funds as of November 9, 1998.

To select two performance yardsticks, at the beginning of this new buy cycle, I reviewed the most recent previous cycle performance for each of the GMIs. That previous cycle covered the time period 9/16/96 to 8/12/98—23 months. Multiplying 23 months by 1.67 percent, (the monthly average growth needed to attain our goal) the result is 38.41 percent. This means any GMI that grew by 38.41 percent or more over that 23-month period attained the goal. During that cycle both the Domestic Fund Composite (42.42 percent) and the S&P 500 (58.52 percent) exceeded the goal. In the example, I chose to use these two indicators as my performance yardsticks.

In selecting the five mutual funds to purchase, I repeated the above process in reviewing the available mutual funds in the Top Performing Mutual Funds listed on the website. After examining all of the funds which had a growth of 38.41 percent or more during the prior cycle, I chose Pro-funds Ultra OTC (enhanced index fund), Safeco Growth (82.93 percent), American Century: Equity Growth (61.19 percent), Columbia Growth (48.47 percent), and Janus 20 (89.78 percent).

The same selection process, as outlined above, would also apply when a new market cycle is generated by the International Fund Composite.

Buying During Mid-Cycle

As a reminder, a mid-cycle period begins 90 days after a buy signal has occurred or after the composite indicator has risen 10 percent or more above its 39-week average. In the example shown in Figure 14-5, I made an additional mutual fund purchase on 3/1/99 using "new money."

On 3/1/99 my existing performance yardsticks were on target to reach the goal for the current cycle. Therefore, they were still appropriate to be used as the performance yardsticks for this new purchase. In addition to the mutual fund prices, it is necessary to record the current readings for

FIGURE 14-3

(A) 11/9/98 – Original Purchase Page 1 of 2
Monthly Bi-Monthly

Symbol	Fund Name	11/9/98 Buy Price	11/16/98 Price	11/16/98 Perf.
SAFGX	SAFECO Growth	21.36	21.04	-1.50%
UOPIX	Ultra OTC	20.23	20.43	0.99%
CLMBX	Columbia Growth	36.56	36.79	0.63%
BEQGX	AmCent: Eq.Grwth	20.56	20.50	-0.29%
JAVLX	Janus Twenty	43.75	43.46	-0.66%
S&P 500	S&P 500	1130.20	1135.86	0.50%
DFC	Domestic Fund Comp.	108778.21	108919.25	0.13%

Symbol	Fund Name	11/9/98 Buy Price	11/30/98 Price	11/30/98 Perf.
SAFGX	SAFECO Growth	21.36	21.54	0.84%
UOPIX	Ultra OTC	20.23	24.71	22.15%
CLMBX	Columbia Growth	36.56	38.10	4.21%
BEQGX	AmCent: Eq.Grwth	20.56	21.07	2.48%
JAVLX	Janus Twenty	43.75	45.71	4.48%
S&P 500	S&P 500	1130.20	1163.63	2.96%
DFC	Domestic Fund Comp.	108778.21	112715.17	3.62%

Symbol	Fund Name	11/9/98 Buy Price	12/15/98 Price	12/15/98 Perf.
SAFGX	SAFECO Growth	21.36	20.89	-2.20%
UOPIX	Ultra OTC	20.23	25.55	26.30%
CLMBX	Columbia Growth	36.56	38.89	6.37%
BEQGX	AmCent: Eq.Grwth	20.56	21.05	2.38%
JAVLX	Janus Twenty	43.75	47.60	8.80%
S&P 500	S&P 500	1130.20	1162.83	2.89%
DFC	Domestic Fund Comp.	108778.21	112543.66	3.46%

Symbol	Fund Name	11/9/98 Buy Price	12/31/98 Price	12/31/98 Perf.
SAFGX	SAFECO Growth	21.36	22.70	6.27%
UOPIX	Ultra OTC	20.23	30.68	51.66%
CLMBX	Columbia Growth	36.56	42.51	16.27%
BEQGX	AmCent: Eq.Grwth	20.56	22.54	9.63%
JAVLX	Janus Twenty	43.75	53.30	21.83%
S&P 500	S&P 500	1130.20	1229.23	8.76%
DFC	Domestic Fund Comp.	108778.21	120925.25	11.17%

Symbol	Fund Name	11/9/98 Buy Price	1/15/99 Price	1/15/99 Perf.
SAFGX	SAFECO Growth	21.36	22.62	5.90%
UOPIX	Ultra OTC	20.23	35.55	75.73%
CLMBX	Columbia Growth	36.56	42.98	17.56%
BEQGX	AmCent: Eq.Grwth	20.56	22.75	10.65%
JAVLX	Janus Twenty	43.75	54.85	25.37%
S&P 500	S&P 500	1130.20	1243.26	10.00%
DFC	Domestic Fund Comp.	108778.21	122189.97	12.33%

Symbol	Fund Name	11/9/98 Buy Price	1/29/99 Price	1/29/99 Perf.
SAFGX	SAFECO Growth	21.36	23.22	8.71%
UOPIX	Ultra OTC	20.23	40.14	98.42%
CLMBX	Columbia Growth	36.56	45.19	23.61%
BEQGX	AmCent: Eq.Grwth	20.56	23.13	12.50%
JAVLX	Janus Twenty	43.75	59.83	36.75%
S&P 500	S&P 500	1130.20	1279.64	13.22%
DFC	Domestic Fund Comp.	108778.21	126524.10	16.31%

Symbol	Fund Name	11/9/98 Buy Price	2/15/99 Price	2/15/99 Perf.
SAFGX	SAFECO Growth	21.36	21.41	0.23%
UOPIX	Ultra OTC	20.23	33.47	65.45%
CLMBX	Columbia Growth	36.56	43.13	17.97%
BEQGX	AmCent: Eq.Grwth	20.56	22.02	7.10%
JAVLX	Janus Twenty	43.75	56.10	28.23%
S&P 500	S&P 500	1130.20	1230.13	8.84%
DFC	Domestic Fund Comp.	108778.21	121351.48	11.56%

Symbol	Fund Name	11/9/98 Buy Price	2/26/99 Price	2/26/99 Perf.
SAFGX	SAFECO Growth	21.36	20.49	-4.07%
UOPIX	Ultra OTC	20.23	31.92	57.79%
CLMBX	Columbia Growth	36.56	43.69	19.50%
BEQGX	AmCent: Eq.Grwth	20.56	22.12	7.59%
JAVLX	Janus Twenty	43.75	57.09	30.49%
S&P 500	S&P 500	1130.20	1238.33	9.57%
DFC	Domestic Fund Comp.	108778.21	122061.86	12.21%

Symbol	Fund Name	11/9/98 Buy Price	3/15/99 Price	3/15/99 Perf.
SAFGX	SAFECO Growth	21.36	20.99	-1.73%
UOPIX	Ultra OTC	20.23	36.53	80.57%
CLMBX	Columbia Growth	36.56	46.29	26.61%
BEQGX	AmCent: Eq.Grwth	20.56	22.93	11.53%
JAVLX	Janus Twenty	43.75	61.25	40.00%
S&P 500	S&P 500	1130.20	1307.26	15.67%
DFC	Domestic Fund Comp.	108778.21	128025.04	17.69%

Symbol	Fund Name	11/9/98 Buy Price	3/31/99 Price	3/31/99 Perf.
SAFGX	SAFECO Growth	21.36	20.59	-3.60%
UOPIX	Ultra OTC	20.23	37.54	85.57%
CLMBX	Columbia Growth	36.56	46.34	26.75%
BEQGX	AmCent: Eq.Grwth	20.56	22.51	9.48%
JAVLX	Janus Twenty	43.75	65.58	49.90%
S&P 500	S&P 500	1130.20	1286.70	13.85%
DFC	Domestic Fund Comp.	108778.21	127011.22	16.76%

your performance yardsticks as of the day you make any purchase. This data is needed for the monitoring process to be discussed in Step 4.

In selecting the additional mutual fund to buy, I reviewed the 3/1/99 Mutual Funds Performance Lists on the website. From the domestic funds listed, I identified those which showed the highest performance during the previous buy cycle, as well as in the current buy cycle and for the past eight weeks.

After weighing the evidence for previous and current cycles and the eight-week performance, you are in a position to select a new mutual fund

FIGURE 14-4

(A) 11/9/98 – Original Purchase Page 2 of 2
Monthly Bi-Monthly

Symbol	Fund Name	11/9/98 Buy Price	4/15/99 Price	4/15/99 Perf.	Symbol	Fund Name	11/9/98 Buy Price	4/30/99 Price	4/30/99 Perf.
UOPIX	Ultra OTC	20.23	38.54	90.51%	UOPIX	Ultra OTC	20.23	37.89	87.30%
CLMBX	Columbia Growth	36.56	46.69	27.71%	CLMBX	Columbia Growth	36.56	46.43	27.00%
BEQGX	AmCent: Eq.Grwth	20.56	23.07	12.21%	BEQGX	AmCent: Eq.Grwth	20.56	23.47	14.15%
JAVLX	Janus Twenty	43.75	65.49	49.69%	JAVLX	Janus Twenty	43.75	64.17	46.67%
S&P 500	S&P 500	1130.20	1322.85	17.05%	S&P 500	S&P 500	1130.20	1335.18	18.14%
DFC	Domestic Fund Comp.	108778.21	129869.90	19.39%	DFC	Domestic Fund Comp.	108778.21	129541.93	19.09%

Symbol	Fund Name	11/9/98 Buy Price	5/17/99 Price	5/17/99 Perf.	Symbol	Fund Name	11/9/98 Buy Price	5/28/99 Price	5/28/99 Perf.
UOPIX	Ultra OTC	20.23	39.00	92.78%	UOPIX	Ultra OTC	20.23	35.77	76.82%
CLMBX	Columbia Growth	36.56	46.66	27.63%	CLMBX	Columbia Growth	36.56	45.27	23.82%
BEQGX	AmCent: Eq.Grwth	20.56	23.60	14.79%	BEQGX	AmCent: Eq.Grwth	20.56	22.96	11.67%
JAVLX	Janus Twenty	43.75	64.06	46.42%	JAVLX	Janus Twenty	43.75	60.23	37.67%
S&P 500	S&P 500	1130.20	1339.49	18.52%	S&P 500	S&P 500	1130.20	1301.84	15.19%
DFC	Domestic Fund Comp.	108778.21	129844.15	19.37%	DFC	Domestic Fund Comp.	108778.21	126370.80	16.17%

Symbol	Fund Name	11/9/98 Buy Price	6/15/99 Price	6/15/99 Perf.	Symbol	Fund Name	11/9/98 Buy Price	6/30/99 Price	6/30/99 Perf.
UOPIX	Ultra OTC	20.23	34.36	69.85%	UOPIX	Ultra OTC	20.23	42.60	110.58%
CLMBX	Columbia Growth	36.56	45.31	23.93%	CLMBX	Columbia Growth	36.56	48.70	33.21%
BEQGX	AmCent: Eq.Grwth	20.56	22.92	11.48%	BEQGX	AmCent: Eq.Grwth	20.56	24.31	18.24%
JAVLX	Janus Twenty	43.75	57.72	31.93%	JAVLX	Janus Twenty	43.75	62.79	43.52%
S&P 500	S&P 500	1130.20	1301.16	15.13%	S&P 500	S&P 500	1130.20	1372.66	21.45%
DFC	Domestic Fund Comp.	108778.21	126249.60	16.06%	DFC	Domestic Fund Comp.	108778.21	134084.52	23.26%

Symbol	Fund Name	11/9/98 Buy Price	7/15/99 Price	7/15/99 Perf.	Symbol	Fund Name	11/9/98 Buy Price	7/31/99 Price	7/31/99 Perf.
UOPIX	Ultra OTC	20.23	47.50	134.80%	UOPIX	Ultra OTC	20.23	39.99	97.68%
CLMBX	Columbia Growth	36.56	50.02	36.82%	CLMBX	Columbia Growth	36.56	47.00	28.56%
BEQGX	AmCent: Eq.Grwth	20.56	25.12	22.18%	BEQGX	AmCent: Eq.Grwth	20.56	23.93	16.39%
JAVLX	Janus Twenty	43.75	65.65	50.06%	JAVLX	Janus Twenty	43.75	60.41	38.08%
S&P 500	S&P 500	1130.20	1409.62	24.72%	S&P 500	S&P 500	1130.20	1328.72	17.57%
DFC	Domestic Fund Comp.	108778.21	137559.27	26.46%	DFC	Domestic Fund Comp.	108778.21	129623.26	19.16%

Symbol	Fund Name	11/9/98 Buy Price	8/15/99 Price	8/15/99 Perf.	Symbol	Fund Name	11/9/98 Buy Price	8/31/99 Price	8/31/99 Perf.
UOPIX	Ultra OTC	20.23	41.38	104.55%	UOPIX	Ultra OTC	20.23	43.93	117.15%
CLMBX	Columbia Growth	36.56	46.13	26.18%	CLMBX	Columbia Growth	36.56	45.71	25.03%
BEQGX	AmCent: Eq.Grwth	20.56	24.08	17.12%	BEQGX	AmCent: Eq.Grwth	20.56	23.78	15.66%
JAVLX	Janus Twenty	43.75	60.41	38.08%	JAVLX	Janus Twenty	43.75	61.37	40.27%
S&P 500	S&P 500	1130.20	1330.77	17.75%	S&P 500	S&P 500	1130.20	1320.41	16.83%
DFC	Domestic Fund Comp.	108778.21	128712.01	18.33%	DFC	Domestic Fund Comp.	108778.21	127908.77	17.59%

Symbol	Fund Name	11/9/98 Buy Price	9/15/99 Price	9/15/99 Perf.	Symbol	Fund Name	11/9/98 Buy Price	9/22/99 Price	9/22/99 Perf.
UOPIX	Ultra OTC	20.23	46.25	128.62%	UOPIX	Ultra OTC	20.23	43.80	116.51%
CLMBX	Columbia Growth	36.56	45.72	25.05%	CLMBX	Columbia Growth	36.56	44.72	22.32%
BEQGX	AmCent: Eq.Grwth	20.56	24.06	17.02%	BEQGX	AmCent: Eq.Grwth	20.56	23.26	13.13%
JAVLX	Janus Twenty	43.75	61.90	41.49%	JAVLX	Janus Twenty	43.75	62.20	42.17%
S&P 500	S&P 500	1130.20	1317.97	16.61%	S&P 500	S&P 500	1130.20	1280.77	13.32%
DFC	Domestic Fund Comp.	108778.21	128156.20	17.81%	DFC	Domestic Fund Comp.	108778.21	127935.71	17.61%

to purchase. Selecting a fund following the steps just outlined will ensure that you will always be buying a fund with a strong current momentum and one that is outperforming the existing performance yardsticks. Experience has shown that when you move into any mutual fund which has a strong uptrend in place, that uptrend usually continues for an entire market cycle.

In the example in Figure 14-5 I purchased Needham Growth. The purchase of this additional fund is monitored separately from those purchased on 11/9/98.

FIGURE 14-5

(B) 3/1/99 – Additional New Money Purchase
Buy Needham Growth
Bi-Monthly Monitoring

Symbol	Fund Name	3/1/99 Buy Price	3/15/99 Price	3/15/99 Perf.
NEEGX	Needham Growth	17.10	17.22	0.70%
S&P 500	S&P 500	1236.16	1307.26	5.75%
DFC	Domestic Fund Comp.	121985.21	128025.04	4.95%

Symbol	Fund Name	3/1/99 Buy Price	3/31/99 Price	3/31/99 Perf.
NEEGX	Needham Growth	17.10	17.85	4.39%
S&P 500	S&P 500	1236.16	1286.70	4.09%
DFC	Domestic Fund Comp.	121985.21	127011.22	4.12%

Symbol	Fund Name	3/1/99 Buy Price	4/15/99 Price	4/15/99 Perf.
NEEGX	Needham Growth	17.10	18.53	8.36%
S&P 500	S&P 500	1236.16	1322.85	7.01%
DFC	Domestic Fund Comp.	121985.21	129869.90	6.46%

Symbol	Fund Name	3/1/99 Buy Price	4/30/99 Price	4/30/99 Perf.
NEEGX	Needham Growth	17.10	18.48	8.07%
S&P 500	S&P 500	1236.16	1335.18	8.01%
DFC	Domestic Fund Comp.	121985.21	129541.93	6.19%

Symbol	Fund Name	3/1/99 Buy Price	5/17/99 Price	5/17/99 Perf.
NEEGX	Needham Growth	17.10	19.92	16.49%
S&P 500	S&P 500	1236.16	1339.49	8.36%
DFC	Domestic Fund Comp.	121985.21	129844.15	6.44%

Symbol	Fund Name	3/1/99 Buy Price	5/28/99 Price	5/28/99 Perf.
NEEGX	Needham Growth	17.10	19.73	15.38%
S&P 500	S&P 500	1236.16	1301.84	5.31%
DFC	Domestic Fund Comp.	121985.21	126370.80	3.60%

Symbol	Fund Name	3/1/99 Buy Price	6/15/99 Price	6/15/99 Perf.
NEEGX	Needham Growth	17.10	21.49	25.67%
S&P 500	S&P 500	1236.16	1301.16	5.26%
DFC	Domestic Fund Comp.	121985.21	126249.60	3.50%

Symbol	Fund Name	3/1/99 Buy Price	6/30/99 Price	6/30/99 Perf.
NEEGX	Needham Growth	17.10	21.64	26.55%
S&P 500	S&P 500	1236.16	1372.66	11.04%
DFC	Domestic Fund Comp.	121985.21	134084.52	9.92%

Symbol	Fund Name	3/1/99 Buy Price	7/15/99 Price	7/15/99 Perf.
NEEGX	Needham Growth	17.10	22.86	33.68%
S&P 500	S&P 500	1236.16	1409.62	14.03%
DFC	Domestic Fund Comp.	121985.21	137559.27	12.77%

Symbol	Fund Name	3/1/99 Buy Price	7/31/99 Price	7/31/99 Perf.
NEEGX	Needham Growth	17.10	22.34	30.64%
S&P 500	S&P 500	1236.16	1328.72	7.49%
DFC	Domestic Fund Comp.	121985.21	129623.26	6.26%

Symbol	Fund Name	3/1/99 Buy Price	8/15/99 Price	8/15/99 Perf.
NEEGX	Needham Growth	17.10	22.75	33.04%
S&P 500	S&P 500	1236.16	1330.77	7.65%
DFC	Domestic Fund Comp.	121985.21	128712.01	5.51%

Symbol	Fund Name	3/1/99 Buy Price	8/31/99 Price	8/31/99 Perf.
NEEGX	Needham Growth	17.10	22.82	33.45%
S&P 500	S&P 500	1236.16	1320.41	6.82%
DFC	Domestic Fund Comp.	121985.21	127908.77	4.86%

Symbol	Fund Name	3/1/99 Buy Price	9/15/99 Price	9/15/99 Perf.
NEEGX	Needham Growth	17.10	23.69	38.54%
S&P 500	S&P 500	1236.16	1317.97	6.62%
DFC	Domestic Fund Comp.	121985.21	128156.20	5.06%

Symbol	Fund Name	3/1/99 Buy Price	9/22/99 Price	9/22/99 Perf.
NEEGX	Needham Growth	17.10	22.73	32.92%
S&P 500	S&P 500	1236.16	1280.77	3.61%
DFC	Domestic Fund Comp.	121985.21	127935.71	4.88%

In Chapter 12, we discussed Momentum Scores. To calculate a current Momentum Score reading, you add the weighted performance for the previous three months for any individual mutual fund or for any indicator. The highest weighting is given to the most recent month. Since you have on the website for the Top-Performing Mutual Funds 4-, 8-, and 12-week performance figures, simply adding these three numbers together could serve as a substitute for the Momentum Score calculation discussed above. Or a simpler process would be to just use the 8-week performance figure, the middle of the range, as a substitute for a Momentum Score reading.

Alert Mode

An *alert mode* is in effect when a composite moves to within 5 percent above or below its 39-week average trend line. After a new mid-cycle period has developed (i.e., 90 days after a buy signal and/or a rise in the composite of 10 percent above its trend line), whenever the Domestic Fund Composite moves into an alert mode, no new purchases should be made. Should the alert mode be canceled because the composite once again moves more than 5 percent above its trend line, additional purchases may be made.

STEP 4. MONITOR EACH OF YOUR MUTUAL FUND PURCHASES

Monitoring

As mentioned earlier, on the day you purchase any individual mutual fund, in addition to noting the price of the fund, you must also note that same day's reading for the performance yardsticks. Both the prices and the yardstick readings are used in the monitoring process.

The examples in Figures 14-3 and 14-4 show the initial purchase made on 11/9/98 and later sold on 9/22/99. A sell signal was given for the Domestic Fund Composite Plan on September 22, 1999.

In the illustration, the performances for all of the purchases made are reviewed on approximately the fifteenth of each month and the first trading day of the next month. The performances for the performance yardsticks are also included.

Portfolio Monitoring Worksheet

In the free section of the Fabian Investment Resources website you have access to a Portfolio Monitoring Worksheet. To create each individual worksheet (you may want to establish several), the following information will be required:

- An identifying Portfolio Worksheet title
- Ticker symbol for each fund purchased
- Purchase date
- Purchase price
- Ticker symbol for each performance yardstick
- Yardstick reading on purchase date

At the close of the market each day, a current valuation is available. It shows

- Ticker symbol
- Name of mutual fund/performance yardstick
- Current mutual fund prices and performance yardstick readings
- Valuation percentage changes for current holdings (+% or –%)

It only takes five minutes a week to determine whether or not your existing holdings are on target to reach the goal. If the performance yardsticks you are using are on target for the 20 percent compounded goal during the current buy cycle *and* if your individual mutual fund holdings are performing equal to or greater than your performance yardsticks during the period you held them, *there is nothing more for you to do.*

If, however, one or more of your existing mutual fund holdings are falling behind the target, you will need additional monitoring. Any individual holding which remains behind the target for two successive months should be sold and rotated up to a new mutual fund which has current performance figures showing strong recent momentum.

A suggestion: Include the ticker symbols at the top of each of your Portfolio Monitoring Worksheets for your chosen performance yardsticks, using the date and their readings from the beginning of the current buy cycle. Following this procedure, you will always have updated current cycle performance for each yardstick available as you are monitoring your existing holdings during the buy cycle.

Refer again to Figure 14-5, which shows the additional purchase, using new money, made on 3/1/99. Note that this new purchase is monitored separately from the 11/9/98 purchases. In each instance, the yardstick indicators are monitored separately showing their own individual performance since the purchase date. These procedures are the same for new purchases from rotating up, which we discuss next.

Distributions

The current income tax laws require each mutual fund to disburse its realized gains to its shareholders. This is called a *distribution.* These payments are usually made in the last six weeks of the year. When a distribution is made, the current price of the fund—its *net asset value* (NAV)—is reduced by the dollar amount of the distribution. Following the plan, the assumption is made that all distributions will be reinvested in additional shares of the fund.

In our monitoring procedures, to compensate for any distribution that is reinvested, you must reduce your original purchase price by the amount of the distribution. Here is an example. Say you purchased one share of a mutual fund for $10. The fund has grown to $11 and your gain would be $1, or 10 percent. A *distribution* of $0.55 is declared. By reinvesting the distribution, you receive an additional 0.05-plus shares. This means your adjusted initial fund price after the distribution would be $9.45. You would now own 1.05+ shares with an NAV of $10.45, which equals a total dollar value of $11.

STEP 5. DETERMINE HOW AND WHEN TO ROTATE UP

Let me remind you again that you are working to achieve at least 20 percent annualized compounded growth on all of our investment dollars. You will be highly motivated to commit 100 percent of your available investment money for two reasons. First and foremost, achieving 20 percent annualized compounded growth actually gives you 52 percent growth per year on the original investment each and every year for 10 years—and even higher growth per year over longer periods. This is the magic of compounding, and this is what will make you a millionaire. Second, the my plan generates both buy and sell signals. The selling rules are your safety valves that prevent you from participating in the losses most investors sustain during market downtrends.

Now, to achieve the 20 percent goal (and even more), you'll need to rotate up when a fund underperforms. Regardless of how selective you are in making your initial purchases, not every fund will fulfill your objective. Therefore, during the monitoring process, should one or more of your mutual funds fail to meet (or exceed) both the goal and the investment yardsticks for a two-month period, *you must sell it and rotate up.*

In Figure 14-6 you'll see that Safeco Growth fell under the selling criteria when it underperformed for two months. It posted a gain of 0.23 percent for February and a 1.76 percent loss for March. While just 1.67 percent per month is needed to meet the goal, note the strong performance by the yardsticks, the DFC and S&P 500 for these months—well above the target. Therefore, on 4/1/99 we sold Safeco Growth and rotated up to Van Wagner VP, which was exceeding the goal and also showed a Momentum

Score higher than the yardsticks. We must now monitor this new purchase along with its performance yardsticks, starting with their readings on 4/1/99.

Summary of Activity for Figures 14-3 through 14-6
(A)   11/9/99 Original purchases
(B)   3/1/99   Additional new money purchase
(C)   4/1/99   Rotating up purchase

STEP 6. KNOW WHEN TO SELL

Sticking with the U.S. domestic market, we knew to buy when both the Domestic Fund Composite and the Dow Jones Composite Index moved above their individual 39-week averages. We know to sell when the Domestic Fund Composite and the Dow Jones Composite Index are both below their individual 39-week averages. When a sell signal is generated, it means to sell all of the domestic equity funds you may be holding, including any nonshorting enhanced index funds. Should any individual fund that you are holding move below its own 39-week average during a current buy cycle, that fund should be sold and rotated up.

When you review the final performance results of the A and B and C purchases in Figures 14-4, 14-5, and 14-6, you can see what the buy cycle growth was at the time of the 9/22/99 sell signal.

CLOSING COMMENTS

This is the moment of truth. So, let me ask you this question: Is there any step in the personalized plan I have just described that you do not understand, or that you believe you cannot follow? If you hesitate with your answer, read Chapter 14 again. Remember that the basic plan essentially has just two rules, one for buying and one for selling.

My next question is this: Do you believe it is possible for this simple mutual fund trading plan to reach a goal of 20 percent annualized compounded growth over the long term? I know that it can, and so do thousands of individual investors who are right now successfully using my plan. But if you have any doubt that you can get this level of growth, pick up a current copy of *USA Today.* Go through the mutual fund pages in the

FIGURE 14-6

<table>
<tr><td colspan="10" align="center">(C) 4/1/99 – Rotating Up purchase
Sell Safeco Growth
Rotate Up to Van Wagner PV
Bi-Monthly Monitoring</td></tr>
<tr><td></td><td>Fund</td><td>4/1/99</td><td>4/15/99</td><td>4/15/99</td><td></td><td>Fund</td><td>4/1/99</td><td>4/30/99</td><td>4/30/99</td></tr>
<tr><td>Symbol</td><td>Name</td><td>Buy Price</td><td>Price</td><td>Perf.</td><td>Symbol</td><td>Name</td><td>Buy Price</td><td>Price</td><td>Perf.</td></tr>
<tr><td>VWPVX</td><td>Van Wagner PV</td><td>19.20</td><td>20.61</td><td>7.34%</td><td>VWPVX</td><td>Van Wagner PV</td><td>19.20</td><td>21.67</td><td>12.86%</td></tr>
<tr><td>S&P 500</td><td>S&P 500</td><td>1293.72</td><td>1322.85</td><td>2.25%</td><td>S&P 500</td><td>S&P 500</td><td>1293.72</td><td>1335.18</td><td>3.20%</td></tr>
<tr><td>DFC</td><td>Domestic Fund Comp.</td><td>127712.83</td><td>129869.90</td><td>1.69%</td><td>DFC</td><td>Domestic Fund Comp.</td><td>127712.83</td><td>129541.93</td><td>1.43%</td></tr>
<tr><td></td><td>Fund</td><td>4/1/99</td><td>5/17/99</td><td>5/17/99</td><td></td><td>Fund</td><td>4/1/99</td><td>5/28/99</td><td>5/28/99</td></tr>
<tr><td>Symbol</td><td>Name</td><td>Buy Price</td><td>Price</td><td>Perf.</td><td>Symbol</td><td>Name</td><td>Buy Price</td><td>Price</td><td>Perf.</td></tr>
<tr><td>VWPVX</td><td>Van Wagner PV</td><td>19.20</td><td>21.47</td><td>11.82%</td><td>VWPVX</td><td>Van Wagner PV</td><td>19.20</td><td>21.97</td><td>14.43%</td></tr>
<tr><td>S&P 500</td><td>S&P 500</td><td>1293.72</td><td>1339.49</td><td>3.54%</td><td>S&P 500</td><td>S&P 500</td><td>1293.72</td><td>1301.84</td><td>0.63%</td></tr>
<tr><td>DFC</td><td>Domestic Fund Comp.</td><td>127712.83</td><td>129844.15</td><td>1.67%</td><td>DFC</td><td>Domestic Fund Comp.</td><td>127712.83</td><td>126370.80</td><td>-1.05%</td></tr>
<tr><td></td><td>Fund</td><td>4/1/99</td><td>6/15/99</td><td>6/15/99</td><td></td><td>Fund</td><td>4/1/99</td><td>6/30/99</td><td>6/30/99</td></tr>
<tr><td>Symbol</td><td>Name</td><td>Buy Price</td><td>Price</td><td>Perf.</td><td>Symbol</td><td>Name</td><td>Buy Price</td><td>Price</td><td>Perf.</td></tr>
<tr><td>VWPVX</td><td>Van Wagner PV</td><td>19.20</td><td>21.13</td><td>10.05%</td><td>VWPVX</td><td>Van Wagner PV</td><td>19.20</td><td>23.50</td><td>22.40%</td></tr>
<tr><td>S&P 500</td><td>S&P 500</td><td>1293.72</td><td>1301.16</td><td>0.58%</td><td>S&P 500</td><td>S&P 500</td><td>1293.72</td><td>1372.66</td><td>6.10%</td></tr>
<tr><td>DFC</td><td>Domestic Fund Comp.</td><td>127712.83</td><td>126249.60</td><td>-1.15%</td><td>DFC</td><td>Domestic Fund Comp.</td><td>127712.83</td><td>134084.52</td><td>4.99%</td></tr>
<tr><td></td><td>Fund</td><td>4/1/99</td><td>7/15/99</td><td>7/15/99</td><td></td><td>Fund</td><td>4/1/99</td><td>7/31/99</td><td>7/31/99</td></tr>
<tr><td>Symbol</td><td>Name</td><td>Buy Price</td><td>Price</td><td>Perf.</td><td>Symbol</td><td>Name</td><td>Buy Price</td><td>Price</td><td>Perf.</td></tr>
<tr><td>VWPVX</td><td>Van Wagner PV</td><td>19.20</td><td>25.39</td><td>32.24%</td><td>VWPVX</td><td>Van Wagner PV</td><td>19.20</td><td>24.38</td><td>26.98%</td></tr>
<tr><td>S&P 500</td><td>S&P 500</td><td>1293.72</td><td>1409.62</td><td>8.96%</td><td>S&P 500</td><td>S&P 500</td><td>1293.72</td><td>1328.72</td><td>2.71%</td></tr>
<tr><td>DFC</td><td>Domestic Fund Comp.</td><td>127712.83</td><td>137559.27</td><td>7.71%</td><td>DFC</td><td>Domestic Fund Comp.</td><td>127712.83</td><td>129623.26</td><td>1.50%</td></tr>
<tr><td></td><td>Fund</td><td>4/1/99</td><td>8/15/99</td><td>8/15/99</td><td></td><td>Fund</td><td>4/1/99</td><td>8/31/99</td><td>8/31/99</td></tr>
<tr><td>Symbol</td><td>Name</td><td>Buy Price</td><td>Price</td><td>Perf.</td><td>Symbol</td><td>Name</td><td>Buy Price</td><td>Price</td><td>Perf.</td></tr>
<tr><td>VWPVX</td><td>Van Wagner PV</td><td>19.20</td><td>24.27</td><td>26.41%</td><td>VWPVX</td><td>Van Wagner PV</td><td>19.20</td><td>25.71</td><td>33.91%</td></tr>
<tr><td>S&P 500</td><td>S&P 500</td><td>1293.72</td><td>1330.77</td><td>2.86%</td><td>S&P 500</td><td>S&P 500</td><td>1293.72</td><td>1320.41</td><td>2.06%</td></tr>
<tr><td>DFC</td><td>Domestic Fund Comp.</td><td>127712.83</td><td>128712.01</td><td>0.78%</td><td>DFC</td><td>Domestic Fund Comp.</td><td>127712.83</td><td>127908.77</td><td>0.15%</td></tr>
<tr><td></td><td>Fund</td><td>4/1/99</td><td>9/15/99</td><td>9/15/99</td><td></td><td>Fund</td><td>4/1/99</td><td>9/22/99</td><td>9/22/99</td></tr>
<tr><td>Symbol</td><td>Name</td><td>Buy Price</td><td>Price</td><td>Perf.</td><td>Symbol</td><td>Name</td><td>Buy Price</td><td>Price</td><td>Perf.</td></tr>
<tr><td>VWPVX</td><td>Van Wagner PV</td><td>19.20</td><td>26.59</td><td>38.49%</td><td>VWPVX</td><td>Van Wagner PV</td><td>19.20</td><td>25.84</td><td>34.58%</td></tr>
<tr><td>S&P 500</td><td>S&P 500</td><td>1293.72</td><td>1317.97</td><td>1.87%</td><td>S&P 500</td><td>S&P 500</td><td>1293.72</td><td>1280.77</td><td>-1.00%</td></tr>
<tr><td>DFC</td><td>Domestic Fund Comp.</td><td>127712.83</td><td>128156.20</td><td>0.35%</td><td>DFC</td><td>Domestic Fund Comp.</td><td>127712.83</td><td>127935.71</td><td>0.17%</td></tr>
</table>

financial section and put a check mark next to every fund that is on target for the 20 percent goal so far this year. Multiply the number of months so far this year by 1.67 percent. The answer is the growth required in the current year to be on target for the goal. When you see the large number of mutual funds that are not only meeting the goal but also exceeding it, you will have your answer.

Next, ponder this question: Has anyone ever told you that it is possible for you, entirely on your own and even with a modest income, to become a self-made millionaire? I am sure no one ever has. But it is possible. And you can do it using the plan. So, the final question is this: Do you want to become a self-made millionaire? If your answer is yes, my plan can get you there.

Let's move on to Part 5. Listen in as I share some thoughts with my grandchildren.

PART 5

A Talk with My Grandchildren (You Are Invited to Listen In)

A Talk with My Grandchildren

QUALITY OF LIFE

Your grandmother and I want to share with you some of our observations from the past seven decades. We are in the latter part of life, while all of you are in the beginning. What follows are some of the things we have learned and believe. One of the things we want to emphasize is the importance of continually striving to enhance the quality of your life.

By "quality of life" we do not mean trying to be extremely happy every minute of the day. Instead, we mean you should always feel that life is worthwhile. Enjoy the present but look with enthusiastic expectation to the future. Be courteous and kind to others and continually find ways to share your good fortune with others.

THREE IMPORTANT BOOKS

I have made reference often to these three books: *Psycho-Cybernetics, Think and Grow Rich,* and *The Richest Man in Babylon.* They contain valuable lessons for you.

To get the most from these books, I suggest they be read three times. In the first reading you will get the essence of what the author has to say. The second time, read slowly, similar to the way you would read a textbook, so that the ideas can sink in. Then, during the third reading, underline the specific thoughts and ideas that you feel have particular significance for you. After that, continue to review each book at least once a year.

Then follow the same process as you read and study my book *The Mutual Fund Wealth Builder.* Reading between the lines, so to speak, you will see I am attempting to get everyone to develop a "financial lifestyle." As the weeks, months, and years go by, you may at times have questions regarding why you should continue to follow the plan. At those times, you'll need a resource to bring you back to the basics. Use my book and the others I am recommending as your resource.

We hope that you will realize early in life the constructive role accumulating wealth can play in your lives and how it can positively influence the quality of your life. We hope our gift of both money and investment knowledge will have a sufficient impact on you, so that you will not only enrich your own life but will reach out and help others. We wish you to share this wealth-building knowledge whenever and wherever you see a need.

One of the easiest ways to share will be to encourage your peers to read the three books mentioned here in addition to mine. However, don't fall into the trap that I did many years ago. I was so enthusiastic about wanting to share this knowledge that I gave away copies of the books to anyone who asked me financial questions or showed an interest in their long-term financial future.

When I gave away the books, however, I found out later that most of the time they were not read. Later I stopped giving the books away and encouraged people to buy them. Those who bought them read them because they valued them more.

THE LIFE CYCLE

Here is my vision concerning some specific segments of the life cycle. You can use it to identify yourself. I use it to understand the actions of others. I can easily anticipate what others will do based on where they are in their life cycle. Your understanding of the life cycle will be helpful when you are considering to whom you will be making your own $50,000 compounding gift.

Age 3 to 5   At this time in our lives, the world is large, exciting, fearful, and boundless. We learn new things and become aware of new concepts almost hourly. Our storehouse of knowledge and life experiences will multiply at a faster rate during this part of our life cycle than it ever will again. Even though our perceptions are increasing rapidly, we do not have very many life experiences to use as a guide to identify what could be important to enhance our quality of life. Furthermore, we really don't care. After all, we are convinced that we can do and have anything. In fact, we forcefully tell the world, in no uncertain terms, not to stand in our way.

Our noninterrupted interest in ourselves makes no allowance for heeding the advice and recommendations of others who try to persuade us that they know what is best for us.

Age 15 to 18   We still find the world exciting, but at this time we are more fearful. We continue to learn new things about the world and ourselves. By now, however, because of our personal experiences, we taint and color the new things we learn, based on our current perceptions.

Because we now have the perspective of hindsight, even though it is still relatively limited, we are absolutely sure we can give thoughtful and worthwhile advice and suggestions to anyone in the 3- to 5-year age group. For ourselves, however, we continue to have a closed mind when it comes to listening to the advice and recommendations of others, who claim they know how to help us to enhance the quality of our life.

Age 30 to 35   We now define the world in our own terms. We will freely admit to anyone who might ask that we believe the world is exciting and full of opportunities. If the truth were known, however, we are more conscience of the fearful things the world contains and also of the doubts we harbor about our own decision-making capabilities.

Our storehouse of personal life experiences has continued to grow. Therefore, we are sure that, with the wisdom we have acquired, we can give thoughtful and worthwhile advice and suggestions to anyone in both the 3- to 5-year age groups and the 15- to 18-year age groups. Interestingly, although it is so easy for us to offer our worthwhile advice to those younger, we only half-hear any advice or suggestions offered by those ahead of us in the life cycle—those older and wiser who want to help us enhance our quality of life.

Age 55 to 60   Virtually all of the attitudes we described during the previous stages of our life cycle are continuing. But now a new perception develops. One day between our fiftieth and sixtieth birthdays, we face our mortality. We do this even if we do not want to talk about it or admit it to anyone. We know the probabilities are high that we have lived more than half of our life. We know whether or not we are satisfied with our existing quality of life. If we are satisfied, we should want to share our advice and suggestions with the younger groups. But if we are not satisfied, most likely we don't know what we can do to make things better yet now at least we are more willing to seek advice.

Conclusion   Not everyone experiences the life cycle exactly as described here. It may not be necessary for everyone to wait until age 50 or older before beginning to ask questions about enhancing their long-term quality of life. At the same time, all is not lost for those who may have delayed this long. There are answers for everyone willing to seek, and also willing to listen.

Becoming a Millionaire

Part of your grandparents' legacy to you is to structure a plan and help you to implement it so that by the year 2022, each of you will be a millionaire. We hope we have also been role models and made you aware of the advantages of being affectionate, helpful, and generous. We hope, too, that we have shown you the benefits of the work ethic. A wise man once said, "Do a good job and be kind." We believe in that and encourage you to practice it.

The table in Figure 15-1 shows how our initial gift to you, growing at 20 percent a year for 25 years, could grow to nearly $3½ million. However, the table does not reflect the impact of the future $50,000 compounding gift you will be making nor has any consideration been given to paying capital gains taxes. I will cover these two items shortly.

As to being millionaires, each of you will have to come to terms with that concept. Some of you may feel you do not deserve or are not entitled to such a large sum of money. Some of you may want to accumulate an even larger amount. Still, some of you will simply ignore the specific amount of money involved and just go on with your life.

I have lived with and without a great deal of money. This gives me the right to have an opinion about the two alternatives. Of course, I believe having an abundance of money is better, but here are some aspects of possessing wealth that you may not have thought about before.

In the early years of our marriage, while your parents were young, your grandmother and I would fantasize about all the things we would buy "if we only had more money." It's funny, but when the money was finally there for us, we no longer had a long "want list." Surprisingly, the want list was replaced by contentment. In fact, we discovered that the contentment of knowing that you can buy anything you want gives greater satisfaction than actually buying and owning things.

Having wealth gives your life a daily uplift. There is an old Yiddish proverb that states, "With money in your pocket, you are wise and you are handsome and you sing well too."

FIGURE 15-1

WATCHING MONEY GROW
AT
20% ANNUALIZED COMPOUNDED GROWTH

	Deposits	20% Growth	Principal Balance
1998	10,000	2,000	12,000
1999	10,000	4,400	26,400
2000	10,000	7,280	43,680
2001	10,000	10,736	64,416
2002	10,000	14,883	89,299
2003		17,860	107,159
2004		21,432	128,591
2005		25,718	154,309
2006		30,862	185,171
2007		37,034	222,205
2008		44,441	266,646
2009		53,329	319,975
2010		63,995	383,970
2011		76,794	460,764
2012		92,153	552,917
2013		110,583	663,501
2014		132,700	796,201
2015		159,240	955,441
2016		191,088	1,146,529
2017		229,306	1,375,835
2018		275,167	1,651,002
2019		330,200	1,981,202
2020		396,240	2,377,442
2021		475,488	2,852,931
2022		570,586	3,423,517
	50,000	3,373,517	

Table does not make allowances for paying capital gains taxes

Go back and reread the pages in Part 1 where I listed many things that I believe. In that list you will find some of the lifestyle problems people experience because of lack of money. Just knowing that your nest egg is continually growing will shield you from the worries that so many others must cope with because they have not taken the steps to build for their own financial future.

During my life, I have met many people who found themselves in jobs they did not like but were too afraid to consider changing because of the possible negative financial consequences. Others have jobs that pay little and do not leave much room for advancement. Many such people live in a state of bare survival. Think for a moment . . . how do you take the time to smell the roses if your primary concern is worrying where the money is going to come from to pay the rent?

Without sufficient dollars, many people will be destined to live in mediocrity, if not downright poverty. Without sufficient money, many people struggle to take care of the basic essentials of life. Without sufficient money, many people argue with their spouses, get into trouble at work, fail to provide for their children, and generally have unhappy days. What a pity this is because, in America, there is no limit to the dreams that can be fulfilled. Money may not buy happiness, but it buys the opportunities to be happy. In other words, it frees up your time and energy to focus on the positive things in life.

If you think about it, wealth has a positive effect on virtually every aspect of your life. This is evident when you consider that the quality of your life is composed of several areas: health, career, personal, leisure, and financial. Success or failure with money influences all these areas.

Obviously, it is important to take care of your health. Eating right, exercising, and having regular medical checkups all contribute to good health. Without money, your diet and basic health needs may not be adequately maintained. And in the event of emergency or serious illness, either for yourself or a family member, you'll want the finest medical care money can buy. But the finest medical care doesn't come cheap. Just the anxiety and stress caused by knowing you can't afford proper medical care can lead to stress and maybe even more serious illness.

More and more we read in the news the startling advances being made in the field of medicine. In the not-so-distant future you can expect to replace worn-out body parts with new ones. Cures will be found for many of today's incurable diseases, and as a result, you can expect to live longer. Indeed, future medical advances will enhance the quality of your life, provided, of course, you have the money to pay for them.

Another area affected by money is your personal life—your relationships with family and loved ones, coworkers, and friends. Everyone's personal life suffers without money. How can you participate in even the most ordinary social activities when you lack money? How can you maintain a happy marriage while experiencing financial problems? Clearly, it is more difficult without money.

Also, when you are short of money, you lack self-confidence and suffer feelings of inadequacy. Life has a way of making us feel like winners or losers, and money or lack of it, in many cases, can be at the root of the problem.

And let's not forget the recreational or leisure side of life. All work and no play makes for a dull, unrewarding life. Leisure activities are important to your sense of well being—it's a time to re-create, to rejuvenate. Do you allow adequate time for leisure activities? How many times are people unable to take that vacation they dreamed of because they didn't have the money to pay for it? How about time for golf, boating, tennis, shopping, travel, or any other leisure activity one might choose? Do you see how money buys all these things, even if you just want to rest in the shade of a palm tree?

Isn't it true that in order to achieve the maximum benefits from most of the important aspects of life, being financially successful helps a lot? For those who say they do not really want to be rich, think again! Everyone wants to eat right. Everyone wants a good doctor when taken ill. Everyone wants to have the time to do what he or she wants to do, when they want to do it. You could say, *money buys freedom!*

The reason for accumulating wealth is to enhance the quality of your life—and the lives of those you love. By now, it should be clear that money is important to your well-being. For this reason, accumulating wealth may be among one of the most important things we can do during our lifetime.

Allow me to give you an adage that I live by which enhances my daily quality of life: *Any problem that can be fixed with money should not cause stress.* And for me it doesn't, or at least not for long. Think about it. Aren't there many little things that go wrong almost every day which, with just a little bit more money, could be easily resolved? If you're short of money, little problems can turn into big ones. But when you have plenty of money, you can simply pay to have the problems corrected. And when you fix these daily problems, you eliminate the stress that goes with them. I speak from experience on this; it is a wonderful thing to be able to live by this adage.

Another advantage of having accumulated wealth is the power it represents without even having to spend any of it. Whenever you submit a financial statement or a credit report, you'll get the red-carpet treatment. Just having a six- or seven-digit amount showing in your investment account will open many doors and give you opportunities that won't even require you to spend a penny.

THE MILLIONAIRE NEXT DOOR

One of the best-selling financial books during 1999 was *The Millionaire Next Door.* Here is an excerpt from an article written by Dr. Paul B. Farrell for CBS MarketWatch in April 1999:

Yesterday I wrote a column about a couple with $1.4 million in assets and a combined income of $175,000. Their living expenses are $80,000. The column drew a couple of very intriguing responses, including a follow-up message from Frank and Jane, the couple in the story:

"Yes, my wife and I do consider ourselves the Millionaires Next Door, but it's not a big deal. There is one common theme in that book which does bother me a bit. All through it, all the people who became millionaires on their own did it by a combination of hard work, saving and not spending. I don't remember them talking that much about enjoying their hard-earned status. To me, the numerical achievement is not the important thing. What is important is what it should mean for us—the ability to retire early and enjoy ourselves after working very hard for the last 30 years. I don't remember much of that sort of thing being in the book. I just hope we haven't forgotten how to have fun after working so hard."

MASTER MIND GROUP

In Napolean Hill's book *Think and Grow Rich,* one of his many excellent recommendations is the creation and implementation of a Master Mind Group. Here are some of his thoughts on why such a group is valuable.

He says that anyone's plans are inert and useless without sufficient power to translate them into action. Power may be defined as "organized and intelligently directed knowledge." Power, using his definition, refers to organized effort sufficient to enable an individual to transmute desire into its eventual fulfillment. Organized effort is produced through the coordination of the effort of two or more people who work toward a definite end in a spirit of harmony. This power also helps in the retention of money after it has been accumulated. Power helps in organizing definite plans and then expressing those plans in terms of action.

The Master Mind may be defined as "coordination of knowledge and effort, in a spirit of harmony, between two or more people for the attainment of a definite purpose." It is not possible for an individual working alone to have this added power assist him or her without availing him- or herself of the Master Mind concept.

So that people may better understand the intangible potentialities of power available to them through a properly chosen Master Mind Group,

Napolean Hill explains the two characteristics of this principle, one of which is economic in nature and the other psychic. The economic feature: Economic advantages are created by any person who surrounds him- or herself with the advice, counsel, and personal cooperation of a group of people who are willing to lend him or her wholehearted aid in a spirit of perfect harmony.

The psychic feature: The essence is, "No two minds ever come together without creating a third invisible, intangible force which may be likened to a third mind." The human mind is a form of energy, a part of it being spiritual in nature. When the minds of two people are coordinated in a spirit of harmony, the spiritual units of energy of each mind form an affinity, which constitutes the "psychic" phase of the Master Mind.

STARTING A MASTER MIND GROUP

Think and Grow Rich points out that a rich life is not only measured in money, but also in lasting friendships, harmonious family relationships, sympathy and understanding between business associates, and inner harmony, which brings peace of mind. It is easy to see why this book is on my must-read list.

A Grandchildren Master Mind Group (GMMG) can serve all of you well for many years to come. As you implement my investing plan and strive to become a self-made millionaire, I encourage you to participate in your very own Master Mind Group. This effort will enhance your chances for success.

I have seen many examples of successful business people—people who had established and run profitable companies during their careers—fail once they retire and devote their efforts to investing. It wasn't that these individuals weren't capable of success; on the contrary, they had previously shown they were leaders. A successful leader, however, who finds he or she is only leading him- or herself no longer is part of a structured environment. This leader doesn't have to answer to anyone else and does not receive input and feedback from others. Always remember that you will receive benefits from interaction with others, especially with those who are sincerely concerned about your well-being. This is the value of the GMMG.

One form of Master Mind Group is an investment club, at which you share your investment ideas with others. In such an environment, you may be forced to explain to others why you bought into some particular investment. You may have to articulate under what circumstances you would sell a particular holding, and you may also have to explain exactly what it is you are trying to accomplish with your investing.

A Master Mind Group, when it includes people who have a reason to care personally about the other members of the group, can offer advice and counsel on investments, as well as other aspects of members' lives. The GMMG fits into this category.

I recommend that you participate in such a group, meet at least two or three times a year, and establish frequent e-mail contact.

FUTURE GMMG AGENDAS

Think about all of the changes that have taken place in the investment world since I wrote *How to Be Your Own Investment Counselor.* Over the past 23 years, for example, the number of available mutual funds has gone from 450 to well over 10,000. During that time the Internet, with all of its ramifications, has had an impact, from where we seek information to actually trading online. I would not attempt to project the things that will happen in just the next five years, let alone what the changes will be over the next 10, 15, or 20 years.

Through the end of 2002, I will be working closely with each of you—both individually and as a group. I have gone through this growth process before and have much of value to share with you. At the beginning, don't concern yourselves about the structure of your future GMMG meetings. Personal events in your lives, along with outside economic events, will give you an abundance of topics.

But when all is said and done, there is one item you must keep on the top of the agenda. There is one question that needs to be answered: What should each of us be currently doing to enhance the probabilities that we will all continue to realize 20 percent growth each year in our investment account, as we strive to become self-made millionaires? The answer is here in my book and the others I have recommended to you.

C H A P T E R   1 6

Advanced Investment Tools

MARGIN: ANOTHER INVESTMENT TOOL

While you are investing for the long term, you want to be aware of all of the investment tools that can help you to reach your goal. One such tool is *investing on margin.*

Investing on margin means taking out a loan from your discount broker and using the proceeds to buy more shares. It is a leveraged transaction in which your loan obligation to the stockbroker is secured by the mutual funds in your account. In other words, your mutual funds are used as collateral.

If the value of the securities you are holding as collateral declines, you may be subject to a *margin call,* in which you will be required to provide additional collateral. Otherwise, all or part of your securities may be liquidated. Therefore, before investing on margin, you must consider current market conditions and your current financial situation. Further on, you will see an example of using margin in the account I am setting up for you.

Margin Requirements

The Federal Reserve Board and various stock exchanges determine margin loan rules and regulations. At Charles Schwab, they will not extend credit unless the equity in the securities you hold in a margin account is at least $2,000.

The amount most stockbrokers may loan is 50 percent of the value of marginable securities purchased or held in your margin account. If the market value of stock held as collateral increases after you've met the initial margin requirements, your available credit may increase proportionately.

You may purchase only certain securities on margin or use them as collateral in your margin account. Most stocks and mutual funds traded on national securities exchanges and some over-the-counter securities are marginable. Equity securities with a market value of less than $5 per share may not be purchased on margin or deposited as margin collateral.

Before using margin with your investment account, you should secure from your stockbroker the most current rules in effect for purchasing and maintenance.

FUNDING YOUR INDIVIDUAL ROTH IRA

As we discussed in Part 3, everyone should maximize the use of qualified retirement plans (tax-advantaged plans). While each of you is working for 20 percent long-term compounded growth, you cannot ignore capital gains taxes on your nonqualified, or taxable, accounts. To fulfill this requirement, a Roth IRA—which is essentially a tax-free account—is included in the accumulation plan for each of you.

Look at Figure 16-1. The table shows that, starting in the year 2003, which is five years after the plan began, there is a withdrawal of $2,000 each year. This withdrawal is being used to make a deposit in a Roth IRA for each eligible grandchild. By the year 2003, most of the grandchildren will be eligible to participate in a Roth IRA. For the younger grandchildren, once they begin earning taxable income, a Roth IRA will be opened for them.

In Figure 16-1, Column 7, you see the growth, at 20 percent compounded, that could be earned by the Roth IRA. This growth will not be subject to capital gains taxes.

Once he or she is over 21 years of age, each grandchild will be eligible for a margin account. Each year when the time comes to make a withdrawal from your start-up, nonqualified account and place it in a Roth IRA, the current status of the market will determine how that withdrawal will be made. If the market is weak and the nonqualified account has

F I G U R E   1 6 - 1

GRANDCHILDREN MILLIONAIRE PLAN
PERSONAL FUNDS AND ROTH IRA

	1	2	3 PERSONAL FUNDS	4	5	6	7 ROTH IRA	8 COMBINED TOTAL
	Deposits	Gift to another	Withdrawal for Roth IRA	20% Growth	Income Taxes 30%	Year-End After Taxes	Value at the end of the year	After Income Taxes
1998	10,000			2,000	(600)	11,400		11,400
1999	10,000			4,280	(1,284)	24,396		24,396
2000	10,000			6,879	(2,064)	39,211		39,211
2001	10,000			9,842	(2,953)	56,101		56,101
2002	10,000			13,220	(3,966)	75,355		75,355
2003			(2,000)	14,671	(4,401)	83,625	2,400	86,025
2004			(2,000)	16,325	(4,897)	93,052	5,280	98,332
2005			(2,000)	18,210	(5,463)	103,800	8,736	112,536
2006			(2,000)	20,360	(6,108)	116,052	12,883	128,935
2007			(2,000)	22,810	(6,843)	130,019	17,860	147,879
2008			(2,000)	25,604	(7,681)	145,942	23,832	169,774
2009		(10,000)	(2,000)	26,788	(8,036)	152,693	30,998	183,691
2010		(10,000)	(2,000)	28,139	(8,442)	160,390	39,598	199,988
2011		(10,000)	(2,000)	29,678	(8,903)	169,165	49,917	219,082
2012		(10,000)	(2,000)	31,433	(9,430)	179,168	62,301	241,469
2013		(10,000)	(2,000)	33,434	(10,030)	190,572	77,161	267,733
2014			(2,000)	37,714	(11,314)	214,972	94,993	309,965
2015			(2,000)	42,594	(12,778)	242,788	116,392	359,180
2016			(2,000)	48,158	(14,447)	274,498	142,070	416,568
2017			(2,000)	54,500	(16,350)	310,648	172,884	483,532
2018			(2,000)	61,730	(18,519)	351,859	209,861	561,720
2019			(2,000)	69,972	(20,992)	398,839	254,233	653,072
2020			(2,000)	79,368	(23,810)	452,396	307,480	759,876
2021			(2,000)	90,079	(27,024)	513,452	371,376	884,828
2022			(2,000)	102,290	(30,687)	583,055	448,051	1,031,106
	50,000	(50,000)	(40,000)		(267,024)			

INCOME TAXES ARE CALCULATED ON THE GAINS PER YEAR AT AN AVERAGE RATE OF 30%
ORDINARY RATES (40% MAXIMUM) AND CAPITAL GAINS RATES (20%)

enough cash available, an immediate cash transfer between the two accounts can be made. However, if the market is in an uptrend and all of the currently invested positions are on target to reach the goal, you would not want to be forced to sell a position to raise the $2,000 necessary to fund the Roth IRA. Under these circumstances, each grandchild can simply request from the discount broker a margin transfer (loan) of $2,000, which shall be placed in his or her Roth IRA.

Following this margin procedure, the existing uptrend positions will not be disturbed. As long as the existing holdings in the nonqualified account continue to grow each month at a rate higher than the interest charged for using the margin loan, the margin position can be maintained.

At some future time, when the market conditions require selling any existing position in your start-up account, then the proceeds of that sale would be used by the stockbroker to pay off the outstanding margin loan.

PAYING CAPITAL GAINS TAXES

The majority of the money in your investment start-up account is nonqualified. This means all of the gains on that money are subject to taxes. Because of the trend-following investment strategy I recommend for you, some gains will be long-term and some will be short-term capital gains.

The tax laws in effect at the end of 1999 required that all long-term capital gains be taxed at a maximum rate of 20 percent and short-term capital gains be taxed at one's ordinary income tax rates. Taxes are required to be paid both to the state and to the federal government. This means the combined rates can range from 20 percent to 45 percent of adjusted gross income. For the illustration example, I assumed an average rate of 30 percent for each of the 25 years. See Column 5 in Figure 16-1.

The following is a description of the data contained in each column in Figure 16-1:

1. The five initial deposits to the nonqualified investment account for each grandchild.
2. The five annual withdrawals of $10,000 that each grandchild will use as their compounding gift. These withdrawals will begin in 2009.
3. The 20 annual withdrawals of $2,000 for deposit into a Roth IRA.
4. The 20 percent compounded growth on the nonqualified investment dollars.
5. The dollars withdrawn from each account to pay the required taxes at a 30 percent rate.
6. The value of each nonqualified account at the end of each year after the $50,000 gift, the Roth IRA withdrawals, and the payment of taxes.
7. The annual growth for the Roth IRA at exactly 20 percent per year.
8. The combined total value for each grandchild's account at the end of each year. As a result of using the Roth IRA and paying the required capital gains taxes, each grandchild's account will have a tax-free value of $1,031,106 in the year 2022, provided the 20 percent compounding goal is attained.

EXTEND THE LEGACY—THE JOY OF GIVING

I have requested that sometime during the 25-year period while your nest egg is growing, each of you give a $50,000 compounding gift to someone of your choice. I am suggesting that the gifting process start at the beginning of the year 2009.

Refer to Figure 16-2, which shows the impact of this gift on the overall accumulation schedule. Each grandchild is giving up $460,764 of growth potential as a result of the $50,000 gift.

FIGURE 16-2

BECOMING A SELF-MADE MILLIONAIRE
NON-QUALIFIED PERSONAL FUNDS

	Start-up Deposits	Gifts	20% Growth	Account Balance
1998	10,000		2,000	12,000
1999	10,000		4,400	26,400
2000	10,000		7,280	43,680
2001	10,000		10,736	64,416
2002	10,000		14,883	89,299
2003			17,860	107,159
2004			21,432	128,591
2005			25,718	154,309
2006			30,862	185,171
2007			37,034	222,205
2008			44,441	266,646
2009		(10,000)	51,329	307,975
2010		(10,000)	59,595	357,570
2011		(10,000)	69,514	471,084
2012		(10,000)	81,417	488,501
2013		(10,000)	95,700	574,201
2014			114,840	689,042
2015			137,808	826,850
2016			165,370	992,220
2017			198,444	1,190,664
2018			238,133	1,428,797
2019			285,759	1,714,556
2020			342,911	2,057,467
2021			411,493	2,468,961
2022			493,792	2,962,753
	50,000	(50,000)	2,962,753	

Table does not make allowances for paying capital gains taxes

Review of Figures 16-1and 16-2.
$3,423,517
− $2,962,753
$460,764

Always be aware of the long-term impact of any withdrawal you may wish to make from your account prior to 2022. Before making such a withdrawal, I ask that you consult with your Master Mind Group. Also, if others in your group should ask about making a withdrawal prior to the year 2022, remind them of the potential growth on the money they will lose by withdrawing it early. Compare the withdrawal to what they would have later if they let their account fully compound over the years. Unless an emergency arises that cannot be resolved by any other means than to make a withdrawal, I recommend that you leave your money alone to compound.

As part of your $50,000 compounding gift, you will also share with the recipient our compounding story, including how to use the plan. This will enable the recipient of your gift to also become a self-made millionaire. With your gift, have them also promise that sometime during the following 25-year money-growing period, they will also make a $50,000 compounding gift to someone else. And have them also promise that they will teach my plan for becoming a self-made millionaire.

MAKE YOUR $50,000 GIFT OVER FIVE YEARS

Have you wondered why each of you received $10,000 each year for five years rather than a single $50,000 compounding gift all at once? My reason for doing it this way was dictated by the human learning process. As a student of people, I know that it takes time for any new idea to become fully accepted. It has nothing to do with the merits of an idea. It is just that everyone must live with an idea for some time before he or she fully understands and adopts it. My experience shows that this acceptance period usually takes at least three years.

As each of you watched your original $10,000 grow by 20 percent, and then watched that initial accumulation plus the second $10,000 grow by 20 percent again, and then again the third time, you have witnessed firsthand the benefits of compounding. Your experience of receiving the investment confirmation statements and seeing the growth in your account brings the effect of compounding to a personal and emotional level. As more time goes by, with continued evidence of successful implementation of the compounding plan, your faith and belief in the process will become stronger and eventually be equal to mine. That is my hope.

One of the stipulations of our annual gift to you is that if any money is withdrawn during the gift period, no future deposits would be made. This is to ensure that the full amount will be given a chance to work for you. When I started your gift, I took it upon myself to be responsible for the stewardship of your funds for at least the first five years. And when you make your gift to someone else, it will be your responsibility to assume the stewardship of their mutual fund account, in order to ensure that your entire gift is put to work for long-term compounding. It will also be your responsibility, for at least the first five years, to monitor the progress of the account and to help the recipient achieve 20 percent annualized compounded growth. With my book as your guide, you know how to do that. And to keep the recipient motivated, the stipulation of your gift should also be no withdrawals during the gifting period, while also working to achieve the 20 percent goal. Otherwise, no further gift deposits will be added. In addition, during the 25-year accumulation period, the recipient will also promise that he or she will repeat the gift process with someone else exactly as described above. In this way, the wonderful gift of wealth creation through compounding will go on and on and on.

You can also keep the legacy going in your daily lives. I mentioned earlier that I feel so strongly about the power of compounded growth that I find myself talking about it all the time. I hope that I will be able to make disciples of each of you. As each of you experience what the power of compounding is doing for you, you will see how it can also enhance the quality of lives for others.

With that said, be aware that the people who will benefit from compounding will not immediately be open to listening to you. If you want to get through to them, it will be necessary for you to have several of the compounding stories at your fingertips, including examples such as an IRA starting at age 40 and investing just $2,000 per year; investing only $113 a year starting at age 25; a 50-year-old with $70,000 to invest all at once. Each of these stories results in the investment growing to $1 million at age 65 with 20 percent annualized compounded growth.

Once you see at least a small amount of interest from your listener, then show them a copy of the mutual fund page from *USA Today*. Explain how the goal can be reached by achieving 1.67 percent per month. Show them the large number of mutual funds, at any time during the year, that are on target to reach the goal of 20 percent. This will help to overcome the common objection that "it can't be done." You and I both know it can be done. This is the message to share with others.

YOU WILL BECOME A FINANCIAL MENTOR

Here is a quote by Algamish in *The Richest Man in Babylon*, which is his reply concerning how to become rich:

> *"I will tell you these things you wish to know because I am becoming an old man, and an old tongue loves to wag. And when youth comes to age for advice he receives the wisdom of years. But too often does youth think that age knows only the wisdom of days that are gone and therefore profits not. But remember this, the sun that shines today is the sun that shone when their father was born.*
>
> *"The thoughts of youth," he continued, "are brighter lights that shine forth like the meteors that oft make brilliant the sky, but the wisdom of age is like the fixed stars that shine so unchanged that the sailor may depend upon them to steer his course. Mark you well my words, for if you do not you will fail to grasp the truth that I will tell you."*
>
> *Algamish then looked shrewdly from under his shaggy brows and said in a low, forceful tone, "I found the road to wealth when I decided that* a part of all I earned was mine to keep. *And so will you. If you did keep for yourself one-tenth of all you earn, how much would you have in 10 years?*
>
> *The answer is: "As much as I earn in one year."*

Heed this advice from Algamish. Make it a part of your personal saving/investment plan to *pay yourself first.* Pay yourself at least 10 percent of your after-tax income and put it to work for long-term compounding. Beyond the money in the millionaire-seeking investment account we have started for you, prove to yourself that you can duplicate the same growth in your own savings/investment account. And in your case, you'll do even better than the example given in *The Richest Man in Babylon*, because your regular savings will growth at 20 percent annualized compounded growth.

As you talk with others and try to encourage them to adopt the 20 percent compounding growth plan, they will ask you what you are doing regarding your savings. When you can document to your "listening students" that you are currently doing for yourself what you are recommending to them, you will have greatly enhanced the probability that they will not only listen to you but heed your advice as well.

In concluding, your grandmother and I want to say, Go forth, enrich your lives, as well as the lives of your children and grandchildren. Be generous and spread the good word on compounding, so that others may share in the bounty.

PART 6

Observations to Ensure Success

CHAPTER 17

Successful Thinking

THERE ARE NO EXCUSES

Even though I do not consider myself a golfer, two or three times a year I walk a golf course with a friend or relative. I participate simply because I want the exercise, and I also enjoy smelling the grass and seeing the beautiful landscape. In addition, watching golfers gives an excellent opportunity to observe human behavior.

One situation frequently observed is what happens after a golfer's ball lands in the middle of the fairway. No doubt you have seen this. Shortly, the player will drive up in his cart to the proximity of the ball, step out of the cart, then walk up behind his ball and sight down the fairway toward the flag. Even though I am not a dedicated golfer, over the years I have read some of the golf books and have viewed some of the golf videos, so I recognize these procedures.

After mentally lining up the path he wants the ball to take, he walks back to his cart and selects a club. He then approaches the ball. He first concentrates on his grip. Next, he positions his feet just the right distance apart. He then bends his knees just a bit. These are the things his instructor has told him to do. For the final step, he wiggles his rear end. You know that once he wiggles, the start-up process has been completed.

Just one more time, he will look down the fairway in the direction of the flag. He will then concentrate on the ground just in front of the ball and take a beautiful practice swing that impresses everyone who is watching. Then he makes the *fatal error.* He moves up a half an inch. He is now in position to hit the ball. Our golfer takes a full swing and almost falls backward off his feet. He has a look of astonishment on his face because he has no idea where the ball has gone. Sadly, there was no resemblance between the practice swing he took and the swing he made when actually hitting the ball.

What does this tell us? It tells us that, in fact, he knows how to properly swing the club when there is no pressure. When the chips are down, however, he responded emotionally and fails to practice what he has been taught. Failing to hit the ball properly doesn't give him license to say "I don't know how to do it." He does know how to do it.

When you talk with individual investors who are not successful, they also claim "I don't know how to do it." From this day forward, if you have read this book through, you won't be able to say "I don't know how to do it." You do know.

As with our golfer, if you allow your emotions to get in the way and do not follow through properly, that is your fault, not the fault of the plan. My point is this: Stick to the rules and don't let your emotions interfere with your potential success.

OUR NEED TO ACCUMULATE MONEY FOR RETIREMENT IS MORE URGENT TODAY

In September 1998, on a one-hour special television program on CNBC entitled "Your Money, Your Dream," Peter Lynch, vice-chairman of the Fidelity Group of Funds, was the special guest. At the beginning of the program, the moderator asked, "Mr. Lynch, you have always advocated that individual investors really have to do their homework if they are going to be successful. Because so many people are not successful, is it that they do not do enough homework or are they simply uncomfortable with the process? What's your best advice to start us out this evening?"

The answer he gave was the following:

The most important thing for all of us to remember is that 20 or 30 years ago it was not necessary to do a lot of investment homework. Now it is, and that is what is remarkably different today. Years ago people would retire with 50 or 60 percent of their last year's salary.

They did not have to worry about where the money was going to come from. That was a problem for their employer. However, today it is different, and it has now become the individual's problem.

Unfortunately, none of us are taught in school about investing. When I was in the eighth grade, I learned about cosine. However, I have not used that knowledge recently. I am not saying anything negative about the study of math. It is very important. But in school you do not learn about bonds. You do not learn about stocks. You could spend a large part of your life in school, could even earn a Ph.D. in chemistry, and not know what a bond or a stock is. There is no structured way for most of us to get this information. The only alternative, therefore [is] . . . you have to learn to do it yourself.

MAKE IT HAPPEN BY DOING IT YOURSELF

I have said over and over again: implementing my compounding plan takes only five minutes a week. And after you spend your five minutes each week, you can walk away with the relaxed feeling that you have done everything you need to do to make it possible for your investments to earn $1 million or more.

By devoting just a few minutes each week, you will be accumulating the kind of money most people strive to attain their whole lives, most often without success. I'm talking about the kind of money that will enable you, along with your family, to participate in the American Dream. In America, being rich is not for just "special people." It is not something that you have to just dream about. It can come true for you and your family, and it will have an enormous impact on your life for the rest of your life.

Many people believe that for them, there is a better chance of getting rich by winning a lottery than from saving and investing. A survey from the Consumer Federation of America found that most Americans undervalue the extent that savings can accumulate over time. The survey found that 27 percent of Americans believe that winning a lottery is their best chance to ever have a half a million dollars or more in their lifetime. Among households with annual incomes of $35,000 or less, those holding that belief jumped to 40 percent.

Don't you agree with me that investing is about enhancing your quality of life and being able to live your life the way you want to live it?

I have planted the seed for you to fantasize about becoming a self-made millionaire. I have told you everything you need to know to make it easy for you to achieve this worthwhile goal. I have told you about the pitfalls to avoid. I have given you step-by-step guidance. In fact, to make you feel comfortable following the plan, I have told you even more than you really need to know. What's more, my plan is available for anyone and everyone who chooses to use it. It does not require years of study. There are no tuition fees.

Simply reading what I have told you in the book and only passing judgement on it will in no way impact your future quality of life.

THREE REQUIREMENTS

1. Understand how the plan works and then believe that the power of compounded growth can convert small amounts of money into enormous sums.
2. Decide you want all of this wealth for you and your family to share for the rest of your lives.
3. Devote five minutes a week to following the plan as you work to achieve your goal.

Following my simple trend-following plan is actually pretty exciting. Sure, the details of the plan are so simple that they may be boring. But living with the results of the plan will be far from boring. Since the plan is simple, it overcomes one of the biggest reasons why people fail at making money: You will not consider this wealth-building process to be a chore. Obviously, you don't want to be doing something regularly that makes you feel you are constantly struggling and making personal sacrifices. Most people can only force themselves to do something that is difficult for just so long. Eventually, they will lose interest. Instead, I am sharing with you now a pleasant hobby that can make you money.

All of us in the Fabian family follow the same investing process that I recommend to you. We have been doing it for many years. After having spent over 30 years in the field of finance, I know what I am talking about. I've done it, I continue to do it, I can't imagine not doing it, and as my legacy, I want to share with you what I have learned so that you can do it too.

Everything you need to know to personally implement my plan was presented in Chapter 14 of the book. I could have just given you those facts and ignored the "human" side of investing. However, I did not choose to do that because, as I've said, I am a student of people. I know that just having the facts would not be good enough to make you successful over the long term.

REVIEW THE PAST

It is important for you to see how and why the plan was developed in the first place. Those 30-plus years of statistical data give you the opportunity to see how the plan has worked during different economic cycles. The charts in Figure 10-7 provide that data at a glance. In addition, it is important for you to see the actual performance results of the plan since it began, more than two decades ago, in April 1977. All of this should convince you of its validity.

In the performance table in Figure 10-6, you see the actual buy and sell dates of every generated switch signal for the entire operating history of the Domestic Fund Composite Plan. Check it carefully and verify for yourself the actual mechanics of the plan. Check the date of each switch signal on the chart pages and see the plan in action. After completing this checking exercise, you have evidence that the plan is as effective and as simple as I have been saying over and over again throughout the book.

I REPEAT AGAIN—KEEP IT SIMPLE

Some people have difficulty accepting the fact that something so simple can produce such outstanding returns. Some believe that adding more complexity will produce even greater returns. Actually, the reverse is most often true. Anyone who feels that way has not yet grasped the significance of why simplicity is needed to maximize the benefits of compounded growth.

To compound money over a short period of time—say, five years or less—will not make you rich. It will not have a significant impact on your long-term quality of life. To experience those results requires compounding over the long term—10, 15, 20 years—or the rest of your life. So let me ask you this: How many things in your life that you promised to stick with years into the future have you actually lived up to? We all know the answer: not many and perhaps even none.

Therefore, to enhance the probabilities that you actually will follow through on the plan because the rewards are so high over the long term, it just stands to reason: *It must be kept simple.*

You may ask, "If it's so simple, why isn't everyone doing it?" Well, most people won't do it because they are too busy eking out a living to make real money. They are too tired and confused and are content to just be part of the herd. Or, they will put it off until "tomorrow"—and, of course, they then never get around to doing a thing.

Another big advantage when working with your money following a simple plan is that you will soon experience the effect of compounding. When you see your money grow, you will find more money to add to your plan. You would be cheating yourself if after you experienced the results of compounding in your life, you didn't have a substantial portion of all your available dollars working to get these magical results. This is the reason why, at the very beginning, I don't insist that you "beg, borrow, or steal" all of the money you can lay your hands on to put to work. If I asked you to do that, you would never get started. And getting started is the most important step in the plan. Therefore, my recommendation is to take it slow at first. Watch it start to happen—then you decide when the time is right for you to do more.

No one cares about your money like you do. No matter how good a broker or friend is, you are not going to get rich listening to what others who are not successful themselves are telling you. I am giving you the facts so that you can decide whether or not my plan is for you. All extraordinary profits from mutual funds flow to those who understand what I have described to you. Most mutual fund investors are not even aware that my plan even exists.

I HAVE ANTICIPATED ALL OF YOUR QUESTIONS

I have been blessed with common sense, plus I have already been where you are now. I remember the questions I asked at that time. I know virtually every question that's been on your mind as you have read through the book. And I know what questions will pop up next as you proceed along each step—all the way to making your first purchase.

No matter where you are—from beginner to advanced—my simple trend-following process will pick you up and take you along on an enjoyable journey to confidence and knowledge. You have seen how my basic process for putting money to work can enrich your life and how compounding is the tool that converts your savings dollars into enormous sums.

STOCK MARKET

My plan is designed to work within the structure of the stock market. It is unfortunate, but those two words put fear in the hearts of many people. When they think about the stock market, many technical terms come to mind—blue chip stocks, small cap stocks, the New York Stock Exchange, the American Stock Exchange, the over-the-counter (OTC) market, puts, calls, options—the list goes on and on. At first, when someone hears that our plan functions within the stock market, they find it hard to accept that none of those "unintelligent" technical terms I mentioned are relevant to what we do.

In the same vein, I would prefer that you not even use the word *investing*. That word conjures up potentially complicated functions to follow. However, we can all agree on what is meant by just "putting money to work." In reality, that is the only thing we are doing. We are putting money to work, striving to get 20 percent compounded growth or better.

PAPER TRADING

To prove that you do not need to know all about the workings of the stock market, I suggest putting make-believe money to work with paper trades. Start right away to follow the Domestic Fund Composite Trading Plan; it doesn't matter where we may be in the investing cycle. Immediately, select five mutual funds to buy on paper only.

If a buy signal is in effect at the time you are making your selections, you know the process to follow to find the individual funds that are on target to reach the goal. You also know how to select a domestic General Market Indicator that is also on target. Once you make your selections, devote five minutes a week to monitor the progress of your funds, starting with the date of your initial paper purchase. As long as each of your paper-purchased mutual funds remains on target with a monthly average growth of 1.67 percent and its individual performance is equal to or greater than the performance of the General Market Indicator you have selected as your yardstick, continue to hold.

Nothing hard or complicated about that, is there? In a short period of time, when you see that the plan works, you'll be ready to make 20 percent growth in actuality.

Question: Almost every month I read about or hear new investment ideas. But I've never heard of your trend-following plan. Why?

Answer: What I am recommending is not something new. It is not a fad. It's a solid, practical method of putting money to work that has been proven in real life use since 1976. I have used it, my family has used it, and tens of thousands of others have used it with great success. And for that reason, the financial press doesn't consider it news. My plan works as well today as well as it did on the day I began recommending it. Financial magazines would go out of business if everyone knew how to make money my simple way.

Question: I have been told not to use the stock market.

Answer: Who ever told you this may be trying to help. But how much do they really know about putting money to work? Don't let people with limited vision stop you from achieving your dreams.

Question: I am too busy to watch investments.

Answer: One of the falsehoods spread by the financial industry is that you need a lot of time, education, or inside knowledge to put your money to work. It isn't true. Just remember one thing: *Making money is not complicated.*

Once you put my simple trend-following plan into practice, you can do better than most million-dollar money managers. And you can learn to do it almost in no time at all without any special education other than the simple facts I have given you.

Question: It seems too good to be true!

Answer: It really isn't. That's why I encourage you to try it out on paper—to make you a believer. Once you're totally confident it works, start making money at your own comfortable pace.

Remember, if any fund you are currently holding does not continue to be on target for the goal, then "paper sell it" and replace it with another mutual fund which is currently on target. We call that "rotating up." And that's also simple, isn't it?

If on the day you decide to start a paper trading plan you find that the Domestic Fund Composite Trading Plan is in a sell mode, then delay purchasing until a new buy signal is generated. That is also simple, isn't it?

As a student of people, I know that once you apply the compounding plan, even if you are just paper trading—and you see for yourself that it really works and that it is as simple as I have been saying, your thoughts about your financial future will start to change. Perhaps they will change slowly at first. But then you'll become convinced that it is working for you, and you will see how the implementation of the plan, with real money, will have you on the road to financial freedom. Even before you are actually rich, you will start to think you are—one of the added benefits of my plan that brings joy and peace of mind.

It Takes Three Years

Let me ask you a question: Do you believe that I believe you can become a self-made millionaire? I think you will answer, "Yes." Now the next question is this: Do you believe it is possible for you to become a self-made millionaire following my plan and will you take the steps to make it happen? Whether you answer yes or no, let me tell you what my experience has been in getting individuals to fully accept both my investment philosophy and my trading strategy.

I have learned that it takes three years for investors to fully accept and then to completely commit to the compounding plan with a large percentage of their available investment dollars. I have talked one-on-one with many Fabian followers to explore this phenomenon. I asked them to describe their acceptance process. Their answers all fell into the following general scenario.

All investors who subscribe to any stock market advisory service subscribe to at least four or five at the same time. Obviously, these advisory letters offer different advice, with varying degrees of complexity. Logic says that the subscriber tries to implement all of the advice he or she is receiving at the same time. As time goes by, the subscriber experiences some level of success with some letters; others are abandoned. With the passage of time, the movement of the market, the changing economy, and the ongoing redefining of the objectives of the individual, and so on, eventually the individual becomes serious about how he or she applies investment dollars. This causes the individual to reevaluate the different types of investment advice he or she has been receiving. Eventually, the relationship between results and complexity takes on a higher importance.

continued

The final determining factor that eventually leads the person to accept my recommendations is the realization of how compounded growth can affect his or her life. The more goal-oriented the individual becomes, the more the simplicity of my plan is appealing. The final determining factor is results. Just talking about a plan which has the potential to attain 20 percent annualized compounded growth does not have the same impact as when you actually see the result with your own investment dollars.

The Rest of Your Life

Allowing three years to pass in order for you to fully accept my premise and then get yourself on the road to fulfilling your goal may seem like a long time. However, when you compare it with the number of years you still have before you, it is a small price to pay. So be patient. Follow whatever acceptance process best fits your temperament and anxieties. Again, for many people, the first step they should consider is to simply do paper trading. Make it a "paper money game." Select five funds. Go through the monitoring and the rotating up process . . . on paper.

Once you are comfortable with your "paper trading," start the process using "real money." I suggest getting started with an IRA. Since an IRA is a tax-qualified investment, there are no tax consequences when you move from one fund to another. As you begin "real money" trading, this is the time to fill out your "Blueprint for Wealth" certificate in the compounded growth section of the book.

SELLING IS PERHAPS THE MOST IMPORTANT PART OF THE INVESTING PROCESS

When some people begin following my plan, I know many of them are going to be reluctant to sell some or all of their existing mutual fund holdings even though the trading and monitoring rules may tell them to do so. Therefore, to relate to those mutual fund investors who ignore this important point, here are some ideas I have taken from an article prepared by Randall J. Schultz of CNN in June 1998:

The current bull market, one of the longest in history, might lead you to believe that it would be difficult for any mutual fund to lose money during that time. Not so.

You may wonder, if some funds are so bad, why do they have any money to invest. Isn't the fund marketplace efficient, with money flowing from poor funds into top-performing funds? In the minds of investors, the bottom line is often ignored due to psychological reasons, according to William Goetzmann, professor of finance at the Yale School of Management.

Mr. Goetzmann studied why investors stick with struggling mutual funds. He found that "cognitive dissonance" played a part. This means Wall Street is telling them one thing but their personal feelings are telling them another. People are selective about the information they believe about their mutual funds. People like to think that they made a good choice in the past and don't like to look at evidence that their fund really did poorly.

In the 1997 study, people were asked how their mutual funds were performing. He found that investors consistently thought their funds' performance was better than the returns actually were.

In some cases the reason why people still have their money in a poorly performing fund is that they're deceased. In 1993, the Unclaimed Property Clearinghouse, a government organization, filed to recover money from mutual funds that belongs to fund holders who are now deceased. Estimates at the time indicated that possibly 20 percent of each fund's assets belong to fund buyers who are no longer living.

FABIAN LEMON LIST (WWW.FABIAN.COM)

When working with individual mutual fund investors for so many years, you learn about their tendencies. As pointed out above, one of these tendencies is their reluctance to sell.

To help overcome this reluctance, 30 days after the end of each quarter of the year, our web page makes available its "Lemon List." This is a group of mutual funds that chronically have shown poor performance. Specifically, the funds listed there have underperformed for over five years. The objective of the Lemon List is to give reluctant sellers concrete evidence to sell any fund they may be holding that is on this list. The most recent copy of this Lemon List can be downloaded, free of charge, at fabian.com.

The web page is designed to make it easy to determine if any fund you presently own is on the list. You simply click on "Search the Entire Lemon List" and then enter the ticker symbols of the fund/s you own.

All open-end mutual funds that are available for purchase have an assigned five-digit alphabetical ticker symbol. When using your computer, the quickest way to access information for any mutual fund is to identify it by its ticker symbol. All confirmation statements you receive from your mutual fund company and/or from your stockbroker will always show the ticker symbol, in addition to the name of the mutual fund.

IGNORE WHAT OTHERS HAVE BEEN TELLING YOU

To be successful, you need to tune out other's advice. Instead, you should simply set your goal, and then everything else falls into place.

I have told people over the years that the less they know about all of the ins and outs of investing, other than the few simple facts I have given about mutual funds, the better off they are. Don't listen to people who

FIGURE 17-1

Source: Copyright © 1999 by Dave Carpenter. Used by permission of Dave Carpenter.

want to complicate things. The less you know, the less you have to unlearn. See Figure 17-1. People who feel they must know everything about the stock market are investment-oriented. People who believe it is important to put money to work to reach their stated goals are investor-oriented.

The investment-oriented individual is constantly striving to find the best investment—an impossible task. The investor-oriented individual is only interested in finding the simplest path to follow, which he or she believes, based on historical precedence, has the potential to reach his or her goal.

Here is an interesting phenomenon. Investment-oriented individuals are never content. They are always searching for the best investment. Investor-oriented individuals can easily find contentment. They only need to know if they are on target to reach their goal.

How Do You Measure Success?

We should all be striving to attain 20 percent annualized compounded growth on our money. We know from studying one of the 20 percent Compounded Growth Tables in the book that 20 percent compounded growth at the end of 10 years produces the equivalent growth of 52 percent each year on our starting investment. And we know that 20 percent compounded growth at the end of 15 years produces the equivalent growth of 96 percent each year on our original investment.

Keeping these facts in mind, let me ask you a question: Suppose that at the end of some future year, you were to review annual mutual fund performance results. Further suppose there were 450 mutual funds that produced performance of 20 percent or more. At that time, let's say, only one fund in this group had performance of exactly 20 percent, while the remaining 449 mutual funds attained higher growth—many much higher.

My question is this: If you owned only that one mutual fund with just 20 percent growth, would you be satisfied? It would be wise to keep in mind that history has shown us that an investor who is not satisfied with a 20 percent compounded growth is far more likely to get stung in the future, rather than get rich. We had already agreed earlier that when you have attained your goal, that means you are a successful investor.

SLOW BUT SURE

My plan is not a get-rich-quick scheme. It is not something that will be here today and gone tomorrow. As mentioned several times, it has been quietly and effectively working for those fortunate investors who have put it to work. And it will always be around because it really does work in all kinds of markets. I know it works because I not only personally use it, but I have taught it to thousands of people who have benefited from it. Here in the book I am giving you the simple lessons that will enable you to use it and reap its benefits.

This is how the American Dream comes true. Small sums of money achieving 20 percent compounded growth—for instance, $2,000 a year in an IRA over 25 years—produces more than $1 million. What's more, my plan works in any economic climate or condition here or abroad. Using it you'll experience small and steady gains; you will never find it boring to watch your money grow. When you know what you are trying to accomplish, and you see that you are making steady progress toward your goal, you can relax.

In time, you will be the self-made millionaire you have chosen to become.

Other Resources

I am assuming that the majority of my readers will take the full three years before they become fully committed to following the my plan. To be continually reminded of my basic premise that 20 percent compounded growth is feasible, I have suggested reviewing the mutual fund listings in *USA Today*.

However, there is another source to obtain similar information available on the Internet:

1. Go to www.morningstar.com. At the Morningstar home page, click on *Fund Selector.*
2. Under Basic Screens, select a Fund Category from the following list:
   All Funds
   US Stock Funds
   International Stock Funds

3. Then select a Screening Field from the following list:

1 Month
3 Month
One Year
Year-to-date

4. After you have made your choices under the two selection headings, click on *View Results.*

A list of top-performing mutual funds, in performance sequence, in whichever category you chose, for whichever time period you chose, will appear. These listings are further evidence that during an uptrend, attaining at least 20 percent growth one year at a time is doable.

Whatever investment plan you decide to follow, look to what independent third-party professionals say about the plan. The Hulbert Financial Digest, Inc., 316 Commerce Street, Alexandria, VA 22314 (703-683-5905), is one source for feedback on financial newsletters.

LET'S KEEP WORKING TOGETHER

I invite you, free of charge, to keep in touch with me on the Internet as you are working to become a self-made millionaire.

In closing this chapter, I would like to say again that my compounding plan is easy to understand and simple to follow. Its simplicity will make it comfortable for you to adhere to over the long term. And by following it over the long term, you will compound small amounts of money into enormous sums. The plan offers you the opportunity to become a self-made millionaire. And once you are a millionaire, you can still use my plan to earn 20 percent annualized compounded growth. Yes, you can do this for the rest of your life. And you life will be greatly enhanced as a result.

ONE FINAL THOUGHT

On the back cover of the book there is a photo of myself holding a copy of *USA Today.* I had that photo taken to remind you:

For the rest of your life, every time you see a copy of USA Today, *you will be know that it contains all of the information you need to make yourself a self-made millionaire.*

INDEX